BIRTH OF THE HOLY NATION

VOLUME 2
ISAAC, JACOB AND SONS

DR. CORBETT GAULDEN

eGenCo

Generation Culture Transformation
Specializing in publishing for generation culture change

eGenCo
824 Tallow Hill Road
Chambersburg, PA 17202, USA
Phone: 717-461-3436
Email: info@egen.co
Website: www.egen.co

facebook.com/egenbooks

youtube.com/egenpub

egen.co/blog

pinterest.com/eGenDMP

twitter.com/eGenDMP

instagram.com/egenco_dmp

Publisher's Cataloging-in-Publication Data
Gaulden, Corbett
Birth of the Holy Nation. Issac; Jacob; and Sons. Vol. 1.;
by Dr. Corbett Gaulden. Steve Nance, editor.
248 pages cm.
ISBN: 978-1-68019-972-7 paperback
      978-1-68019-973-4 ebook
      978-1-68019-974-1 ebook
1. Religion. 2. Old Testament. 3. Patriarch. I. Title
2016900589

Cover design and page layout by Kevin Lepp, www.kmlstudio.com

DEDICATION

I first became a father quite some time ago with the birth of our first daughter. In time another daughter was born. Soon after that, my wife and I decided we had "plenty" of kids, as the saying goes. These two spent their growing up years very busily teaching me what it means to be a father. I learned a lot from them over the years of their preparation for life. Much of it was hard to learn, but they were patient—and diligent—to teach me the lessons. They were also particularly keen to provide me with a laboratory within which to observe how sibling relationships work. In later years, I began to acquire sons of a spiritual kind. When that came to be, I already knew a lot about how to be a father. This book places a major emphasis on Jacob and his twelve sons, as well as the sibling relationships among those sons. With this in mind, it is my pleasure to dedicate this volume to Krista Burns and Rachel Gaulden, those great "teachers" whom their "Dad" loves so much.

Watch Corbett Gaulden's additional
teachings on the Birth of The Holy Nation, Volume 2
at The Raven's Food website. Each chapter's video
is meant to be viewed prior to reading the chapter.

TABLE OF CONTENTS

FOREWORD

In his first book, *Birth of The Holy Nation vol. 1*, Dr. Gaulden introduced us to the promise of God given to Abraham, to build a nation out of a seed. From Isaac, born through a miracle, the nation of Israel was founded. The consummate purpose for the creation of this natural nation was to nurture and bring forth yet another seed to fulfill an even greater promise; namely, to reconcile all of the sons of Adam to Himself. From Christ, God started another nation, a holy nation, in the image and likeness of God Himself. Dr. Gaulden showed the consistency of the greater promise governing all aspects of the lesser promise. The nation of Israel was formed to enable the greater promise of redemption of humankind through Christ. "God was in Christ reconciling the world to himself" (2 Cor. 5:19). He continues the development of this central theme in this current book, *Birth of The Holy Nation, vol. 2*.

Why did God choose to create a holy nation as a central part of His plan to reconcile man to Himself? Was it not enough that Christ died on the cross to save mankind, and is it not enough just to believe in Him?

Whereas the popular gospel emphasizes the message of salvation, meaning going to heaven when we die, the biblical gospel centers on reconciliation to God. They are not the same thing. One message focuses on obtaining a destination upon death while the other recognizes that there was a prior existing reason for the creation of mankind, and man

i

is saved to be reconciled to that original intent. God announced that His purpose for the creation of man was to make a being "in (God's) image and likeness." When He created this being, He called him "Son" (Lk. 3:38). A son is designed to be "the radiance of God's glory and the exact representation of his being" (Heb. 1:2). The invisible God intended to become visible by putting His nature and character on visible display through His Son. Such a son, of course had to be a spiritual son. Flesh begets flesh, and spirit begets spirit. Since God is a Spirit, any being that is designated as His Son must also be essentially spirit. Yet, if His intent was to display His "likeness," such a son must also be visible. That is the only way the world could see what God is like. The first Adam was a spirit clothed in flesh. So also was the last Adam. In the first son, God was meant to be seen in the natural creation. Adam was meant to interpret the natural creation as the means of showing the nature of God through the physical order of creation (Rom. 1:20). Christ, the last Adam, was meant to show God as God is. "Anyone who has seen me has seen the Father" (Jn. 14:9. "I and the Father are one" (Jn. 10:30). The spiritual Son, though he appears last, is meant to carry the fullness of the representation of God.

The Body of the natural son is limited by physical factors such as time and space. The spiritual is timeless and transcendent. The shadow and type of the representation of God is carried in the natural order, which typically appears first. The nation of Israel is such a type and shadow, and is the best picture of God that was available until Christ.

In studying the birth and development of the nation of Israel, one is looking into a mystery relating to the coming forth of a holy nation whose purpose is the full disclosure of the nature of the invisible Father. Dr. Gaulden does a forensic examination of this developing phenomenon and reveals the secrets of the divine nature of God hidden in the story of the patriarchs.

Just as it required an entire nation functioning over time to reveal the secrets of God as Father dealing with sons whose understanding of Him was as one seeing through a veil, so also it requires a corporate man who is assembled as the spiritual body of Christ to present the many facets of the glory of God. The natural order precedes the spiritual order (2 Cor. 3:1-18). Volumes 1 and 2 of *Birth of The Holy Nation* are essential for the complete understanding of God's original intent to bring forth a Son in whom He intended to disclose Himself fully. "For God so loved the world that He gave His only begotten Son, that whoever believes in Him should not perish but have everlasting life" (Jn. 3:16 NKJV).

God's motivation for revealing Himself is rooted in His essential nature—His love.

Dr. Samuel Soleyn

FOREWORD
FROM VOLUME 1

Today it is common to relegate the Bible to the realm of history, allegory, and myth, an ancient relic belonging exclusively in the genre of religious thought and discussions of faith. Many today make a clean and sharp distinction between the realms of faith and reason. In doing so, they advocate distinct forms of "truth," presenting reason as "real truth" while regarding spiritual insights as "religious truth." Reason purports to hold the keys to the mysteries of how the world works while "religious truth" is seen as optional and limited to the realm of belief and faith. In this bifurcation, two distinct forms of thought exist side-by-side, and each individual chooses what constitutes truth to him or her. This is a consumer-based approach to truth, in which everything is by definition subjective, and the popular will is the standard by which all things are judged to be true or false. Reason views each human being as a creature whose task is to determine whether or not he or she has a spiritual component or is purely a material being. The outcome of this inquiry is purely optional, exclusively personal, and has no effect on the way anyone else might resolve the issue. Biblical characters and stories are interpreted through a linear process that considers them to be of little value beyond the narrative itself. Reason, therefore, regards the Bible as being largely without value in establishing standards for human life and conduct. At the same time, however, it recognizes the Bible's usefulness to some individuals. Truth, then, is not absolute but highly personalized, and the individual may elect between the process of reason and faith to determine what works for him or her.

A contrasting point of view considers that man was created by God, who put into one being both heaven and earth. This view holds that man contains within his physical body both his spirit and his soul. He is connected to God and to the eternal realm through his spirit, while he is equipped to function in the earth through the investiture of his soul. His soul is meant to be submitted to his spirit so that the wisdom of the heavens may be received through his spirit and translated into functional activities in the earth through his soul. Anyone who in this way is connected to the heavens through the Holy Spirit is capable of speaking the wisdom of the eternal over all the circumstances of the earth. Such a person sees the Bible as a book containing the wisdom of the heavens to be decoded through the Holy Spirit. All the stories and sayings of the Scriptures contain mysteries to be revealed in this fashion. While a linear approach to Scripture is the superimposition of reason upon the process of interpreting the Bible (a practice that continues to acknowledge the supremacy of reason over revelation), this revelation-based approach considers the eternal point of view to be preeminent and therefore the superior standard by which truth is to be established. This standard inherently conflicts with the present process of determining truth on the basis of personal choice.

Dr. Corbett Gaulden has taken one of the central figures of the Scriptures, Abraham, and presented his life as one that contains profound insights into aspects of the nature of God in his dealings with man. Abraham stands out as a man who determines to seek and to understand the true God against the background of the polytheistic society in which he lives. God responds by choosing him to be the one from whom the Messiah will come. At the inception of this relationship, God establishes foundational principles by which He will act, and through which His nature is disclosed. These principles continue to function throughout both the Old and New Testament Scriptures and form a basis for the understanding of God Himself. This process of revelation introduces us to a transcendent order of being, which by its very nature is superior to the present order of determining truth through reason. The time of the conflict between reason and revelation was prophesied many centuries ago in Zechariah 9: 13: "(I) will raise up your sons, O Zion, against your sons, O Greece, and make (Zion) as the sword of a mighty man." The Scriptures, as interpreted through revelation, are described as "the sword of the Spirit" (Ephesians 6:17).

Dr. Gaulden has revealed rare and valuable insights into the nature of God as viewed through His dealings with Abraham. His reexamination of covenant in its formalities and intentions are invaluable benchmarks for determining truth not just for that day but for all time. In the end of humanity's time, God will restore divine order as the basis of both truth and judgment. This book by Dr. Gaulden has come at the appropriate time and is of foundational value.

Dr. Samuel Soleyn

PREFACE

When I began this work, I was still employed at a university. In fact, it can be said that I have been at this for several decades, taking notes and formulating various ideas for understanding the underpinnings of the Jewish and Christian faiths. It never escaped me that the message of the Christ, JESUS the Son, was prefigured in so many ways by the revelations of truth that were provided in the Old Testament (**OT**). In fact, the New Testament (**NT**) quotes the **OT** extensively to demonstrate to us that the story is continuous. Now that I am retired from the academic life, I can turn my attention even more fully to matters of truth to be found in holy writ.

Volume one was published before I retired. With the publication of volume two at this time, the two volumes together provide fitting bookends to the end of that life and the beginning of whatever may lie ahead for my wife and me. In the same sense there is a significant shift in the patriarchal narrative between the two volumes. Volume one laid much groundwork for understanding why Abraham was so important to the plan of GOD. I also spent considerable time developing a paradigm for consideration of the eternal nature of the relationships that make the holy nation a possibility. This was necessary to strip away the ambiguity through which we typically filter our perception of important matters in scripture. In the end, each individual is in a distinct and unique relationship with GOD and with His will in that person's life. Volume one revealed how deeply this relationship was worked into the life of Abraham, that great **patriarch** of the faith.

In this second volume, the focus shifts from Abraham to his successors. GOD's work didn't end with Abraham. In a sense, because Abram was the first man to whom GOD began to enunciate the "great nation," we might consider him its founder insofar as human efforts are concerned. But one man does not a nation make; it takes an entire people to make a nation.

We find ourselves living in a time when there are many ideas about what it takes to make a nation or to be a people. Ideas concerning political management of peoples are quite varied in our world. None of these, it seems to me, are of the stuff of GOD's actual interest, although many purport to be. How often men appeal to the authority of GOD's name to justify their own sense of how men ought to be organized at the "national" level. It turns out that GOD, too, has ideas about nationhood, and He selected the family of a nomadic herder to begin to bring those things to be in the earth.

The process was difficult because whatever form of nationhood we have faces the question of longevity. GOD has in place a Kingdom that is eternal in nature. Because His Kingdom is eternal, He seems to have thought it a good idea to make it visible in the Creation. In order to do that, He needed people to be its citizens. Thus began that work, which is still in the mind of GOD and was still under discussion at the end of the time of writing of the **NT**.

It seems GOD did not desire to borrow a culture for His great and holy nation from the nations of man. By selecting Abram to be the first human seed of that nation, He selected a man into whom He could place a culture that was not like the culture of the peoples among whom he lived. In order to accomplish this, GOD required from Abram everything that was his original culture and began to build the new, desired culture into him. In this way, GOD's nation would have GOD's culture at its core. When the one man was ready, GOD began to populate that which was to come.

Sinai, the Levitical system, and the compromises of the Christian church have so obscured this original culture that it can no longer be recognized. But the seed is present and eternal. We know that JESUS is THE "Seed" of Abraham. In Him, in the fullness of time, I know that we will see what the Kingdom of GOD, the Holy Nation (the great nation promised to Abram) looks like. We will experience the tangibility of *its presence in the earth*. Perhaps this will not be very far advanced within my lifetime, but it will be seen and inhabited in the earth. The dawning of that truth in my mind did not happen at an early age, nor did it come easily. Only with great effort over many years has the Spirit of GOD placed these things in my conscious mind.

In the preface to volume one I went into some of the personal history that got me here. That story continues. As I suppose is true of many writers, the capture of the thing in written form is not the end of its revelation to the spirit. The ways of GOD are many, and often mysterious to our minds.

It is to that end that I live. There is a role for me to play in the revelation of the culture of the Kingdom. It is my great blessing to bear, and live under, the grace granted to me to be a party (in however small a way) in the revelation of the ways of Our GOD. I pray that you will receive my work with that motivation in mind.

ACKNOWLEDGMENTS

As I have said before, my frailties are many. Only the grace of GOD has prompted and sustained me in this work. It simply would not be possible otherwise. I have only recently come to know that the Holy Spirit can "inhabit a keyboard." It is His constant revelation to me that makes this work feasible. Praise GOD for this grace!

GOD did not make us to be sole sources of His revelation and wisdom. Many who have gone before me and many who have gone along beside me have contributed considerably to the understandings that have been built into my mind's frame. In truth, they are innumerable. Some of them have been very actively and indispensably involved in the tangible work that this book has become. The "them" in this case are the same as for volume one. However, some of the readers of that now published work have been very encouraging that what this work is makes it of value to them. Those encouragements added to the whisperings of the Spirit sustain me in continuing this labor.

In particular, Mary Ellen Green, Colleen Stegall, and Judy Gaulden have been "right there" as this endeavor has moved along. Joshua Chambers continues to amaze in making the electronic aspects of this project integral and important components of it. As before, the eGenCo staff are great people. It is my great pleasure to call them friends. Another published writer, Dr. Elijah Morgan, was also very kind to share with me recently some valuable insights and encouragement.

Please scan the QR code or go to the web address to view Corbett's video introduction to the book.

Introduction

THE FIRST SONS
OF THE HOLY NATION

http://bit.ly/1ZhaMh9

Please go to ravensfood.everykindred.com for access to additional supplements to the book. Content will be added from time to time as desirable to support this book.

Introduction

THE FIRST SONS
OF THE HOLY NATION

The basic purpose of this book and its predecessor, *Birth of The Holy Nation, volume 1*, is to explore the scriptural, and therefore spiritual, concept that inherently resides in the earthly and visible phenomenon in which fathers and sons interact. In volume one we examined the idea of father and son relationships from both normative and practical perspectives. The normative perspective required that we extract the principle directly from scripture, and we attempted to do so. The result of such an exercise, however, sometimes appears dry, distant, and unattainable. The practical perspective is different. To pursue the matter practically, we examined scripture as well, but we performed our analysis on what is the most complete descriptive treatment of the topic of father and son in human terms. In this volume we shall continue to examine the development of family phenomena as found in the narratives concerning the patriarchs, Isaac and Jacob and their families.

Generally, we may use the term *patriarch* to describe the specific four-generation phenomenon of Abram/Abraham, Isaac, Jacob/Israel, and the twelve "sons" (*b'nai Yisrael*) of Jacob/Israel. Abraham, in his relationship with GOD as his Father, was the focus of volume one.

While Abraham, Isaac, and Jacob were the patriarchs of the *nation* of Israel, the twelve sons of Jacob/Israel came to be known as the "fathers" of the twelve *tribes* of Israel. The historical range of this current volume extends from the time of Isaac's life to the naming of the twelve tribes of the sons of Israel. While we will consider many things as we pass through the historical narrative, our focus will be on the passing down from father to son of the promises GOD originally gave to Abram. The relationships themselves will enable us to arrive at both practical and normative conclusions.

In the New Testament, JESUS almost always uses the dyadic term "Father" to refer to GOD. He also uses the term "Son" to refer to Himself. In so doing He implies a father and son relationship in much the same sense that Isaac had a father and son relationship with Jacob. JESUS could have referred to GOD as the Creator or the Ineffable One or some other such theological term. He did not fail to recognize the magnificence of GOD, but He normally referred to GOD as "Father" both in second and third person references. The familiarity inherent in this form of address humanizes for us the relationship found within the Godhead. It helps make GOD approachable. In its absence, GOD would remain far off from us; someone we could only address indirectly. The relationship JESUS portrayed for us enables us to come near to GOD, just as any son should approach his father. This, in turn, enables us to approach a study of the lives of the patriarchs from a normative perspective to accompany the simple historical narrative.

In order to make our examination complete, we will also take into consideration relationships between brothers (the sons of Jacob). Relationships between brothers are important to us, but they are, in and of themselves, only one generation deep. They have other properties that often lead to their crowding out of serious, long-term considerations. The Kingdom of GOD is an eternal phenomenon. It cannot be confined to a generation. Relationships between brothers occur simultaneously with relationships between a father and the persons who are brothers, but are of a different kind.

Birth of The Holy Nation, volume 1, provided an in-depth examination of the **FATHER-SON** dyadic relationship that exists between GOD (The Father) and JESUS (The Son), which is unique and exists outside such considerations as time, except in the instance(s) of JESUS' appearance(s) on the earth. It turns out that the New Testament is a one-generational phenomenon. Only one generation was needed to present the updates to the revelation of GOD that were needed to launch the Kingdom through the sons of GOD. It was not necessary to present the full pattern of father and son relationships in the New Testament because they had already been presented in the patriarchal narrative. Even more so, the patriarchal narrative covers the evolution of one **father-son dyad** into a nation of promise. The patriarchal narrative was necessary because it produced the revelation of the nature of the Holy Nation from its inception by way of an address to a sheepherder in Syria.

The patriarchal model of relationships consists of several distinct phenomena that are useful to us as we seek to gain an understanding of who we are and how we can best relate in any of our human relationships. It does this by presenting its principles in real flesh and blood. These fellows ate and drank and slept and worked and sweated and stubbed their toes and everything else that **normal** flesh and blood encounters. They were right and they were wrong. They were righteous and they were wicked. They exhibited a wide range of qualities in their relationships with one another and with the folks around them as they lived out their lives. Herein we will examine a wide range of humanity through the life experiences of these persons. We can then effectively integrate these experiences with GOD's pattern for humanity.

There is a specific kind of relationship paradigm in scripture that permits us to look at the "male and female thing" as containing differences. That phenomenon, called marriage, is the focus of my book *Marriage: Finding GOD's Design*, although the subject enters into the present discussion from time to time. The patriarchal family, of course, included females as wives, mothers, daughters, and sisters. Again, gender is not the point. The biblical narratives primarily concern themselves with relationships among male personages to carry the spiritual message of interest to us in this study. Of course, certain of the females add necessary richness to the narrative, and we will include them as we go along.

For sons of GOD the most important attribute of sentient existence can be summed up in the simple statement, "GOD is love." Left alone, the statement presents love as a somewhat ambiguous phenomenon. For certain political and theological purposes this might be alright. Folks often claim that "a loving GOD wouldn't" do this or that, appealing to the ambiguous nature of an isolated idea to make their case. But for the purpose of understanding who we are, the statement is inadequate. Love needs to be personalized to be real. These fantastic patriarchal folks do that for us. They present relationships in a rich matrix of kind and quality. We intend to make much of that because who we are has a lot to do with the fact that we are not simple, completely isolated phenomena. We are part of something that is ongoing, even eternal. This study argues that the glue that holds that something together is love–particularly, the love of GOD.

The particular relationships of interest to us are quite special. They occur in the matrix of the call to being of GOD's Holy Nation in the form of its type and shadow. The very human nature of the central characters–you can almost see the sweat on their faces–provides us with the prefiguring type and shadow of the eternal phenomenon. This founding of the type and shadow of the Holy Nation takes place in the context of very fallible persons. Their potential chaos is held at bay by the very loving will that determined that there would be a nation to begin with. And human beings are the raw material in the call, development, and manifestation of the type of the nation. These real human beings provide us a context in which to understand that we are currently graced to carry that same call in the bosom of that same love so that such a nation in its fullest manifestation will come forth.

We will use these relationships and the history of their ups and downs to point to a significant battery of life principles that can enable us to get through the process of being human in a divine context.

The early chapters of the first volume laid groundwork and defined terms to help us understand the nature and significance of the various dyadic relationships that comprise the human experience, with particular emphasis on the singular prominence of the **father-son** dyadic relationship in the passing on of GOD's promises from generation to generation. Included in that discussion was the importance of love and the principle of "first-ness," or **primacy** (rank, if you like), to the overall dynamic of the **father-son dyad**. The focus of that examination was the man known as Abram/Abraham, the prototypical **patriarch**, the "father" of the Holy Nation of Israel; the one with whom GOD established His covenant and to whom He gave the promise of land and nationhood. We examined Abraham's relationships with his two sons, Ishmael and Isaac, but with particular attention given to Isaac, the "son of promise." The final chapter of this first volume examined Abraham's trans-generational influence.

Volume two opens with Isaac and his son Jacob, but the primary focus will be on the sons of Jacob because they present us with a rich fabric of all kinds of relational phenomena. Their sheer number guarantees this. In the generations before Jacob's sons, we get a look at certain brother pairs and we learn from them. However, the twelve sons of Jacob bring a lot to the table in terms of understanding the great diversity of the sons of GOD. They enable us to examine both trans-generational and intra-generational phenomena simultaneously. How very real that makes life! We can really relate to these guys, not just as titular heads of some group of people, but as men who had to work things out among themselves.

To summarize, the goal of this two-volume work is to examine the lives of the patriarchs in their many dyadic, human phenomena in an effort to discover how a man became the first human mover in prefiguring the Kingdom of GOD in the earth. We will accomplish this by looking at the real relationships and their underlying phenomena of four generations of nomads. In so doing, we will see anew the humanly-reciprocated love of GOD as the essential condition for producing the manifestation of His will in our time and forever, in spite of the frailties of men. GOD got it done whether Simeon and Joseph got along well or not.

Please scan the QR code or go to the web address to view Corbett's video introduction to the book.

CHAPTER 1

ISAAC: THE SECOND PATRIARCH

http://bit.ly/1JGoVCC

Please go to ravensfood.everykindred.com for access to additional supplements to the book. Content will be added from time to time as desirable to support this book.

ISAAC: THE SECOND PATRIARCH

(Genesis 17-28; 35:27-29)

Having examined in volume one the person of Abraham through scripture, we will begin this second volume by turning our attention to his son, Isaac. We know that Isaac was not the only son-in-the-flesh of the man who came to be named Abraham. We know that Ishmael was born to Abraham by Hagar (Gen. 16:4, 11) and that Keturah bore him several sons (Gen. 25:5-6). However, Isaac was the only son of Sarah. He was the **firstborn** and possessed the **birthright**. Abraham gave all his flesh-sons, except Isaac, gifts and sent them away (Gen. 25:5-6). When Abraham died, Isaac inherited his herds and flocks and water wells and campsites and custody of the properties he had possessed and oversight of his servants and so forth. When Abraham died, Isaac became very wealthy. Interestingly, he had lived his whole life in that wealth with full access to it, but now it was his to dispose of as he would. None of the other sons of Abraham received a portion of the **inheritance**. We may imagine that the gifts they all received were rich, but were limited in time. Only to Isaac went the perpetuity of the property and identity of Abraham. He was now the chief man and de facto "king" of a nation that would become the "great nation" about

1

which GOD had spoken to Abraham way back there at the beginning of this whole thing (Gen. 12:1-3). Isaac was the heir and sole keeper of the promise GOD had made to Abraham.

It is not that the other persons born of the flesh of Abram/Abraham just fell into the abyss. No, several of them in fact became the fathers of groups of people known to the descendants of Isaac later on. Ishmael is considered to be the father of the groups of people generally referred to as "Arabs." The word speaks to whole groups of people generally lumped together as Arabs in ancient times. In more modern times, the definition is more specific, but still directly related to Ishmael. Scripture records the names of thirteen sons of Ishmael (Gen. 25:12-18). Esau, the **firstborn** son of Isaac married one of Ishmael's daughters. This is not the place for a full discussion of Ishmael, but we must note three essential facts: he was not an heir to Abraham; he became very success-ful demographically in his own right; and his descendants mattered to the Israelites. In fact, when Joseph's brothers sold him into slavery, it was to a band of Ishmaelites (Gen. 37:25-28).

Two of the six sons of Abraham by Keturah were named Medan and Midian (Gen. 25:2). Descendants of these two fellows show up as troublesome groups to the Israelites later in history, particularly during the period of the judges of Israel. In fact, some seem to think these guys were the original Arabs. It is possible there was a mingling of all of the Ishmaelites and "Keturahites" (not a proper term) into the Arabic tribal groups.

But Isaac was the *son of promise* and the *heir* of Abraham. He was to be reckoned the **firstborn** because of who his mother was, and he was the possessor of the **birthright** through the same mechanism. The **father-son dyad** Isaac inhabited with Abraham was significantly dif-ferent from any of the other **father-son** relationships that Abraham inhabited. It is as though Isaac were an only son (Gen. 22:2). In a way he was because he was the only issue through the womb of the barren woman Sarah. In fact, Sarah and Abraham took specific, deliberate steps to make sure that Isaac's **inheritance** was secure. We can eas-ily imagine that the servants of the chief man were well aware of his wishes regarding the succession upon the event of his death. They knew decades in advance that this man Isaac was the eventual chief man.

We should consider it a foregone conclusion that Abraham taught Isaac all that he could learn about tending herds and flocks, about caring for the needs of the servants in the camp, about relating to the Canaanites among whom they dwelt, about water and pasture and weather cycles and so forth. In the particularly intimate relationship between the father, Abraham, and the *b'c⁴or*, Isaac, there would have been no effort spared to make Isaac a fully functional replacement for Abraham at the time of his death. The basic skills involved would have been passed down from Terah to Abram years earlier in *Aram Naharaim*, and even before that. But the context completely changed between the time of Abram's youth and the youth of Isaac. Sheep were still sheep and goats were still goats, but the land and the neighbors and the watering holes and so forth were not of Terah - they were of GOD. GOD was the Father of Abraham in his subsequent fathering of Isaac. In time, GOD would become the *de facto* Father of Isaac after the death of Abraham (Gen. 26:2-6), but we shall save that for now.

It is clear that Abram longed for a son. He wanted an heir. Let's consider what might well have occurred had there been no son. At the time that Abram could no longer care for his animals (the bulk of his wealth) or when he died, the questions would emerge: Who shall care for all these things? To whom will be assigned their possession? These were very real and important questions. The animals represented real wealth. The servants relied on Abraham (or someone) to provide for their care and protection. In such a system as existed at the time, the only two possible answers were either a capable heir or the chaos of each man taking what he wanted.

Obviously, for the sake of all, the capable heir was the better choice. In Isaac, Abraham found that capable (and qualified) heir and trained him to be exactly what was needed for the estate. Of course, this meant that Isaac was to some degree a copy of Abraham; an extension of Abraham into the future. As such Isaac could rely on the retinue of servants to remain loyal to him. He could rely on the treaties and agreements

Abraham had forged with the peoples in Canaan and the Philistines. He would be in a position to carry out his father's wishes with respect to such matters as the welfare of any of his father's surviving relatives. Had his mother, Sarah, outlived Abraham, Isaac would have had the power to see to it that his mother was cared for in a way that was pleasing to her. And most of these things would be exactly as Abraham would have done them. For all these reasons and more, Abraham had the proper and undisputed heir in Isaac. Furthermore, GOD Himself had specified that it be so.

SON OF PROMISE

While it may be somewhat repetitive to review those parts of GOD's interactions with Abraham to gain an understanding of who Isaac was and why he was so important, it is also worthwhile. Let's remember that GOD unfolded the fullness of his promise to Abram/Abraham over some considerable time, twenty-five to thirty years. Only in the last year or so before Isaac's birth did GOD inform Abraham regarding the name he was to give to his son and the specific womb that was to bear him. Abram knew that he would eventually become a great nation and that he would produce progeny in order to do so, but only after he had been renamed Abraham did GOD provide to him the full revelation of Isaac. Prior to that time, Abram had received the promise without that specificity and had brought about the birth of Ishmael. But GOD had the specific son of the barren woman in mind in His promises (Gen. 17:15-16). The result of that intervention is that we know for certain whom the son of promise was. The promise was included in a covenant, so it had the mark of GOD all over it.

As the **firstborn** with the **birthright** and the property of being the son of promise, Isaac came on the scene with a great deal of status with men and with GOD. He was born with it. God arranged his birth in such a way as to permit no ambiguity as to who he was. Patriarchal **primacy** was installed in the **father-son** relationship Isaac inhabited with Abraham. This **primacy** was of the kind found in the **FATHER-SON** relationship. In the absence of any other priesthood, Abraham was to act as father and priest to Isaac, who then was to act as both father and priest to his sons. This sequence of **father-son** relationships served as the vessel of eternity for the Kingdom in that time.

Let's remember that Abram had been very concerned about his heir. Sarai too had exhibited considerable concern. Each of them had different but related reasons for their concern. Abram greatly desired continuity. He had built quite an estate and had the promises of GOD, but no heir. Sarai wanted the things her husband wanted with the additional desire to be cared for should she outlive Abram. Only an heir could provide what was needed. Lot had disappointed, in a sense[1] And Eliezer was a servant (Gen. 15:2-4), not a son. It is not clear whether Eliezer's status precluded **inheritance**, but if it did, Abram still would have had to formally adopt Eliezer in order for him to inherit. Even then, Eliezer would have held dubious status in the eyes of the rest of the camp, not to mention Abram's political and business partners.

Then there was the "make your own heir" plan that Sarai concocted (Gen. 16:1-2). That plan produced Ishmael, which worked out badly even for Sarai, whose idea it was. Abram loved Ishmael (Gen. 17:18), but that was not a viable solution to the heir problem. The story of Isaac begins at that point even though he was included eternally in GOD's plan for Abram and the great nation to follow. This son came unequivocally from GOD without human concoction.

There was a certain drama that accompanied Isaac's birth because Abram had already set his heart on the fact that his son Ishmael was the son of promise and that he would be the heir. As far as we know, the status of **firstborn** with the **birthright** was assumed for Ishmael. The matter of his having been born to a slave was apparently resolved in Abram's mind. Technically, the son of the slave woman was born a slave, but Abram surely had some method to resolve that problem. In some format, he would manumit Ishmael and perhaps even his mother Hagar. This would change Ishmael's status from slave to son and all would be well. Perhaps Ishmael's manumission had already occurred. We will never know because scripture is silent on the matter. Apparently Hagar was never manumitted. By the will of GOD, these things were not to be (Gen. 17:17-22).

Ishmael was obviously Abram's choice to be his heir. He was from Abram's own body. But GOD had chosen another to carry the mantle of eternity into the context of the **father-son** relationship of Abram. This mantle of eternity was to include the designation of being **firstborn**, the **birthright** of the **firstborn**, and the son of the promises of GOD. However fine a man Ishmael was, he was not the chosen vessel for these things.

ISHMAEL AMONG THE CAMP'S PEOPLE

What might the people of the camp have thought about the matter of Ishmael as heir? Certainly, when Hagar carried Ishmael in her womb, her status among the other servants in the camp must have risen considerably. After all, she was carrying the son of the chief man in her womb. No other woman in the camp except, possibly, some unspecified concubines, had ever walked in such honor. The other servants probably assumed that this son was to be the heir of the chief by the design of Abram and Sarai themselves. Still, though, a son born to Sarai would have been held in greater honor because she was a free woman and the "full" wife of the chief man. Hagar would always only be the mother of Abram's child, not his free or full wife. Had it been the case that Sarai/Sarah never bore a son, Ishmael would have been acceptable to the people in the camp if Abram made it so. However, he would always only be just slightly different than the folks in the camp. His mistakes in their management would be magnified in their eyes. No matter his personal capabilities, he would have lived his life on the edge of acceptability in his role as the chief man.

Were Sarai/Sarah to bear a son herself, however, Ishmael's credentials would simply cease to be adequate to the people. The son of the chief man and his free wife would show up with more prestige. The people would quickly attach themselves emotionally to this son over Ishmael. By the time he was held in his father's arms, all would expect his leadership and would dedicate themselves to his success on their behalf. Remember that Abram meant "beloved father" and the people would expect the same from his son by his wife.

THE CHOSEN WOMB

However, GOD had chosen that a specific womb would be the carrier of this particular son, the **firstborn** and heir. This womb could not be the womb of a slave woman. The proper womb would be that of a free woman who had a choice in the matter. This womb could only be the womb of the full wife of Abram/Abraham. Proper order was required. No other solution would work. In GOD's own economy, He demanded that this birth and the subsequent **father-son** relationship possess the characteristics and persons of His own choosing. It is of interest that the chosen womb was kept barren until the woman was well past the age of childbearing. Sarah's womb was barren until all other "natural" possibilities for a son were exhausted. This ensured that Abraham and Sarah both were aware that the birth of the heir was not solely of their own doing. The miraculous enters the picture with great clarity in this matter. Sarai/Sarah was barren and past menopause (Gen. 17:17-19; 18:11) and would bear the son of promise to a man who would be one hundred years old at the time of birth. In a manner known only to GOD, He awakened this quiet womb from its barrenness for His purpose.

The name of this heir was also predetermined by GOD. That name is associated with the surprised, almost scornful, laughter of each of his parents (Gen. 17:17-18; 18:10-15), but it was given before their responses were manifested. Again, GOD was in complete control of the rollout of this, the first **father-son** relationship that was intended to represent in the earth the divine **FATHER-SON** relationship. These two fellows, Abraham and Isaac, were to be an important part of building the presence of the Kingdom of GOD in the earth. Their relationship was also the vehicle for building the practical model of the eternal through **father-son** relationships in the earth. The existence of the Abraham-Isaac **dyad** was of critical importance to GOD.

Abraham's misstep with the Philistines (Gen. 20:1-3) notwithstanding, things occurred according to GOD's plans and Isaac arrived in a timely manner. From the time of their awareness of Sarah's pregnancy, everyone in Abraham's camp knew this was to be the heir. One can only imagine their excitement about this arrival and their concern for the health of their mistress—except on the part of Hagar, who was teaching her son Ishmael to be contemptuous (Gen. 21:8-10). It could have been otherwise, but this was the route Hagar had chosen years before and it would be continued now. Obviously, this birth meant the loss of almost everything to her and her son. Everlasting bitterness and enmity was to be its fruit by the prophecy of GOD Himself (Gen. 16:7-12).

By the time of Isaac's weaning, probably on his fifth birthday,[2] conditions had again become intolerable between Sarah and Hagar. This time Sarah asked Abraham to handle the matter (Gen. 21:8-10), and she stated in particular the need to maintain great clarity concerning the identity of the heir. The only apparent solution so far as Sarah was concerned was the expulsion of Hagar and Ishmael from the camp. Abraham didn't like that idea very much, but the LORD assured him it was okay and that Ishmael would be okay (Gen. 17:20). Now the nuclear family at the heart of the camp could be in proper order for the work of GOD to commence. There was no ambiguity as to the **inheritance** and continuity.

SCHOOLING THE HEIR

We know very little of Isaac's life after Ishmael's dismissal until the time of Abraham's sacrifice of Isaac in Genesis 22. It seems quite reasonable, though, to suppose that most of his time was spent learning how to be the true son and heir of Abraham. Once the contender Ishmael was banished from the camp, it had to be apparent that the heir was present in the person of Isaac. We can only imagine the doting of his parents and the smiles of the servants as the toddler went about getting into everything. Many of the servants probably received assignments relating to his care and his education. It is likely that to be selected as one of Isaac's helpers was something desirable among the servants. Only the best persons in each skill set would be allowed to attend to his needs.

The "prince" was born and the whole camp had the responsibility to see to it he was cared for and well trained. We may imagine Isaac interrupting a meeting between Abraham and his chief herdsmen as they discussed which pasture to scout or the best place to find water at that time of year or any other of the numerous decisions that had to be made. Surely he was allowed to attend any such events and to learn how to take care of the animals and the camp and its people by way of authentic involvement.

Over time, the proud father Abraham would encounter his trade and treaty partners. Given the lifestyle of the camp, these meetings were infrequent enough that a great deal of formality must have been involved when such encounters occurred. As Isaac grew old enough and strong enough to be with his father, he would be there to observe the rituals and to get to know his father's trade partners and friends. They would come to know him as well. This would give Isaac the commercial education he needed to be the chief man of the camp. Surely, before he was even a grown man he would have been permitted or encouraged to engage in some of that commerce himself on behalf of his father, his mother, and his own future. He would learn to be *about his father's business*[3] in these experiences.

We may imagine also the times when Abraham took quiet time to teach Isaac who he was and about his ancestors; about who GOD was and about the covenant GOD had made with Abraham; and helping Isaac to understand who he was in the whole thing. Surely, the **patriarch** carefully instructed his son in these important matters. They were such important matters that Abraham had uprooted his entire camp and followed GOD into a land he had not known. They were important enough that he had expelled Ishmael from the camp.

Isaac's education must have been quite extensive because all of everything was to be left to him along with the responsibility to walk in the knowledge of the covenant and its promise and requirements. This young man was to carry the promises forward and preserve them in his own progeny until all was fulfilled. From Abraham's perspective Isaac was, in essence, the vessel of eternity.

ROAD TO MORIAH

Some years pass before we encounter Isaac again in scripture. Using the biblical narrative as our guide, the next event occurred when GOD instructed Abraham to take Isaac to Mount Moriah (Gen. 22:2). This happened before he was thirty-seven years old, but beyond that we don't know when. It seems likely that Isaac was grown or nearly grown at the time, but that is uncertain. However old he was, he made the trip with Abraham with two of the younger servants to meet their needs along the way. It appears that Isaac was not familiar with the instructions that GOD had given to Abraham. It is also unlikely that Abraham had informed Sarah of his instructions. Given the duration of the journey, it is probable that they set out from Abraham's headquarters at Beersheba. It appears that by that time in their lives Sarah lived full time in the more temperate climate of Hebron. This also argues for a more advanced age for Isaac as they set out on this journey.

For Isaac, this was merely a journey with his father, probably one of many they had made together. The small number of servants and burden beasts would indicate a short journey. Perhaps Abraham even informed Isaac of the destination and that the trip was for a sacrifice. It would be natural for Isaac to go along to continue to learn how his father served his GOD. In any event, the narrative suggests Isaac did not know that death awaited him atop Moriah. It appears that only Abraham had that information.

When they got near the place, Abraham and Isaac separated themselves from the young servants (Gen. 22:5) and proceeded to the actual place where the altar was to be built. Isaac played an active role. It seems quite natural that any son would ask the question he asked of Abraham regarding the sacrifice (Gen. 22:7-8). Abraham's answer was satisfactory to a son who trusted his father, and they got on with the preparations for the sacrifice. The gathering and piling of the stones that were to be the altar went on apace. The wood was arranged atop the stones. Still, though, GOD's provision had not appeared and Isaac must have begun to wonder, but at any rate he did not question his father further on the matter.

At some point, when all was prepared, it became necessary to deal with the purpose of the journey. Isaac would have to be placed on the altar and the sacrifice enacted. Somehow Abraham bound Isaac. How he went about such a thing is not specified. Nor, as noted before, are we informed as to Isaac's age at this time. Abraham's emotions at that moment must have been almost overwhelming. How could he give up his beloved son, the heir from his own body that GOD had promised him so many years before? Why would GOD require such a thing of him? Likewise it is hard to imagine that Isaac remained calm any longer either as his father began to bind him to place him on the altar. If Isaac was a grown man, as this writer believes, there might have been some sort of struggle between them as the reality of the event sank fully into Isaac's awareness.

Perhaps not. It may be true that Isaac submitted willingly to what his father Abraham began to do. Perhaps the **filial** love of the son for his father was such that he willingly played his part in spite of his emotional state. If Isaac was a grown man, as is likely, he could have easily overpowered his father who was himself in horrible agony at that moment. We simply do not know how this transpired. However it transpired, the event of the sacrifice was upon the two of them, these two parties to such a carefully arranged **father-son** relationship.

Textual evidence indicates that Abraham fully intended to sacrifice Isaac. This would be done by cutting his throat as he lay bound on the wood on the altar. Abraham's agony was at its peak. We must surmise that Isaac as well was as fearful as he had ever been in his life. Scripture indicates that the death of Isaac was only one quick movement away

11

(Gen. 22:10-11)–the movement that would draw the knife across the blood supply in Isaac's throat, thus ending his life in a very short period of time. Abraham had sacrificed animals before. Isaac had surely been with him at some of those sacrifices; he knew what was coming. Neither of them any longer had any reason to doubt the outcome or to delay it.

In that instant (not before) GOD's requirement was met. The Provider provided the substitution (Gen. 22:12-18). Abraham quickly cut the bonds that were on Isaac and he and his beloved son captured the ram caught by his horns. Try to imagine the unthinkable relief both Isaac and Abraham must have felt as the ram gave his life and GOD received the sacrifice. Isaac was at that time as near to death as he ever would be again until the end of his life many years later as an old man. What power must have entered the relationship between Isaac and Abraham that day as they experienced together this most graphic example of the provision of GOD! They must each have rejoiced in the other as never before. Their fellowship must have been almost not-of-this-earth after these events. When they were together later, words must have failed them as they remembered that day at Moriah. We take it for granted. They lived it to its last moment. They were there to shed the tears of thanksgiving as they embraced one another on that lonely hilltop.

In this event Isaac learned the full extent of his father's love for the LORD. Surely he already knew the history of Abraham's relations with GOD and of the promises and the covenant. Now he had the most intimate knowledge imaginable of what these meant to Abraham. Abraham was fully qualified now as a father because he was fully qualified as a son to his Father.

It is probable that when these things occurred Isaac lived with Abraham at Beersheba rather than with his mother at Hebron. When Sarah died in Hebron, Abraham journeyed there to see to her resting place. If it is true that Isaac lived with his father during those days, being employed in his father's business, he would have traveled to Hebron with his father. Their journey together to Sarah's funeral would have been a time of mourning, but they could console one another.

It is not likely that Isaac was absent when his father purchased the cave in the field of his friend, Mamre, for her tomb. By now, Isaac being thirty seven years old, the people of Hebron would be very familiar with him and he would be quite welcome as a witness to the formal proceedings. Likewise, he would be a participant at the funeral itself with his father. This would further solidify his identity.

ENTER THE WIFE

There seems little doubt that Isaac loved his mother. Scripture states that he mourned for her for three years[4] until he took Rebekah as his wife. In Rebekah, Isaac took consolation from the loss of his mother. While his mother was an important component of his past, his wife was to bear the sons who carried his future.

There is no indication in scripture that Isaac sought a wife. And unlike his father, there is no indication that Isaac ever took to himself a concubine. In time his father Abraham made arrangements to secure a wife for Isaac from among their relatives in Padan Aram, which is another name for *Aram Naharaim*. This woman would be of similar status to her great-aunt and mother-in-law Sarah, now deceased. Fetching a wife for Isaac was a serious mission with conditions set down by Abraham and entrusted only to his most faithful and capable servant (Gen. 24:1-9). His servant was successful and returned with Rebekah after having paid her family a proper bride-price.

For some time before this Isaac had made his home at *Beer Lahai Roi*. While waiting for his father's servant to return with his bride, he apparently moved to Hebron where he was waiting to meet her. They married as soon as they met. Isaac did not choose his bride. As we have just seen, his father had made all the arrangements. We can be sure, however, that all the preparations for her welcome and comfort were in place when she arrived. This was not a determination of mutual suitability. This was the consummation of the thing that had been already determined and awaited fulfillment.

Nothing is known of the early years of Isaac's and Rebekah's married life except that she apparently was barren (Gen. 25:21). Isaac prayed that she might have children and the LORD heard him. After twenty years of marriage, Rebekah was finally with child. Abraham was still alive at the time. Having reached one hundred sixty years of age, we must suppose he had had some concerns about having grandchildren, but the time had finally come.

After twenty years of longing for children, Rebekah finally found herself pregnant with twins. This troubled her pregnancy in some mysterious way. Scripture seems to say it was not the presence of the twins that was the problem. The problem in this view is that the twins had already begun to struggle with one another,[5] and it was this that caused the stress she was experiencing. When she sought the LORD, He consoled her with the knowledge that there were twins, and He told her what was going on with them. In doing so, He assured her that the pregnancy would be successful. He also made promises with respect to the nature and destiny of the two sons.

In the course of time, Isaac's two sons were born; the first was named Esau and the second, Jacob. The manner of their birth is of interest and is prophetic in its own right. When Jacob reached out of the birth canal and grasped Esau by the heel, he was already acting out the matters of the prophecy the LORD had given to Rebekah (Gen. 25:24-26). There are some differences of opinion about the meaning of his name, but most agree it means something like "supplanter." That is, he was to supplant his slightly older brother. As we know now, this proved to be the case.

Scripture tells us that Isaac formed a stronger attachment to Esau than he did to Jacob (Gen. 25:27-28). On the other hand, Rebekah favored Jacob over Esau. This dynamic undoubtedly added to the troubles between the two boys in the years of their maturing.

In any event the sons of Isaac were born and Abraham saw in the flesh the next generation of the promise after his son. The fulfilment of the promises could now continue. We must assume that from time to time the two boys were in the presence of their revered but aged grandfather. After all, they were about fifteen years old when he died.

Isaac was the **firstborn** of Abraham and the possessor of the attendant **birthright**. That **birthright** contained the **inheritance** of all the herds and flocks and campsites and wells and contracts and everything else that Abraham had accumulated over his lifetime. It came to include also custody of the very covenant that GOD had made with Abram/Abraham (Gen 25:5, 26:2-6). Upon his death, everything that had been Abraham's that he had not given away or spent would go to Isaac.

The timing of these things is not clear, but we do know that somewhere in this timeframe Abraham died. With his passing, all his wealth transferred to Isaac. Big brother Ishmael returned to the land to be with Isaac as they saw to the disposition of Abraham's body in the cave-tomb near Hebron (Gen. 25:9-10) where Sarah had been interred some thirty eight years earlier.

At some point as Abraham's two grandsons approached adult status, the events surrounding Esau's repudiation of his **birthright** occurred, probably after Abraham's death (Gen. 25:29-34). Up to that point in time, we must assume that Esau was the heir apparent. Isaac preferred him, and Esau seems to have had more in common with Isaac than Jacob did. And he was the **firstborn**. Whatever the full set of circumstances, Esau was laboring with some task in the fields and was quite fatigued when he returned to the camp. Jacob, who seemed to prefer to stay inside the camp (Gen. 26:27), had prepared some reddish lentil stew. When Esau became aware of the stew, he asked his brother to share some of it with him. This is the first of two instances in which Jacob "supplanted" Esau. When Esau requested the stew, Jacob bargained with him, offering to give him some stew in exchange for his **birthright**. Esau made the pledge and Jacob gave him some stew.

Let's consider what happened at that time. Esau was the **firstborn**. He clearly held the **birthright** as his property. There was only one such **birthright**. Hence, at this point in time, Jacob had no **birthright**. They both had inheritances coming as the sons of Isaac. Each of them would receive a portion of the wealth that Abraham had passed on to Isaac and that Isaac had added to prior to his death. Both were to be wealthy men. Both were living their lives in the largesse of being the sons of the chief man. As we have seen, though, the **birthright** was more than the **inheritance**. First, it was a double portion of the **inheritance**. Before the stew trade, Esau was set to receive two-thirds of Isaac's wealth at the time of Isaac's death. Jacob was to receive only one-third of the estate, which was still quite an **inheritance**. Esau, in addition to the two-thirds **inheritance**, was also to receive the position of chief man. He would have authority over his brother Jacob and their mother, as well as everyone else pertaining to the estate. He would become the business partner of his father's business partners. He would be the negotiator of treaties. He would be the host, however generous or not, of his brother. He was set to be the key character of the next generation insofar as the promise was concerned. He gave all that to his brother for some stew.

After this trade, Jacob owned the **birthright** along with everything that came with it. Henceforth, Esau would receive only one-third of the estate and would watch his younger brother take his place as the authority in all that pertained to the continuation of their father's and grandfather's place in the world. It was that cut and dried. It seems that everyone in the camp knew of the new arrangement. In any event, Esau could not retract the bargain. He, the **firstborn**, had surrendered the **birthright** of his own accord and with more than a modicum of contempt. This was an enormous insult to his father, but we have no record that Isaac ever said or did anything about the slight. For the time being things remained the same inside the family. This affront to Isaac, by the way, was even more horrendous than the affront of the prodigal son of New Testament infamy (Lk. 15:11-32). The reason is that the "prodigal son" requested his **inheritance** but he was not **firstborn**. Therefore his **inheritance** was a minor share of the wealth of his father. His request implied that he could not trust his father or that he was too impatient to stay under his father's care while his wealth increased. Rather, he chose to harm his father to follow his own dreams. Esau, in *his* actions, despised his father in every way when he traded away the **birthright**. It was as though he declared in that moment that everything his father was and all that was his in the future was worth no more than a bowl of stew. While we might tend to feel sorry for Esau, the harsh reality is that his actions were indefensible and unforgivable.

LIKE FATHER LIKE SON WITH THE PHILISTINES

The time came when there was a famine in the land. Abraham had gone to great lengths during his lifetime to make sure Isaac stayed in Canaan or in the uninhabited Negev. However, when there was another famine in the land of Canaan after Abraham's death, Isaac departed and moved to Philistia (Gen. 26:7-11). Here he repeated his father's sin of misrepresenting who his wife was because of his fear of the Philistines. The woman Rebekah was she from whose womb had sprung forth the nation in their generation. He dishonored that womb when he placed it at risk among the Philistines. One can only wonder how Rebekah felt about this behavior. But she went along with it nevertheless. When Isaac's deception was revealed, the Philistine king again acted honorably and disallowed the violation of Rebekah. The king's edict was clear: she was to be respected—or else.

It was here in Philistia, early in his stay, that we have a record of GOD's first contact with Isaac to discuss the future and the continuation of His arrangements with Abraham (Gen. 26:2-5). In this instance, GOD repeated many of the things He had committed to Abraham and was very clear that these things were now passing on to Isaac for their continuation. The LORD also made it clear to Isaac that in so doing He was honoring Abraham's obedience.

It is not clear exactly how long Isaac remained in Philistia, but there were two additional events of notice. First, the LORD Himself warned Isaac not to go to Egypt (Gen. 26:2-5, 24). Second, Isaac planted crops and reaped a bountiful harvest, and he was a shepherd.[6] This implies a sojourn of some significant period of time, probably several years at least, although it is impossible to determine this with any accuracy

Finally the Philistines became aware that Isaac had grown more prosperous than they and demanded that he be sent away from their midst. At this point the text preserves a curious fact. After Abraham's death, the Philistines had filled in a number of wells he had dug during his time among them (Gen. 26:17-22). It appears that Abraham had remained on friendly terms with the Philistines after the treaty with King Abimelech that was signed before Isaac was born. However, after Abraham's death, the treaty was repudiated by the Philistines. They voided the treaty by filling in Abraham's wells. It is clear that by allowing Isaac to settle among them at the time of the famine they were still on friendly terms, but no longer felt bound by the treaty.

These things matter because they give us a glimpse at a couple of interesting phenomena. First is the fact that at the level of man-to-man or **brother-brother**, death ends a relationship and any vows associated with it. This is in contrast to the eternal nature of **father-son** relationships when those follow the standard. The second interesting phenomenon is that a new treaty was reached between Isaac and the Philistines even though they wanted him gone. This came about as he traveled back toward the home of his father Abraham. As he was on the road to Beersheba, his servants unstopped one of the wells the Philistines had filled. The Philistines claimed it for themselves, so Isaac moved on easterly. As he moved, his servants dug two additional wells that the Philistines then insisted were theirs (Gen. 26:19-21). Isaac obligingly moved on and his servants dug a third well that the Philistines did not quarrel about (Gen. 26:22). That was pretty much the nature of the negotiation over the boundary between Philistia and Isaac's own territory.

After this, Isaac returned to Beersheba, where Abraham had lived much of his life. The LORD spoke to him again in Beersheba (Gen. 26:23-25). This was a reaffirmation of the promises He had made to Abraham. On this occasion Isaac built an altar near Beersheba as his father Abraham had done many years earlier. This was an interesting event in that it nailed down Isaac's understanding of the promises in the same way and in one of the same places where Abraham had also marked his understanding with GOD. Also, Isaac's servants found new water there. The finding of water was very important in that country as there were no nearby rivers. Only flowing, productive water wells could provide what was needed for Isaac's camp.

Just as had occurred with his father Abraham many years earlier, the Philistine leaders came to Isaac there at Beersheba. They told him that they had noticed that GOD was with him and wanted to formalize with him an agreement of friendship and, more importantly, the boundary between their territories of influence. The Philistines departed peacefully and there is no sense that any violations of the treaty ever took place. Nor, in fact, did Isaac ever again go into any country other than his own.

Scripture records that some while after this, when Esau and Jacob were forty years old, Esau took two wives (Gen. 26:34-35). These women were Canaanites, specifically, Hittites. Sixty years earlier, because of Abraham's concerns about Isaac, Abraham had sent a senior servant to *Aram Naharaim* to fetch a bride for Isaac so that he would not marry a Canaanite. Surely, Esau and Jacob knew this story. But, for whatever reason, Esau chose to marry Canaanite women. Perhaps it was because no provision had been made for wives for himself and Jacob. We cannot be sure of his reasons of course, but he had married women from the race with the curse of slavery on it. We see later that this was unacceptable. The Canaanite daughters-in-law were not popular with Isaac and Rebekah. Of course, Esau had already repudiated his **birthright**. It seems he made unfortunate choices, even though his father still preferred him over Jacob.

JACOB'S DECEIT

The biblical narrative records that sometime later an event occurred that finally precipitated the crisis between the sons of Isaac (Gen. 27:1-40). It appears that Isaac's eyesight became significantly diminished over the years until he became fairly inactive in the matters of the camp because of it. On a certain occasion he sent his favored son, Esau, on a special errand. It was Isaac's desire to have some game in his diet rather than the same old sheep and goat. Esau was to fetch the game for his father and to prepare it using some special recipe Isaac favored. Esau seemed quite willing to go and carry out his father's wishes in the matter. Isaac was concerned about what he felt was his impending death. His intention was to bless Esau upon receipt of his food. This was to be a rich blessing, as we shall see.

Rebekah became aware of this arrangement as it was being made (Gen. 27:5-6) and decided to use it to the advantage of her other (and favored) son, Jacob. If Jacob could receive the patriarchal blessing instead of Esau, it would firmly and unquestionably position Jacob as the heir in every sense. After all, the patriarchal blessing was in essence a prophecy. In pursuit of this outcome, Rebekah instructed Jacob in carrying out a ruse on his father that would result in a father's blessing for his son; in this case a patriarchal blessing including the installation of **primacy** (Gen. 27:5-13).

At this point it is pertinent to examine the relationships involved. Isaac inhabited two **father-son** relationships. One of these was with Esau his **firstborn** and the one with whom he had the closer relationship. There were dimensions in this relationship that were not present in his other **father-son** relationship with Jacob. The Esau relationship not only involved the **firstborn**, but also had originally involved the **birthright** that normally accompanied the position of the **firstborn**. Even after Esau ceded his **birthright** to Jacob, Isaac was still strongly attached to Esau.[7] Esau was simply more like his father, which probably had something to do with the preference.

The other **father-son** relationship, the one with Jacob, was one that we may be sure was also filled with **paternal** love, but it was not as close as the one with Esau, even after the affair with the **birthright**. The sons thus presented Isaac with a kind of split loyalty. On the one hand, he had a closer relationship with Esau, while on the other hand Jacob was now to be the chief heir and the one who inhabited the position of leadership of the camp and the emerging nation. Isaac likely continued to spend time and do chummy things with Esau, but he also had to prepare Jacob to be the chief heir. Perhaps, though, Isaac was not really tending to these things yet, even though his sons were now past forty years of age.

The ruse Rebekah concocted and helped Jacob carry out consisted of three parts (Gen. 27:8-17). First, they had to disguise some goat using the recipe that Isaac liked so well. Then a disguise had to be constructed for Jacob himself in such a way as to convince his nearly blind father that he was Esau. These things had to be done quickly, as they did not know when Esau would get back to camp with a deer or whatever. This they did.

When his son Jacob came to him, Isaac was uncertain who it was. He asked for the unknown person to identify himself. Then came the third part of the ruse. When Jacob claimed to be Esau, he probably didn't sound right to Isaac, who asked to touch him to verify his identity. He thought he heard Jacob's voice, but his physical inspection suggested Esau. This too was the result of Rebekah's careful planning. Even after the physical inspection, Isaac was still unsure, so he asked again for verification. Jacob lied again and verified that he was Esau. Then Isaac tried one more time to verify which son was before him. He smelled Jacob but perceived the smell of Esau because Jacob was wearing Esau's clothes. In four things Isaac had failed to expose the ruse, even though he was suspicious. Really, there were five things, in that when Jacob presented himself as Esau, Isaac was surprised at the quickness of his successful hunt (Gen. 27:18-27).

Having concluded that Esau was indeed before him and that he had the delightful meal to look forward to, Isaac proceeded with the patriarchal blessing (Gen. 27:27-29). The first part of the blessing Isaac uttered had to do with *prosperity*, something he himself was well familiar with. The second part of the patriarchal blessing promised his son ***primacy*** in the affairs of life, to include even national influence. As we know, this was irrevocable. Even though Isaac had been deceived, he had pronounced the blessing and it could not be changed even in spite of the deception. This is what Esau soon discovered, to his strong disappointment.

When the ruse was exposed soon after, Isaac was upset along with Esau at the trickery of Jacob, but he maintained that the blessing was final (Gen. 27:30-40). It is not clear how he had intended to separate the **primacy** from the **birthright** to begin with, but it appears that he had intended to do just that. But now it was impossible to separate the two. Our Father is constant in what He does, and Isaac had learned this principle from his father. Both the **birthright** and the patriarchal blessing belonged to Jacob, as both Isaac and Esau realized quickly. Jacob had supplanted or replaced Esau twice, and Esau ranted about it, but it was too late.

Isaac did provide a blessing for Esau, but it did not include any sort of **primacy**. In fact, while it was generally positive, it placed Esau in a secondary status to Jacob, just as the LORD had specified to Rebekah during her pregnancy. Isaac could not or would not undo what GOD had done.

Esau was quite angry as these matters were concluded, and he determined to kill Jacob in revenge (Gen. 27:41). His plan was to strike as soon as Isaac died, which he believed would be very soon. As it turned out, though, quite a few years passed before the death of Isaac. He was already past one hundred years old by that time, but lived to be about one hundred eighty years (Gen. 35:27-29). Other passages indicate it was at least another fifty years, probably more like sixty, before his death. Had Esau carried out his plan, he would have had a long wait.

We don't know how much time transpired, but Rebekah soon learned of Esau's intent to kill his brother. This probably was inevitable because of the close-knit community in which they all lived. Interestingly, it seems she did not tell Isaac of Esau's plan. Rather, she used yet another ruse to thwart Esau's intent, a ruse she knew would appeal to Isaac: finding a wife for Jacob (Gen. 27:46 – 28:5).

Abraham had brought his wife with him when he came to Canaan. She was a free "Aramaen," as he himself was. So important was this to him that when it came time for Isaac to have a wife, Abraham went to great lengths to be sure she was not a Canaanite. In fact, his efforts focused on a wife from his own kinsmen in *Aram Naharaim*. This bride was purchased with a great bride price and considerable effort. She was Rebekah herself. Neither of them could have forgotten these facts as they contemplated wives for their sons.

Esau had disappointed them both in this matter. At about age forty he had married two Canaanite (Hittite) women. Surely he knew his family history and the story of the heroic effort to gain a proper bride for his own father years earlier. In all fairness, Esau was the same age when he married the two Canaanite women as his father had been when he married Rebekah. But he had disappointed his parents nonetheless (Gen. 26:34-35). We can wonder whether he discussed the matter with them before marrying his two wives.

Nevertheless, these wives supplied Rebekah the pretext for saving the son of her own preference, Jacob. It is interesting that she did not tell Isaac what her real motivation was in the matter. Surely he would have wanted to save his own son, but it is not clear what he could have done in order to bring that about. After all, Esau's plan was to wait until Isaac was dead.

First, Rebekah prepared Jacob for his departure and told him to go among his kinsmen back in her original home. The purpose, she told Jacob, was so he could escape Esau's wrath. Next, she brought a complaint to Isaac concerning Esau's wives, claiming that they vexed her and she wanted no such wife for their other son. Again, given their own history, she knew this would strike a chord with Isaac. Isaac then sent for Jacob and sent him on the journey to *Aram Naharaim*, or Padan Aram, as the area is sometimes called. In commissioning Jacob, Isaac instructed him to find a wife after he arrived at his mother's family (Gen. 28:1-2).

One component of the commission with which Isaac sent away his son Jacob was another significant blessing (Gen. 28:3-4). While it was similar to the blessing given when Jacob deceived him, it was an even stronger blessing. It was also more explicit concerning the land itself. One suspects that Isaac feared that he would not see Jacob again, and that he wanted to be sure Jacob was reminded of where his destiny lay.

This is pretty much all we know about the life history of Isaac, although he lived for at least another fifty years. He did eventually see Jacob again, as well as all of Jacob's sons after the family returned to Canaan from Padan Aram about twenty years later. In fact, Isaac lived for about thirty years beyond that, which meant that he even got to know Benjamin, the youngest son of Jacob.

Surely Isaac rejoiced to see the promises of GOD coming true in the lives of Jacob and his twelve sons. He was still alive when the various misfortunes befell Joseph, his death coming about thirteen years later. In fact, Joseph was released from prison about the time Isaac died. It had been Abraham's desire that Isaac not leave Canaan because of the prophecy of the LORD concerning the bondage of Abraham's descendants. From Abraham's perspective it would be good if Isaac never left so that thing could not come true. The LORD honored that desire of Abraham and, as far as we know, Isaac went nowhere outside Canaan other than the area occupied by the Philistines and slightly into the northern reaches of the Negev. His death then opened the way for Jacob's journey to Egypt that awaited the positioning of Joseph in that kingdom.

Isaac himself was witness to the fact that the patriarchal anointing was going to Jacob and that a large number of descendants was on the way so that the occupying of the land was nearly within reach. Of course, he probably also had opportunities to visit with Esau from time to time even though Esau had moved a ways away. In fact, we know that at the time of Isaac's death, Esau was able to aid his brother Jacob at the funeral in Hebron (Gen. 35:29). They buried Isaac together and the threats of Esau were forgotten.

In the great silent period between Jacob's departure from Canaan to gain a wife who would please Isaac and Rebekah, Jacob is definitely the star. There was not anything else for Isaac to do with his part of the fulfillment of the purposes of GOD. As was the case with Abraham, scripture is quiet regarding the latter years of Isaac's life. Surely, he was able to rest. We may infer that the time at which Jacob moved his family to Hebron was well before the death of Isaac, at least fifteen years. During that time, Isaac surely clarified his estate in such a way that at the time of his death everything was in order. It is likely that Esau visited from the south on occasion and that full peace was insured between the two sons of Isaac well before his death.

WHAT ABOUT ESAU?

Isaac had two sons, Esau and Jacob. They were twins, with Esau arriving a few minutes earlier than Jacob. By definition Esau was the **firstborn** (Gen. 25:25). By expectation he possessed the **birthright**. The **birthright**, which Esau received by default, contained a number of elements. The realization of virtually all of those **birthright** elements was a matter of the future. Other than an acknowledgment that he was the **firstborn**, the *b'c*ʰ*or,* who possessed, in trust, the **birthright**, the *b'c*ʰ*orah*, there was not much tangible *property* at the time of his birth and childhood.[8] The full nature of the **birthright** was in its future value. While Esau would be trained and educated for his **birthright**, most of it would come in the form of **inheritance** and position at the time of his father's death.

We know, of course, that the LORD Himself spoke to Rebekah some time before the birth of her twin sons (Gen. 25:23-24) and specified the nature of the relationship between them. However, it was possible to hope that the **birthright** would remain intact anyway. Perhaps the conditions of the prophecy of the LORD would not come to pass. Perhaps they would not be onerous. Perhaps Esau would be the prime actor in Isaac's estate and the conditions of the prophecy still be met. Who knew specifically? There were difficulties, however, in that He mentioned that the younger would rule over the older. That would be hard to get around if it manifested itself as GOD had said it would.

In any event, we do know that over some time after the day of birth alignments were made inside the household of Isaac. Whereas before he had been the father of no one, he now had two sons. As a result, he inhabited two **father-son** relationships, one with each of the two sons. Esau and Jacob now inhabited a **fraternal**, or **brother-brother**, relationship. Each relationship had its own dynamics. The **fraternal** relationship of Esau-Jacob was difficult even from the time they were in Rebekah's womb (Gen. 25:22-24). In fact, their conflict was the source of the distress Rebekah experienced during the pregnancy.

Isaac's camp must have been an interesting place. His preference for Esau over Jacob probably led to more emphasis on the broad range of skills needed to run things. Esau's tutors probably helped him learn to govern, to shepherd, to know the land and so forth. Jacob was probably given similar training, but the emphases would have been different. Esau was trained to rule while Jacob was trained to be useful. Esau was to be chief man with Jacob as more or less a prince in the camp. As prince, he would not rule, but would have rights to the things of the camp. Perhaps this is the reason that scripture emphasizes the different temperaments of the two sons. Esau was a hunter, while Jacob preferred to hang out in the camp. Esau was aggressive and unafraid, while Jacob was taught to remain in the background and defer to his brother.

The personality and skills that Esau developed were attractive to his father. He was apparently the natural leader to whom Isaac wanted to leave his estate. It seems that Esau returned his father's affections. This **birthright** contained not only **inheritance** and leadership; it also contained a closeness to the father in the Isaac-Esau relationship. Certainly Esau knew that he was the favorite of his father. Esau knew he was the **firstborn** and he knew that he possessed the **birthright**. This might well have led to some degree of contempt on his part for his brother Jacob.

The ill feelings Esau probably had for his brother undoubtedly were magnified by the prophecy the LORD had pronounced to Rebekah (Gen. 25:23). How could he possibly "serve" this camp-boy? What characteristics did Jacob possess that could make such a thing possible? Even if Isaac had not been partial to one son over the other, he still had the **birthright** and position of **firstborn**. This "other son" could in no way be superior to him. Things like these must have resonated in Esau's mind and heart. Isaac's behavior did little to assuage such feelings because, we may infer, Isaac probably agreed with him.

Of course Isaac knew perfectly well the content of the "conversation" between Rebekah and the LORD, but we may safely infer that this did not dissuade him, either in his feelings about his sons or in the way they were trained and educated. Esau received every encouragement from his father and proceeded through his formative years fully expecting to be in charge in the fullness of time. He was ready to be the chief man and there were no contenders, certainly not Jacob.

There were no other brothers or sisters revealed to us in scripture. Given the rather thorough biblical discussion of this nuclear family, we can safely infer that none existed. This means that the camp consisted of four free persons, or "citizens," at its core. Abraham was still alive but lived elsewhere. Everyone else was a servant of one kind or another. As Esau and Jacob learned to understand the covenant that GOD had made with Abraham and its extension to Isaac, they became informed about relationships as GOD was building them into their family. From time to time they were probably in the company of their grandfather Abraham, who reinforced their knowledge and understanding of GOD Himself. Including Abraham, there were still only five citizens of the "great" nation GOD had spoken of. Hence, there were no other persons in the third generation to whom Esau would pay great attention. How much more sure of his position in the scheme of things could he have been? Everything was in place for his accession as the third **patriarch** of this nation GOD was building from the old man Abraham. What could go wrong? When the boys were fifteen years old, Abraham died.[9] Then there were only the four citizens of the great nation.

At some point in time, probably after Esau and Jacob had become grown men, an incident occurred in Esau's life that changed everything for him (Gen. 25:29-34). This was the event of his infamous trade of his **birthright** for a bit of stew. At the time this event happened, Esau's position was such that whatever affected him affected everyone else in the camp. As **firstborn**, and second only to his father, Esau's needs and doings were focal points to this group of people. We have no way of knowing what he was doing "in the field" that day, but he was really hungry when he got back to the camp. Apparently, as he came into the camp he quickly came across Jacob's tent. It is not likely that was where he was headed, but that's where he found himself. Perhaps it was the aroma of the stew combined with his hunger that led him to his encounter with Jacob. Perhaps Jacob's stew was famous in the camp.

That would be consistent with Jacob's image as a camp boy. Who knows? Whatever the reason, Esau found himself in Jacob's area of the camp.

Not surprisingly, Esau asked for some of the stew. Surely he was right to assume that he would get some of the stew simply for the asking. Perhaps he had eaten Jacob's stew many times before. On this occasion, however, a strange thing occurred. Rather than simply share the stew, Jacob asked to make a bargain with Esau: Esau's **birthright** for a bowl of stew. This was a very bold request. Perhaps Jacob had planned for it for years. Or, perhaps, it was completely spontaneous. Jacob may have sensed vulnerability in his hungry brother and quickly took advantage of the situation. In any event, had we been there observing, we would not have expected much more than scornful laughter from Esau. After all, Jacob was requesting virtually the whole world in exchange for the bowl of soup that Esau wanted.

Esau might have thought something like, "What an outrageous request!" Surely Jacob did not expect such a transfer to occur. It was too far beyond reasonable to be real. Esau could, at that point, have broken off the encounter. Surely there was some other food at another tent nearby. It was his camp, after all, and almost no one was more important or revered than he was. He quickly would have come upon other food that would have been quite acceptable.

But that is not what Esau did. In the condition of his deep hunger of the moment, he made a disastrous calculation. He concluded that he would accept the transaction proposed by his brother. In front of witnesses, he said out loud something like, "Aw, what difference does it make. I'm so hungry I will agree to this outrageous bargain so I won't starve." That is paraphrased, but it captures the spirit of his speech at the moment. Jacob provided Esau a bowl of stew, which he ate and went on his way, no doubt refreshed from his serious hunger. It was probably only later that he really took time to think about what had transpired. Apparently, he did not take it very seriously at first. Only later, when the implications of his actions became clear, would the realization of his error begin to sink in.

What is really important is what this event tells us about the character of the man and the importance of the spiritual aspects of his life as far as he was concerned. At the spiritual level, Esau had just thrown his whole life in his father's face. On the spur of a careless moment, Esau spat upon everything that Isaac had done for him and prepared for him. In an instant, nearly all of what had been perceived as his great destiny was gone. Now he would be as Jacob had always been. Jacob had gained from him virtually everything at very little cost. Some stew was received in exchange for the status of chief man in the third generation of the great nation. Esau's status in the camp began to diminish greatly as people realized the import of what had happened.

Apparently, the event came to be widely known. In such a tight-knit community it would have been impossible to keep such a thing hidden. It seems to be the case, though, that Isaac continued in his favoritism toward Esau. We cannot speak to whether other things changed, but that, at least, remained constant. A reasonable scenario is that the change of Esau's status was generally known and accepted. In this case, the camp shifted its allegiance to Jacob but remained wary of the favored status that Esau retained with his father. If this was the way of it, there would be tensions in the camp, but the revere in which Isaac was held would keep the peace as long as he was alive.

The family went and lived among the Philistines for a time after the **birthright** transfer occurred (Gen. 26:1). The sons are not mentioned during the sojourn but were surely there. In a sense, the family members were refugees. During that time, Isaac had great favor from the LORD and became significantly wealthier. And Esau had to endure the fact that his share was the smaller, half as much as that of his brother. We may safely assume that his resentment of Jacob grew significantly.

Some time passed after the triumphal return of the Isaac family and camp to Beersheba on the borders of Canaan. Eventually, we encounter Esau again when his father sent him out for his favorite food. Isaac felt that his life was near its end and wanted a special treat from the hands of his favorite son (Gen. 27:1-4). Esau complied and was quickly successful in his quest. When he returned to the camp in a sort of triumph, he soon learned that Jacob had received a patriarchal pronouncement from their father. Then Esau was in a kind of mental agony. Isaac had given a significant spiritual benefaction that Esau had always believed was his. There was really nothing else that Isaac could give to him in terms of the future of the great nation. All of that was lost.

In his lament, Esau asked his father to give him something as well (Gen. 27:38-40). Isaac, in great agony of heart himself, prophesied for his son. All that the LORD would permit was that Esau would eventually become free of subjection to his brother. He would be free, but Jacob would be the heir.

Having lost so much, Esau's ire overflowed at that point. He vowed that at the time of Isaac's death, he would kill Jacob (Gen. 27:41). His love for his father would preserve Jacob's life until then, but that was all that held him back from his vengeance. But, as we know, mother Rebekah heard about his vow of vengeance and conspired to save Jacob.

Please note, we have just concluded that the **filial** love of Esau outweighed his poor level of **fraternal** love. As **filial** love is a response to **paternal** love, this is perfectly reasonable. It warns us again, though, that the absence of proper **paternal** love weakens the power of **fraternal** love.

ISAAC ben ABRAHAM – THAT DAY

At Moriah, as we have seen, GOD completed the process of making of Abraham a father in whom the fullness of human fatherhood could be seen. The LORD's testimony after he stopped Abraham from sacrificing Isaac is a very powerful testimony concerning the work that had been completed in him. *But Isaac was there too.* He too was a part of the scene involving the sacrifice of the only son. He *was* that son.

There is little doubt in my mind that Isaac was a grown man at the time. He easily could have overpowered his father to prevent the events that seemed to go forward that day. Scripture is silent on the matter because the task was the final shaping of Abraham. *But Isaac was there.* He had already asked his grieving father about the identity of the sacrifice.

It appears that Isaac willingly submitted to what was happening. If so, he offers to us the finest expression of **filial** love in scripture except for that of JESUS. He never sought to exercise power or authority in respect to his father Abraham. Imagine the love that transacted between the two of them before that day. Imagine the love between the two of them and the admiration of the LORD from that day forward. Isaac was the obedient, **firstborn** son of his father. He inherited thereby the full promises of GOD regarding the great nation.

In Isaac we see the son who was obedient to his father up to the point of his own death. This qualified him to become the carrier of the national destiny given by GOD. The path of his life was to oversee the coming to destiny of his son Jacob even though Isaac seems to have not been able to see that.

Please scan the QR code or go to the web address to view Corbett's video introduction to the book.

CHAPTER 2

THE THIRD PATRIARCH: JACOB IN THE SHADOWS

http://bit.ly/1ZhaJSA

Please go to ravensfood.everykindred.com for access to additional supplements to the book. Content will be added from time to time as desirable to support this book.

THE THIRD PATRIARCH: JACOB IN THE SHADOWS

The last of the three capital patriarchs was Jacob *ben* Isaac. By the time we arrive at the story of Jacob much of what was needed by way of groundwork for the "great nation" was already in place. GOD had established the necessary patterns and doctrines to make that possible. Patriarchal **primacy** was in place. **Father-son** relationships which were eternally purposed were now established in the earth. The stature of these three generations of men was firmly entrenched. Now came the time of the peopling of the promise. After all, for the first two generations there was only one qualified son in each. Ishmael and Esau were each dismissed in their own generations and would no longer cloud the issue.[10] Thus, the **father-son** patterns were kept fairly simple while the necessary order was developed. The time for the descendants to begin to grow in number had come. Growth in numbers gives us the opportunity to explore quite complex sets of **father-son** and **brother-brother** relationships for the purpose of gaining insight into how a larger system of GOD's promise in human beings looks and functions.

Let's say up front that Jacob was never "not-in-the-picture," as per the title of this chapter. He was just the second son as far as his father was concerned. Jacob became preeminent when his mother constructed a plan by which she convinced Isaac that it was good to send Jacob away to fetch a wife for himself. Her real motivation, as we have seen, was to protect him from his brother Esau's vow to kill him at a specific time. As it turned out, Jacob spent twenty years in a foreign country, during which time things changed back home in Canaan. Jacob met his father's requirements for return as soon as he married Leah and Rachel. However, his mother would not have been satisfied with his return at that time because of the continuing possibility of his murder at the hand of Esau. Not to worry; Rebekah's brother Laban kept Jacob in servitude for quite a while.[11]

Jacob spent the first half of his life in the context of the life of his father Isaac. Much of what we previously examined in Isaac's life we will consider again from Jacob's point of view in order to assess the impact of those events on his development. This is important because Jacob was a distinctly different character from his father with a significantly different destiny[12] in terms of its details, even though that destiny was the continuation of Abraham and Isaac. The herds Abram brought from *Aram Naharaim* survived and flourished under his care and then under the care of Isaac. They both, each in his turn, added other wealth to the estate they were passing along. When Jacob received that rich estate at the time of Isaac's death, it was added to the great wealth he had himself brought back from Abram's country of origin many decades after Abram arrived in Canaan.

SON OF PROMISE

When we considered the life of Isaac, one of the most cogent points was that he was the son of promise and had to be sorted out from Lot, Eliezer, and Ishmael for the sake of clarification as to **birthright** and **inheritance**.[13] Jacob was born to Isaac along with Esau. Before their birth, GOD had given very specific information to Rebekah concerning them (Gen. 25:22-23). However, Jacob's destiny was rendered somewhat ambiguous by the attachment his father felt toward his brother Esau. Isaac had a very strong **father-son** relationship with Esau that contained an assumption of the rights of the **firstborn**. One may even infer that Isaac intended to ignore GOD's "advice" when the time came for passing things on. In this case, the elimination of ambiguity came, in part, at the hand of the brother in question. Esau's surrender of his **birthright** (Gen. 25:31-34) took much of the ambiguity out of Jacob's destiny. His mother's arrangements rounded things off by inducing Isaac to confirm the prophecy of GOD given to her before the birth of her sons. While the outcome was inevitable, these matters had still needed clarification and were now clarified by the actions of Isaac, who was the **patriarch**.

Let's summarize the matter. Abram/Abraham was *selected by GOD* out of his generation to carry the weight of the Kingdom of GOD as it began in the earth in its typological format. Abram, after his positive response to his selection, was given the *promise of a son*[14] to carry on that identity. After Abraham's destiny passed to Isaac in the form of the covenant that GOD moved him into (Gen. 26:2-6, 23-25), he too needed an heir to carry matters forward. GOD caused him to wait for quite some time, but eventually the heir was on the way. The complication of twins required yet further *divine intervention*, which came in the prophecy to Rebekah. At the time that the LORD spoke to Rebekah, it became clear that Jacob was to be the son of promise in the next generation. Of course, the matter of the older brother now had to be resolved. It is in this matter that we see clearly the distinction between **paternal** and **fraternal** love.

In both cases, these "sons of promise," Isaac and Jacob had to be produced from the womb of a woman who had previously been barren. Why? Because this was GOD's work, not that of any man. Subsequently, in each case, a kind of sorting needed to occur so that all understood clearly the identity of the selected son of promise. This highlighted the divine selection process and removed the matter of selection from the hands of fallible men. We shall see that this promise-and-selection phenomenon will continue to carry forward in the succeeding generations, and even down to the kingship of Solomon.[15] How better to highlight the divine selection of the Only-Begotten so many years later?

JACOB'S EARLY LIFE

As I mentioned before, Jacob's early life was caught up in the complexity of the lives of his father Isaac and his older brother Esau. This complexity actually began with Rebekah's struggles during her troubled pregnancy with the twins after twenty years of barrenness. When she sought the LORD in the matter, He told her that it had to do with the nature of the future relationship of the two sons in her womb. Specifically, He informed her that the outcome of their struggle would be that the older of the two brothers would serve the younger (Gen. 25:23). In fact, the struggle for **primacy** was already under way in her womb as a precursor of what was to come. It is unusual for us to think that the future of children would be so strangely marked already before birth. Perhaps that was necessary as a sign to Rebekah that she should seek the LORD and that what He said in return was underscored from the very beginning of the lives of her sons. (Consider John the Baptist in Elizabeth's barren womb—Lk. 1:41-45).

These conditions, then, pre-dated the birth of Jacob and Esau: Esau was born first, yet Jacob was the son of promise, in this case, the bearer of the **birthright**. The significant complication was that the **birthright** went with the status of being the **firstborn**, and that was Esau. Some things had to change and some formal, public event had to take place to remove the **birthright** from Esau to Jacob. Although certainly not a **typical** phenomenon, it was not altogether unknown.

Let's suppose for the moment that Isaac had embraced the prophetic word that Rebekah received from the LORD as somehow binding on him. He could then have begun the lives of his sons from birth in such a way as to train Jacob for the **birthright** and Esau for the secondary role. In time, no doubt, Esau would come to resent this due to his having been born first, but the conditions for his acquiescence would have been set and managed in such a way as to insure the best outcome for the camp.

Unfortunately, Isaac did not choose to go that route. Instead, he allowed the individual inclinations of his sons to guide his actions, rather than the Spirit of GOD. Most likely there was an element of lethargy or non-decision-making in his actions. Esau was **firstborn** and the **birthright** was expected to go to him by default. No other person in the camp, not even Rebekah herself, could change that. Only Isaac had the authority to reassign the **birthright**. It may be that his natural inclination toward a close relationship with Esau caused him to permanently delay taking any actions to change the *status quo*. In the absence of any instructions from him, the camp's residents naturally would move in the direction of continuing to reckon the **birthright** to be Esau's. To do otherwise would be to offend the chief man. If we assume this was a matter of postponement, the longer it was postponed the harder it would be to make the changes necessary. So, the camp operated in such a way as to prepare for Esau's future rule. There just was not a "Jacob option" in play. Hence, Jacob remained in the shadows.

We may wonder about Rebekah's silence in these matters. Given what we may easily infer from scripture of her character, there was no silence between her and Isaac. Surely, she regularly reminded him of the announcement (Gen. 25:23) the LORD had made to her, especially considering her relationship was closer with Jacob than with Esau. It appears that Isaac simply disregarded it or postponed any actions related to it.

There can be little doubt that Esau and Jacob themselves knew of the promise. Each would, in his own way, bear the knowledge of those pronouncements. The import of those promises was very different to each of the two of them. Esau undoubtedly was not happy with the portent, while Jacob likely viewed it with growing anticipation. It is further very likely that the entire camp knew of GOD's pronouncements in the matter, but Isaac still needed to take some action for these things to become manifest insofar as the servants were concerned. Isaac's **primacy** was absolute for the people. The camp was largely ambivalent or unconcerned in the matter except for the personal servants of Rebekah, Esau and Jacob. Folks operated on a business-as-usual basis year in and year out. And nothing changed. Esau was still the **firstborn** with assumed **birthright** and was the choice of Isaac, at least by default. At the same time, Jacob was the chosen of GOD (and of his mother). Some sort of uneasy stalemate in these matters must have pervaded the camp. There is no information that Abraham was aware of these matters or that he ever spoke concerning them. These boys were his grandsons and that was good stuff. The situation was Isaac's to manage. In reality, this was to be perhaps *the* test of the exercise of his patriarchal **primacy**, which came from GOD. The test was not from man.

In fact, as we can see after the fact, the **father-son** relationship between Isaac and Jacob was destined to be the vessel of the eternal Kingdom. The Isaac-Esau relationship could not be that vessel. While Isaac determined essentially all things for the people of his camp, it was GOD Himself who determined how the great nation was to be identified. It was not, as we often assume by default, that Jacob was available at the right time. It was that Jacob was chosen in eternity by GOD to be the third **patriarch**. Isaac could not derail that. The sons of Esau were not to be the fourth generation in the great and holy nation. The **birthright** transfer was inevitable (Gen. 25:33).

To put it simply, Jacob was born into a difficult situation and he and his twin brother had already been struggling in the womb. The outcome of that struggle to become the **patriarch** after the pattern of Abraham and Isaac hung in the balance, but the outcome was pre-determined by GOD. It was the dynamics of arriving at that outcome that consumed so much of the energy of the family and the camp. The stakes were, after all, monumental and of eternal consequence.

So life began for Jacob as for Esau. Probably at first the *de facto* celebration of the end of the years of Rebekah's barrenness was tremendous and lasted for some time. Also, the care of the two boys jumped to the top of the list of priorities for the entire camp. Of course, most folks would not have a direct hand in that but it would be a focal issue for some time nonetheless. Perhaps there was even a need for wet-nurses to assist in the feeding. In time, the sons of Isaac would be weaned and begin to move about in the camp as they chose. The servants would be aware that the sons of the chief man were to be tolerated and cared for in every possible way. As soon as practical it would be made clear they were to be free to observe and to be involved in everything they wished as long as their safety was carefully protected. The two young masters would be allowed to express interest in whatever interested them. When Jacob inquired of a servant in some matter of skill, it would be the great honor of that servant to instruct and train him in that area of expertise, with the help of the most masterful members of the camp. Cryptically, the biblical text indicates that Jacob was interested primarily with what went on inside the camp environs, while his brother was more interested in the activities outside the camp. There is no indication that this was by any design of any person. It appears from the text this was simply a matter of individual inclinations (Gen. 25:27).

Of course, Isaac and Rebekah required that certain specific elements be included in the education and training of each of the two young masters. Isaac, operating in the belief or hope that Esau would succeed him, would be sure that matters of leadership were included in Esau's curriculum. On the other hand, it also seems certain that Rebekah would see that Jacob observed and received much of that same training as well. Certainly Isaac would not preclude Jacob learning of these things, but he would *insist* that Esau learn them.

That's about all we know of the early years. When the boys were fifteen years old, their grandfather Abraham died. Their father, along with "uncle" Ishmael, worked together to see to his funeral at the cave of Machpelah near Hebron. This might have been the first, or even only, time the two teenagers ever saw their uncle. Certainly after those events Isaac would have reminded the young men very carefully regarding their identity in the house of Abraham.

THE BIRTHRIGHT

Some years after grandfather Abraham's death and burial, the event that marked the basic change in the way the camp worked took place (Gen. 25:29-34). One might construct a scenario in which Jacob watched every time Esau left for an extended period and made sure to have a stew ready when Esau returned to the camp. That would be a strange proposition. It is much more likely that the **birthright** encounter was one that simply happened, from Jacob's perspective. It would have been too hard to contrive.

Being a man of the camp, it appears that Jacob gained some skill in food preparation. This undoubtedly was true for Esau as well. One might make a very weak case for some sort of plot but, again, the events of that fateful day, from a purely human point of view, appear to be simply coincidental. It is not likely that Jacob expected to possess the **birthright** before the day was out. He was just preparing some stew as he often did. Esau's arrival in the state of exhaustion in which he arrived was simply what it was. We cannot know why Jacob chose exactly that time to propose the **birthright** bargain, short of some sort of divine intervention. In that case, it was simply time for the transfer to occur and the LORD arranged the events to suit that purpose.

However it came about, when Esau requested some stew from his brother, Jacob presented the proposal right then and there. He must have been quite surprised when Esau accepted it. Whoever else in the camp witnessed the exchange must have been quite surprised as well. But the bargain was made and word must have spread through the camp in an instant. There is no record that Isaac or Rebekah said or did anything, but they must have soon known of the bargain. It was irrevocable, and it appears that everyone accepted that. Isaac would not undo the bargain. Even had he attempted to do so, the LORD would have intervened. In fact, hearing about the bargain must have been very painful to him because in it Esau so thoroughly despised all that his father had prepared and done for him.[16]

Jacob must have felt quite strange from the moment the bargain was proposed and accepted. It is easy to imagine that as Esau ate the stew, Jacob was in a sort of daze. It had come to pass at last. There can be no reasonable doubt he knew of the prophecy, but now it was coming to pass right there in front of everyone. As of that evening, Jacob possessed the **birthright**. It was simply his from that point on. Most of the implications of that were probably things he already knew about, but the reality of the change in his perceived future must have been almost shocking. He was not—and then he was—*that* son. The promise was on him. The entire camp had to begin to adjust to this new reality. Attitudes must have rapidly shifted for everyone. The identity of the new future chief man was now known among them and the validity of the prophecy of GOD (to Rebekah) was established, or at least mostly so.

The biblical narrative provides no information as to the continuing interactions between Jacob and Esau after the **birthright** transfer. We may suspect there was some unhappiness on Esau's part. We hope that Jacob was kind. How might Rebekah have reacted? Esau was also her son and no doubt she loved him as well, but her attachment to Jacob was stronger. And how would Isaac react over time? He loved Esau and was more attached to him. Now, though, the **birthright** was lined up with the word of the LORD spoken to Rebekah. The shift in his thinking toward Jacob as primary heir probably took some getting used to. However, he could look back on his own life and how his birth had confounded the hopes and expectations of Ishmael and his mother Hagar to see that GOD would have His way.

However the principals worked out their own adjustments to this foundational change, life went on in the camp. Duties were performed. Animals were born. Journeys to pasturage were conducted. Wells were probably dug. Kings and their representatives were negotiated with. Celebrations of birth and death were conducted. Life went on.

But Isaac had to adapt to the fact that his son Esau had rejected his identity for nothing more than a bowl of stew. There must have been times when Isaac pondered this unexpected event and found context for it. Perhaps he was tempted sometimes to try to undo the exchange. He could not. Had he done so it is likely that he would evermore have had to concern himself with other superficial behaviors in which Esau might engage, further threatening the estate. That estate was the seed of a Kingdom designated by GOD. These saner reflections surely guided Isaac as he made his psychological adjustments to the new reality. In time he must have moved on in his thinking to an understanding that this was the will of GOD.

Rebekah was surely happy when the transfer came about. To her way of thinking this was entirely what had been promised to her. The fact that she liked Jacob better than Esau was surely a bonus to her as she adjusted. It is likely that she was the main force in the changes in the camp's ways that would accommodate the transfer of birthright. Isaac likely left those matters to her.

Esau, after reality sank in, was surely devastated by what he had done. His dreams of the future were largely shattered. He now had to determine how to live in the presence of his brother. Further, he probably faced some real ego challenges as the story of his surrendering his **birthright** circulated through the camp. He really had very few options. He could rebel, but that would be foolish. He could decide to move on from the camp. At least initially, this does not appear to have been his decision. He could decide to adjust and hope for the best. He may have decided that he needed to be more careful of his brother's feelings from that point on. We simply do not know what his disposition was on the matter because scripture has not revealed it to us. At any rate, there was no hurry; the time for a final decision was still some time off in the future.

We cannot be sure of the timing, but at some point in time before Jacob and Esau were forty years old, there was a famine in Canaan. This particular famine was severe enough that Isaac decided to move his family and camp into Philistia until it passed (Gen. 26:1). Having made that move, Isaac was visited by the LORD, who first confirmed the covenant with him and then forbade him to move further down to Egypt (Gen. 26:2-3). An interesting component of this reaffirmation of the oath is that it was given when Isaac was not in Canaan. He was in Philistia, and the Philistines were not Canaanites. They were related to another son of Ham named Mizraim, which means Egypt.

While he was in Philistia, Isaac disrespected the sacred womb of Rebekah just as his father had done twice to Sarai/Sarah. The outcome was the same. The king was offended by Isaac's behavior and went about making sure the Philistines respected Rebekah (Gen. 26:10-11). When Isaac became quite noticeably rich with new wealth, the Philistines drove him away. His expulsion prompted new negotiations with the Philistines over the boundary between them, and a well at Beersheba. This marked the beginning of a new phase in Isaac's life. The twins were no doubt present as things were going on, but the narrative does not mention either of them during this period.

When Esau was forty years old, he married two Canaanite women. Scripture tells us that these weddings upset both Isaac and Rebekah (Gen. 26:34-35). There is no mention of Jacob marrying.

We are not informed how much time passed before the narrative resumed, but some number of years went by without significant event. Life went on. Animals were born and died and so forth. The time came when Isaac began to consider his mortality. Apparently he became nearly blind and thought his death was near even though it wasn't. So he sent for Esau and charged his oldest son with fetching him some spicy game and then prepare it in a special way he liked. Isaac proposed this in the form of a bargain (Gen. 27:1-4): if Esau would prepare him some tasty game dish, Isaac would bless Esau. The specific blessing of a **patriarch** has great power. It would not replace the **birthright**, but it had merit in itself. This bargain suggests that the relationship between Isaac and Esau was intact. Esau responded that he would comply with his father's wishes.

It is here where Rebekah's scheming came into play. Hearing the charge Isaac had given to Esau, she determined to hijack the patriarchal blessing and gain it for Jacob instead (Gen. 27:5-10). While this was not necessary for the **birthright**, it likely would place even greater distance in authority between Jacob and Esau. So, she took action.

Rebekah sent for Jacob and divulged her scheme to him. Jacob was skeptical because of the physical differences between he and Esau. They were **fraternal** twins, not identical twins. He rightly feared that Isaac might detect the ruse even though he was very blind. His concern was drawing down a curse upon himself rather than a blessing if his father discovered that he was not Esau . After all, Isaac's word was law. Rebekah assured Jacob that in that event she would take the curse upon herself should there be one.

Finally Jacob relented and fetched the goat for the meal along with the elements of the disguise he was to wear in his father's presence. When all was prepared, he took the spicy dish and presented himself to his father (Gen. 27:18-19). Isaac asked who he was, and the lies began. As Jacob had feared, Isaac recognized that his voice was not the voice of Esau When Isaac sought to confirm his son's identity, Jacob lied. We may infer that Jacob was quite nervous about the matter by then, but he was committed. There was nothing to do except see the entire thing through. Any other course of action would absolutely reveal the deceit.

Isaac, understandably suspicious, continued the interview by inquiring how it was that Esau had finished his errand so quickly. In his second lie of the evening, Jacob reported that he had experienced extraordinary success in the hunt. This appeared to further deepen Isaac's suspicions. After all, he had not yet heard Esau's voice, only Jacob's. In addition, he had not expected such quick success. So in order to satisfy his mind, the nearly blind Isaac sought to use his other senses to determine whether it was Esau or Jacob who was standing before him. His sense of touch did not give away the disguise because Rebekah had prepared Jacob for that. Still suspicious, however, Isaac asked Jacob again to verify who he was. Once again, Jacob lied and affirmed that he was Esau. At this point Isaac, apparently convinced, gave in and asked for the food. It was prepared just as Esau would have prepared it, so Isaac was satisfied upon eating it. Isaac then asked Jacob to come and kiss him. In this exchange, Isaac made one last attempt to detect whether there was a deception, and failed once again. Jacob was wearing Esau's clothes, which bore smells that Isaac would associate with Esau and no one else. The deception had succeeded. It's safe to assume that Jacob was extremely relieved at this point. He and his mother had set out to deceive his father and had succeeded. Now there would be no curse.

Isaac blessed Jacob at that point, believing he was blessing Esau.[17] It was a true prophetic, patriarchal blessing that he gave to Jacob. The blessing was a rich adjunct to the provisions of the **birthright** he had already acquired. Perhaps Isaac thought the blessing would compensate

Esau and ameliorate his loss of the **birthright**. In any event, he blessed Jacob in such a way as to reinforce his already considerable authority in the future. Jacob left his father that day without revealing that he had deceived him. He walked away with the patriarchal blessing that contained **primacy** in it.

Isaac was very agitated when, shortly thereafter, he discovered he had been deceived. Esau showed up with the meal of game he had prepared at his father's request, only to learn what had just transpired. The next few moments were dramatic for Isaac and Esau as they dealt with what had happened. In addition to losing his **birthright** some years earlier, Esau had now lost the primal authority in a patriarchal, priestly pronouncement. There was no remedy. It could not be undone (Gen. 27:37). Esau asked for and received another blessing, but it was only secondary in nature. The only real benefit it gave Esau was that it allowed him to leave and live outside the authority of his brother. There was no chance of ascendancy in this pronouncement.

Surely Jacob reported to his mother concerning the success of the deception even while Esau was in Isaac's presence. Undoubtedly, Jacob's and Rebekah's time together was considerably happier than the goings on between Esau and Isaac. At last, things had come together as Rebekah had hoped.

THE VOW OF ESAU

This drama set in motion the next set of significant events for the nation. Esau's first reaction was anger and a request that he still receive something from his father (Gen. 27:38). This being accomplished, Esau still had to deal with his feelings, which were even stronger than before. He had lost his **birthright** to his brother some years earlier and now he had hoped for a strong prophetic word from his father. He had lost that as well due to Jacob's deception and had only a subordinate prophecy that smacked of having to leave his father.

Before long, Esau vowed to kill Jacob as soon as Isaac died (Gen. 27:41). As did they all, Esau believed that time would come soon.

Somehow Rebekah found out about Esau's vow and determined to set things in motion to save Jacob from his brother's wrath. Informing Jacob of Esau's intentions, she instructed him carefully as to how to escape the threat by fleeing to her homeland. We can be sure Jacob immediately began to prepare for his escape, at least secretly.

This created another problem. If Jacob suddenly departed without warning, he likely would be pursued. After all, he was the heir apparent and his presence in the camp would continue to be expected whether Esau was angry or not. Not wanting to reveal to Isaac how serious the situation was, Rebekah concocted a scheme she knew would be attractive to Isaac: they would send Jacob off to find a wife. This would explain his absence to all and sundry and would not leave Isaac in a bad way.

We saw that some years earlier (probably 30) Esau had taken to himself two Canaanite (Hittite) women as wives. We noted earlier that they were a grievance to both Isaac and Rebekah. This was quite logical. After all, Abraham had gone to great lengths to find Rebekah as a bride for Isaac. There being no other free women in the camp, they could be expected to seek a wife for Jacob from somewhere else. The best place, they both knew, was Rebekah's homeland. There Jacob could find a free woman who would produce grandchildren for Isaac and Rebekah who would be citizens of the nation that was beginning. Esau's wives could not produce children who would be of equal status. This would be a final victory for Jacob in a sense. His children would be those expected of the son of promise. Among them would be the son(s) of promise for the fourth generation of this divine enterprise.

So it was decided. Isaac would send Jacob to Padan Aram to find a bride from among the kindred of Rebekah specifically (Gen. 27:46 – 28:2). In the short run, this would also remove Jacob from Esau's reach. Secretly, Rebekah proposed to send for him to come home when the troubles with Esau had faded somewhat. Altogether this plan would preserve Jacob's place but take him out of harm's way with no threat to his status or his **birthright**. Isaac would not have to be informed of Esau's vow, which would only add to his grief. For everyone except

Esau this was a good plan. Even for Esau it had advantages because he would not be reminded daily of his struggles with his brother and he might eventually get over his desire for revenge.

Isaac sent Jacob off with yet another blessing regarding his errand to find a suitable wife. He was specifically to go to his great-uncle Bethuel for the purpose of the covenant. We have no information as to the company with which Jacob left. It appears he did not leave with a bride price.[18] In any event, it appears that the whole thing was fairly quickly arranged, as Esau didn't know about it until after Jacob had departed.

Poor Esau. He learned of the displeasure of his parents in his Canaanite wives, so he arranged to marry a daughter of Ishmael, (Gen. 28:6-9) probably to please them. But once again he missed the mark.

THE ROAD TO THE KINGDOM

Jacob began his long northeastward journey and soon came to the region of Bethel, where his grandfather Abram/Abraham had built an altar so many years before.[19] In some ways, we may say that Jacob had led a fairly peaceful life. His early training was important, but was not particularly challenging. Isaac had likely seen to it that Esau was challenged because of the expectation he would become the leader. Jacob was not expected to have to carry the burden of leadership, so his curriculum would have been more passive. This was echoed in his general lifestyle, at least until he acquired the **birthright**. He had been present whenever he wished in most of the things that went on, but Esau's role had been prominent. Even as late as the encounter involving the blessing of Isaac, he had played the role of one yielding to his brother, having to resort to trickery rather than interacting with his father in a straightforward manner involving the future of the people.

But there were many things in his favor. He was one of the two sons of the chief man of the camp. He was one of only four "citizens" of the nation to come. He had acquired the **birthright**. He had not married among the Canaanites, a thing that both his grandfather and his father would have discouraged. He had, at least, observed his father caring for the camp. He now had a blessing, the contents of which included an implied **primacy**. Finally, he had a charge from his father to go and find an appropriate wife: as Eve to Adam, as Sarah to Abraham, as Rebekah to Isaac. In so doing, he was also avoiding a showdown with his brother.

Now he was to go and become the man who could wear the mantle of leadership of this people, not so much of the servants as of the citizens of the nation in the making. This was not known, of course, to the persons in the conversations that led to his departure. Nonetheless, it was now underway. In the adventures to come, Jacob would be alone to work things out, to learn to lead.

When Jacob left Beersheba that day, he was headed for a place of safety in which he would hopefully find an appropriate wife. He had never been apart from his mother and father. He had always been in a place of privilege. Now he would be alone for a time except for a small number of personal servants. There were no tents for him to wander about in. This was a real adventure with real dangers. Neither his mother nor his father would be there to help him. The large encampment he was accustomed to, basically a moveable village, would be traded for a very small number of tents that had to keep moving. He might have taken a few animals, but only for food. Jacob was stripped of nearly everything he had ever had or known and was going to a place he had never been.

AT BETHEL

Assuming the small party was riding animals, the stop at Bethel would have occurred on the second or third night after leaving home. It is noteworthy because Bethel was, as it were, the spiritual entry point for grandfather Abraham into Canaan. It was also the place Abram went to in order to renew his relationship with GOD after his return from Egypt. The area was not called Bethel yet, but it had become significant as a sort of focus for being in Canaan. Perhaps Jacob was not even aware that his grandfather had been there twice and had even built an altar there. Nevertheless, it was already, in some sense, holy ground.

At home in Beersheba, Jacob had enjoyed a very comfortable life. Now, at Bethel, he was reduced to using a rock as a pillow. This symbolizes the significant change that was underway in his life. Jacob was not a boy any more, but this kind of change would upset a person at most any age. Jacob's famous dream (Gen. 28:10-13) occurred that night in the area of Bethel. The dream also seems to have marked the passage he was going through.

The first recorded occurrence of contact between GOD and Jacob took place that night in the context of the dream. The LORD Himself spoke to Jacob in the dream and reinforced the direct link of his life with those of Abraham and Isaac. The announcement was about the same in content to those Abram and Isaac had received at the key times in their lives. The one distinct difference was that Jacob was leaving the land. Therefore, the LORD assured him that his departure was not permanent. He promised both to remain with Jacob and to insure his return to Canaan (Gen. 28:13-15). We cannot know how comforting this might have been to Jacob, but he now had GOD's word on it. This was more than an escape from Esau's wrath or a journey to acquire a wife. This was now a kind of mission for his GOD and the GOD of his fathers.

Jacob was impressed. The text makes it clear that he was in awe of the experience he had that night. He considered it a holy place. Jacob is the first person in scripture to call the place *Beth-el*, the house of GOD. There was a city nearby called Luz, but Jacob gave the place its new name of Bethel. This was due to the awesomeness of the experience of that night. Consider the other things he did before he left Bethel (Gen. 28:16-22). He made a pillar of the stone he had slept on. To him it seems to have been a holy pillow stone because of the dream he received on it. He anointed the pillow stone and gave the spot its new name. He then made a vow that if the LORD would care for his needs while he was away in a foreign land, he would honor that provision. He would further consecrate the place itself. Finally, he would give to GOD a tenth.

The last part of Jacob's vow is interesting. First, Levi was still in his loins[20] and Sinai was a long way off in the future. The Levitical tithe could not, then, have been what he was thinking of. Second, he would give the tithe to GOD. How was that to be accomplished without the Aaronic priests to receive it? Perhaps he thought back to the story of his grandfather handing over his tithe to Melchizedek. Considering the treatise on the matter of Melchizedek in the book of Hebrews, this is an interesting question for us. We must assume that Jacob at least intended to find some entity to whom to give his tithe so that he accountably gave the tithe that was the fruit of his vow. Using the Abraham and Melchizedek event as a model, he would find a person of suitable priestly authority to whom he would provide that tithe. That would be the accountability required. We are only left with the question of the identity of that accountability entity.[21]

We know that Jacob was the father of the men after whom the tribes of Israel took their names. These twelve, yet to be born, became the building material of the nation. The man Jacob was their source. From him they were to receive their preparation to be a nation. His preparation was not yet adequate for that purpose. That night on the stone pillow was the beginning of that. But with that night came the assurance of who he was and who GOD was. The camp boy was beginning to become the father of the nation of GOD's promise. The promise of GOD had elicited the vows of a man from him for the first time.

The love and care of the Father were given in the promise. The proper response of a son was given in the vow. While the word covenant is not used in this passage, this was a true covenant entered into by two parties, with requirements on each. Thus began a true **Father-son** relationship between GOD and Jacob.

The stone pillow had become a stone pillar. (That will only be funny in English, but I couldn't resist.)

Please scan the QR code or go to the web address to view Corbett's video introduction to the book.

CHAPTER 3

JACOB IN HIS STRUGGLES

http://bit.ly/1ne4cMv

Please go to ravensfood.everykindred.com for access to additional supplements to the book. Content will be added from time to time as desirable to support this book.

CHAPTER 3

JACOB IN HIS STRUGGLES

We observed earlier that Jacob was not technically in exile, but it was important for him to leave home in order to save his life. There is another dimension to his departure that we need to consider. Jacob also needed to leave home so he could learn to be the leader he would need to be. For most of his life he had lived in the shadow of his brother Esau. As Esau was groomed to lead the family camp, Jacob was groomed for a more secondary role. When the LORD arranged for him to have to leave the comforts and safety of his home, everything began to change. In fact, his uncle Laban's somewhat treacherous behavior would require much of Jacob until he was ready to be the chief man. In the meantime everything would change back home as well.

Leaving Canaan stretched Jacob farther than he had ever been stretched before. But that was just the beginning of his stretching process. He was going to the country of his relatives to seek his maternal grandfather's house. That should be almost as good as home. But the LORD had a new curriculum for him which he would soon engage and which, in time, would take much of the weakness out of him. We could call this GOD's "twenty-year plan" for Jacob. At its end, the new chief man would emerge. In fact, the leader of a nation would emerge per the commitments of GOD.

Let's remember that the commission Jacob's father had placed on him was that he was to find a wife among his kinsmen (Gen. 28:1-2). This woman would then be of a kind with his own mother and grand-mother, which would be good in the eyes of both Isaac and Rebekah. As it turned out, Jacob met the woman of his desire almost as soon as he arrived at the proper location in Padan Aram. In fact, she was the first named person he met. Unquestionably, she fit the requirements his father and mother had laid down. Had he been there only for that purpose, and had he brought along with him a bride price, Jacob's mission would have been over fairly quickly. Of course, GOD had other purposes for Jacob, so things did not happen quickly. Although Jacob found the wife he desired almost immediately, he had to wait seven years for the wedding.[22] And when the wedding day finally arrived, his uncle's deceit further complicated matters.

A WIFE FOR JACOB

Upon his arrival in Padan Aram, Jacob met Rachel right away (Gen. 29:16-18). Of course, there was the journey to Padan Aram after crossing the Jordan valley, and that took some time, perhaps weeks. But we know nothing about that journey other than its begin-ning and end. It was successful in the sense that he reached the home country of his relatives in that part of the world. There, a **typical** pastoral scene unfolded that had to do with the care of the flocks. While Jacob was learning of the customs of the area in this mat-ter from shepherds who had gathered with their flocks at the local well, a young woman appeared. Jacob immediately rolled away the stone covering the mouth of the well for her. In so doing, he met Rachel. Upon learning who she was, he rejoiced in the success of his wife-finding venture. Smitten with the young woman, he seems to have decided quite quickly that she should become his wife. It is interesting to note that the text here suggests that Jacob was of above average physical strength and that he sometimes was willing to take the initiative in a very straightforward manner.[23] These aspects of his nature and personality were more subdued in the years spent in his brother's shadow.

Having enabled and sheltered Rachel in the watering of the flocks, Jacob was invited home to meet her family, who were his relatives. In fact, her father came out and made the invitation himself. Laban affirmed the kinship, and Jacob had a new home. After a short period of time Jacob's uncle Laban (his mother's brother) made an offer of employment (Gen. 29:14-15). The implication was that although Jacob had been a guest upon his arrival, after a month it was time for him to move on or go to work for his uncle. Even the bond of kinship carried with it some limitations on hospitality.

Because Jacob had fallen in love with Rachel (and because he lacked a bride price), he suggested an employment contract of seven years for the hand of Rachel in marriage. Of course, room and board and common expenses would be included as well. This seven year period of servitude would at once be both his wages and his bride price. We cannot know what a typical bride price was in those days, but this was probably a very generous offer that Jacob made to his uncle. Because of his affection for Rachel, it seems that Jacob also liked this bargain. After all, it was he who had suggested it.

Uncle Laban liked the deal also. He stated this was a better match for his daughter than any other he was likely to encounter (Gen. 29:19-20). It was done. There is some lack of agreement as to whether he actually worked the seven years first or if it was only a matter of making the contract before he made the request to receive Rachel as his wife. The stronger argument is that he performed the work for seven years and then asked for the wedding. In any event, Jacob asked for the wedding to take place. Laban agreed, and then deceitfully married Jacob to his older daughter, Leah. Deceitfulness seems to have been a family trait.[24].

By the light of the next day Jacob discovered that his uncle had deceived him and confronted him on the matter (Gen.29:21-25). Laban presented a plausible defense and requested two things from Jacob. First, he would remain with Leah alone for one week and then he could have Rachel. However, the bride price for Rachel herself had just doubled to a total of fourteen years. Jacob agreed to the new contract terms and received Rachel as his wife a week later. His uncle drove a hard bargain.

At this point two things had occurred. First, Jacob had met his father's request that he find a bride from among his mother's kindred. Second, he had acquired the bride he wanted as well. From the standpoint of his father's requirements, he was "eligible" to return home. While this also met the stated requirements of his mother, she had placed a second, secret requirement on him as well: to remain in that faraway place until the danger from Esau's threat was over, ostensibly by way of Esau calming down. She would then send for Jacob (Gen. 27:45). Of course, Jacob had now obligated himself to seven more years of servitude. Was seven years long enough that Esau got over being angry? We will never know. What we do know is that there is no record of Rebekah's come home-message. Jacob had already been away for seven years. Now he faced an additional seven years before he could think of returning home.

We do have evidence that there was at least occasional news (Gen. 22:20-24). This probably happened as a result of commerce. Trading caravans were constantly on the move in that part of the world. These caravans were often commissioned to take messages from place to place. They were generally allowed to move about freely because of services like this and because they brought products that were not locally available. A family as important and prominent as Isaac's would have ready access to such services, probably multiple times in any year. Of course, things could easily go awry, but it is likely that such a message could be successfully sent.

At the same time, it is also true that we do not know the duration of Rebekah's life. Because of her absence from the narrative after Jacob's departure, it appears that Rebekah died before Jacob's eventual return home, but scripture does not record her death. In any event, the text never mentions any other contact between Jacob and Rebekah. So far as we can tell, they never again saw one another. However, she could die knowing that her goals for her favorite son had been met. In the meantime, Jacob was employed and married in Padan Aram. The time for him to return to Canaan had not yet come. By way of a postscript, when Rebekah did die she undoubtedly was buried in the family tomb with Sarah and Abraham.

THE BABY WAR

The biblical narrative is very plain in stating that Jacob favored Rachel over Leah (Gen. 29:30). Earlier we examined the fact that children, and sons in particular, were very important in these ancient cultures. A son was not only the continuity of his father's identity and estate; he was also the guarantor of his mother's future should she outlive his father. This became even more important when multiple mothers were in the picture. For example, Sarah was keen about seeing to it that her son was Abraham's heir. Rebekah likewise favored Jacob over Esau and needed Jacob to be the heir, partially to insure her influence in the encampment. She knew it was highly unlikely that Esau would turn her out, but she also believed that Jacob would be more careful of her welfare.

Jacob now had two wives, one of whom would bear his **firstborn** son. As we have seen, the **normal** expectation was that the son born first would be the heir and the possessor of the **birthright**. We have already examined the importance of the **birthright**. Although the possessor of the **birthright** could be changed by the father, under **normal** circumstances, and without some extraordinary reason, no son other than the **firstborn** would get the **birthright**. And where the **firstborn** was concerned, it did not matter who the mother was, as long as she was the wife of the chief man rather than a slave or servant.

Jacob preferred Rachel, but the LORD showed early favor to Leah, and she became pregnant first. When she had borne her son, she was very happy that he was not a she. Now she would have more of a claim to her husband's esteem (Gen. 29:31-32). She had borne for him the **firstborn**. From that moment, Reuben possessed the **birthright**. In time to come, he would be first among his brothers in everything. He would be trained to be the chief man after Jacob's death. He would be in a position to ensure that his mother was treated well regardless of what Rachel might have wanted to do to her. He would naturally be a magnet for his father's attention and affections and thus immediately enhance his mother's position in the family. Leah more or less had the prize. In this dimension at least, she had moved ahead of Rachel.

The LORD continued to see to it that Leah's womb was open and Rachel's was closed.[25] Before long, Leah had borne more sons to her husband. In naming the next three sons, she chose names that specified how things were going in the "baby war" as far as she was concerned. She obviously wanted to win Jacob's primary affections away from Rachel. It is also clear that this was not working out as well as she hoped. Rachel was still barren, but Jacob still preferred her to Leah. Leah, though, was assured a safe future.

Leah's successes with pregnancies aggravated Rachel and she blamed her husband, who was not happy with that accusation.[26] Eventually she decided to resort to a trick to gain some standing in the baby war. She concluded to send her maid Bilhah to Jacob. If Bilhah could bear a son to Jacob, Rachel would gain some standing if only because it was her "side" of the family that was now having babies. In fact, Bilhah did have a son, and then another. These two births seem to have satisfied Rachel's need. She now had sons to see to her welfare in the future. They would also attract some of her husband's attention back toward her tent.

Apart from this "baby war" between the sisters Leah and Rachel, this contest to command the primary affections of their husband, we really don't know much about what was happening in Jacob's family. It does appear there were shifts in one direction or another at various times. We also do not know whether Jacob continued to have a sexual relationship with Bilhah after Naphtali was born. There was some point of satisfaction for Rachel after that particular birth, and she might have ended that.

In any event, after Leah had given birth four times and was not getting pregnant again, she sent her maid Zilpah to Jacob to see whether more sons could be had on her "side" of the family. This was a success-ful venture, as Zilpah also bore two sons (Gen. 30:9-12) before that phase of family history also faded into the past.

Another thing we do not know for certain is the actual order in which the sons were born. It does not seem likely that Rachel waited so long that Leah had four sons before she sent Bilhah to Jacob. Therefore, Dan might have been born before Judah, for example. We simply do not know. Beyond the **firstborn**, Reuben, the text is more focused on the groups of sons than in their birth order. But at some point, after eight sons had been born into the family, Leah again became pregnant. She had two more sons after the two Zilpah had born on her behalf. In addition, she bore Jacob a daughter named Dinah. Ten sons and a daughter later, Rachel was still barren.

Rachel had even tried the use of mandrake (Gen. 30:14-15) to enhance her likelihood of pregnancy, but she was still unsuccessful. She seemed to have lost the baby war. Even so, Leah was unsuccessful in attracting Jacob's preference away from Rachel. This is obvious in the continued use of names that reveal Leah's insecurity in this matter.

Finally, in His own time, GOD permitted Rachel to bear a son (Gen. 30:22-24). Notice that the name Joseph was given to him because she felt she had previously been reproached in the great baby war with her sister. Now she would be on equal footing with Leah. She had the preference of her husband and had born him a son. Finally, the struggle between the sisters was over.

LABAN'S CONTINUED TREACHERY

By this time, well over fourteen years had passed since Jacob had left his parents' home. There are no indications in scripture of his receiving any message from home, but Jacob began to desire to return anyway. Having fulfilled his contract conditions, he approached Uncle Laban with a request to that end. But Laban had decided that Jacob's labor was too profitable to him and wanted to retain that labor. Jacob even verified that he felt he had made Laban wealthy through his labor.

But Laban wanted Jacob to stay on to continue to make him even wealthier.

In order to keep Jacob with him, Laban asked for a new contract (Gen. 30:29-30). In this instance, Jacob asked to begin to share in the wealth. Rather than asking for a share of the profits or some such thing, though, Jacob asked for an unusual provision. He would take from the herds and flocks of Laban only certain unusual kinds of animals, some not yet even born. This placed a kind of unknown element into the mix. Apparently Jacob felt these unusual animals would occur often enough to be worth the bargain.

Uncle Laban agreed to the bargain and then immediately attempted to subvert the deal (Gen. 30:31-36). Jacob had asked for speckled or spotted young animals from the current herds and any such offspring who appeared later. Laban agreed and then saw to it that there were no such animals for Jacob to take. He removed them and sent them away with his sons so Jacob would not be able to take them when he came for them. Jacob's cousins took the "stolen" animals to a place three days journey away from the rest of the herds. Inherently, this implies the belief that there would be no more such animals born in the future because of genetic factors. Laban, however, left the bulk of the herds in Jacob's care because of the superior care they would receive. He only took away that which would have been Jacob's pay.

Jacob had been raised in the knowledge of GOD. It could not have escaped him that his grandfather and father were possessors of a very important covenant and that he himself was soon to be its keeper. In fact, he had even made the vow to GOD to that effect (Gen. 28:20-22). What he began to do after he detected the perfidy of his uncle looks peculiar to us. It is almost as though he was attempting some kind of magic. Perhaps he received this commission from the LORD. We simply don't know its origin. Whatever the source of the plan, Jacob began to systematically build his own flock from the best of Laban's flock and to leave its lesser animals to Laban and his sons. This was accomplished through the peeling of the sticks to be placed in the watering troughs. It produced the desired results. He then separated his animals from

Laban's, thus building the quality of his own herds while allowing those of Laban to degenerate in quality. Any time Laban wanted to inspect Jacob's herds he found only animals of the type specified in the agreement, but of a higher quality than those in Laban's own herds. In this way Jacob became very wealthy fairly quickly at the expense of his dishonest uncle. Family traditions have two edges.

Laban's sons, who were Jacob's cousins, eventually noticed that their herds were weakening while the animals in Jacob's herds were vital. Their wealth was diminishing and Jacob's was increasing (Gen. 31:1). In a family where deceit was common, this undoubtedly raised alarms. As a result, friction arose between Laban and Jacob. The phenomenon of change was obvious whether they could detect the method or not, and Laban began to resent Jacob and was suspicious of his success. After all, he had dominated his nephew and kept him poor ever since he had arrived in Padan Aram nearly twenty years earlier.

The timing of GOD had arrived. When the LORD commanded Jacob to leave Laban, He was very specific (Gen. 31:1-13). He reminded Jacob of the vow taken at Bethel and told him specifically to return to the land he had come from. When he recounted his dream to his wives, he might have modified the details concerning the gains he had made among the herds, or that might be the more detailed explanation for his methods. We cannot be absolutely sure, but he was in essence asking his wives to approve of his plan to return to Canaan.

As an aside, both times when the wives are mentioned in the text, the order is Rachel and Leah. The baby war was over and Rachel was still the preferred wife. On the other hand, Leah was quite well off, as she had given Jacob eight sons; six from her own womb and two others by her handmaid Zilpah. Rachel, on the other hand, still had only the one son (plus two others by her handmaid Bilhah).

Apparently the two sisters were somewhat emotionally estranged from their father (Gen. 31:14-16). Jacob told them that Laban had changed his wages ten times in the years he had been with them. Obviously, his wives were in a position to verify the veracity of that assertion. They agreed with their husband that Laban had poorly used him and, as a result, had kept from his daughters and grandchildren much of what they could have expected from him. As far as they were concerned, the fact that God had enriched their husband Jacob at their father's expense was as it should be to right past injustices they had collectively borne. They were in complete agreement with Jacob in the matter of leaving their home and family to go to his.

The matter decided, the family simply gathered together what they were taking and left. Sending no message to Laban, perhaps in the understandable fear that he would stop them, they departed quickly, quietly, and without warning. (Gen. 31:17-18). These were nomadic people and moving was something they did well. It may be that Rachel and Leah had always lived in a more stable environment, but they had gone out into the fields when Jacob sent for them. Hence, all that they needed they had with them. Everything else, the animals and the servants, were there as well because that is where they lived anyway. The whole family and whatever they had by way of personal property just left for Canaan, leaving no forwarding address. The utility companies were not even notified.

Jacob quickly got the traveling party across the Euphrates River and headed for home. It appears he intended to cross the Jordan River below the Sea of Galilee. Hence, he made for the area known as Gilead (Gen. 31:21), a region of low mountains just east of Galilee and the Jordan valley. From there he could cross the Jordan relatively easily and be home. This was the most straightforward route for his goals. Jacob certainly would have desired the easiest path he could find because of the makeup of his camp. The animals would have young with them and the women and children needed careful consideration as the journey progressed. This was, though, no nomadic meander. They would make the best time they could, given the need to care for the weaker members of the party.

Laban was probably with his sons at the time of Jacob's departure (Gen.31: 19-23). Their camp was a goodly distance from that of Jacob; initially three days travel for the animals. Or perhaps he was in a site of his own where his permanent dwelling was. In any event, it took three days for Laban to hear the news of the departure of Jacob and his family and herds. This no doubt infuriated Laban. There was the simple discourtesy of leaving with no farewell. There was the reality that Jacob was his very best herdsman. There might have been a fear that he had been robbed in some way. After all, he was already very suspicious and jealous of Jacob because of the complaints of his sons. Whatever the case, he got together a pursuit party and headed out after Jacob.

It took Jacob about ten days to reach Gilead (Gen. 31:22-23, inferred number of days). It took Laban seven days to catch up. He could travel much faster than Jacob because he did not have the same concerns. We don't actually know what was in Laban's heart to do. His anger probably caused him to consider all sorts of things. The extreme would be something like forcing Jacob's camp back to Padan Aram and keeping him under arrest. We simply don't know, and it is likely Laban wasn't sure himself what he intended. Whatever his considerations were, the LORD Himself warned Laban in a dream (Gen. 31:24) not to do much of anything either good or bad.

So Laban and his pursuit party caught up with Jacob and his camp there in Gilead, in the mountains east of Galilee. Probably the men with Laban were armed and prepared to cause trouble, but the LORD's warning was enough to defuse the possible confrontation. Laban, however, could not resist fuming a bit and scolding his son-in-law. In so doing, he brought up the only real offense he had left after the LORD's warning. All else having been said, and having grudgingly excused the departure, Laban was left with the accusation that Jacob had stolen his gods. These would have been small, probably fired-clay figurines of various deities that were popular in the area of Padan Aram. Some of these votive figures would have been of general purpose, while others likely were figures that he related to specific events in his life. For this reason they were very important to him, at least some of them. In his mindset, these figurines protected his house, his family, and his property. If he believed they were stolen, he would definitely want them back. This collection of objects was not like the GOD who had spoken to him in a dream, but he wanted them nonetheless.

We know that Jacob was innocent of the theft of Laban's household gods, so we can imagine how he must have felt. This accusation would, to him, look like a fake provocation designed to justify some unpleasant course of action on Laban's part. Jacob offered a basic defense (Gen. 31:31-32). He had fled secretly because he was afraid that Laban would take his family and property from him if he asked for permission to return to Canaan. That does seem to be quite a logical conclusion given what we know of the character of Laban. On the other matter, Jacob was more forceful. He told Laban there were no gods of his in the camp and, that if there were, punishment would be meted out to the thief. In any event, he told Laban to search the tents, find his gods if they were there, and then go away and leave him alone.

Rachel surely knew Jacob's stories of his life from before they met. She knew of the GOD of his grandfather and father. She knew of his vow to serve GOD if he returned successfully to Canaan. In the thinking of the times, though, gods were local phenomena. Any given god had a geographical area of influence, and was generally limited to that area. Hence, the GOD of Abraham and Isaac might very well have had no meaning for her as that GOD was in Canaan, not in Padan Aram, where she had grown up. While she knew of the GOD of Abraham and Isaac, she also knew the stories of the gods of Laban. They had been near her all her life. It is likely that she was in some way devoted to some of those gods. And now her husband was taking her away from where they resided in her father's house. These gods would be vestiges of the culture from which she was being taken. While it would be troublesome to her father, it is likely that her theft of the gods was for her own comfort and, perhaps, protection on this very unusual journey. Whatever her reasoning, she had taken some or all of the gods from Laban's collection and had hidden them. Jacob did not know this.

The theft of one's household gods essentially consigned the victim to a life of mischance. All kinds of things could go wrong without the little deities to prevent them. In some cultures this would also be an unforgiveable insult. In some cases, the insult would be so severe that death for the thief was the justified penalty in the minds of the people in those cultures. Jacob, in light of this, suggested just such a course of action, so sure was he that the little gods were not in his camp. He went so far as to suggest that Laban carry out an unimpeded search of his own throughout the camp to verify the absence of the god figurines. Had he known that his beloved Rachel was the thief, surely he would have taken a different course of action.

However, the beloved Rachel had stolen and hidden those little gods in her own camel saddle (Gen. 31:34). It seems that she alone knew of the theft at the time. A probably tense Laban carried out the search. He had no choice, as Jacob had really given him none. In this way he could save face with his companions and still get away having done no harm. For whatever reason, Rachel's tent was the last one he searched. She sat upon her camel saddle and told her father that she was menstruating. Would he please excuse her for not arising? There was little Laban could or would do about that, so he went about searching the rest of her tent. Having not found his gods, Laban could now depart from Jacob's camp with no shame. Jacob still knew nothing about the thefts Rachel had carried out. His innocence and the innocence of his party were proven as far as he was concerned. He should be free to continue his journey. At this point there was virtually no likelihood that Laban would demand anything else from him.

With a clear conscience Jacob then demanded a full reckoning from Laban. He required that Laban demonstrate evidence or be done (Gen.31:36-42). His frustration apparently boiled over and he took control of the situation. Basically he scolded his father-in-law for the way he had treated him for the last twenty years, pointing out that he had been a faithful servant to Laban. He was outraged that Laban had pursued him and made such accusations. He still didn't trust Laban and told him so. This was a kind of squaring of accounts for Jacob, and was probably necessary because the two would never see one another again. Laban, not to be outdone, replied that he had little respect for Jacob himself, but he realized there was really nothing he could do because of the family. He again laid claim to everything, but he was going to let Jacob be on his way.

The two men having expressed themselves, it was time for some sort of truce to end the encounter. Laban suggested they enter into a kind of treaty (Gen. 31:44-54). And so they did. There in the mountains of Gilead, Jacob erected a testimonial stone and the fellows in his camp helped him build a mound of native stones. This mound then became the site of the formalities of their agreement. In the formalities two main matters were established. First, Laban charged Jacob concerning the welfare of his daughters and grandchildren. He specifically called upon the LORD as the guarantor of that agreement. He also announced that the mound and the pillar were the markers of the boundary between them. Jacob would remain on his side and Laban on his. In this case, he called on the GOD of his grandfather Nahor, and of Abraham and of Terah as the witness to this boundary agreement. Jacob took the oath proposed by his uncle, and things were thus settled. It was now possible for them to part in peace. Jacob would go to the home of his father a wealthy man. Laban would return to Padan Aram with the assurances of future peace between them.

Laban and Jacob hosted a meal together for all who were with them, and Laban and company spent the night in Jacob's camp. Those acts sealed the deal. The next morning Laban kissed his daughters and grandchildren, blessed them, and went home. He probably kissed Jacob as well, as they had made peace. The crisis was over. Laban was gone and would never be heard of again in scripture. The twenty-year exile was over and now it was time to cross over into Canaan proper.

ESAU

Leaving Gilead, Jacob camped near the Jordan.[27] Soon he would cross the river. In that camp, the LORD sent messengers to him. This was consistent with the fact that when Jacob had departed twenty years earlier he had had a vision of angels shortly before he crossed this same river going in the other direction. So Jacob named this place *Mahanaim*, which means "a pair of camps." It appears he was referring to the proximity of his camp to a place in which there were angels of

GOD. Scripture makes no reference to a purpose for this encounter, but it was a significant event nonetheless. The vows he had made to GOD at Bethel were about to come into operation.

But one last hurdle remained: his brother Esau. There are a couple of things to remember here. Esau had sworn to kill Jacob some twenty years earlier. The other is that the reason Rebekah wanted Jacob to leave was specifically to save him from Esau's wrath. Of course, the cover story of the wife-hunt accompanied that. The wife-hunt had been successful. In fact, he had two of them and two concubines and eleven sons and at least one daughter. And he was rich, with many animals and servants. But there was still Esau.

The message to "come home" never came from his mother. He was returning because the LORD had told him to go home, and he was done with his mother's brother. But there was still Esau. Somehow, Jacob knew that Esau lived in the south in an area called Seir. There is no explanation in the text as to why this was the case, but that is where Jacob sent messengers with a somewhat contrite message to his brother announcing his return to Canaan (Gen. 32:3-5). His messengers found Esau and brought back word that Esau was coming with a veritable army. Certainly the body of men Esau brought was more than sufficient to destroy Jacob and all that were with him. These must have been very tense days for Jacob as he awaited his brother there in the Jordan valley. Jacob's preparations for the reunion were made in fear of what would happen. Esau's vow still stood as far as Jacob knew. As he re-entered the land of his home, he once again entered the shadow of his brother. It wasn't clear in his thinking yet, but in order to be who he was in GOD's reckoning, he would have to break out of that shadow.

It's not clear how long Jacob and his company spent beside the river, but it would have taken a few days for his messengers to reach Esau and return with a response. On the other hand, it would not be long after the messengers returned before Esau's band reached him, perhaps the next day. Preparations had to be made (Gen. 32:3-23). As a precaution, Jacob decided to divide his camp into two parts so that one part could escape if the other was attacked. He also sent to Esau several gifts of animals across the river ahead of himself and the camps. The gifts were to proceed in a series of offerings, each with a message of conciliation for Esau in the hope that the gifts would soften his attitude toward Jacob. He himself and the two camps would remain for the night on the east bank of the Jordan, his last night as an alien. For everyone else in his camp, this was their last night before entering the land of their new home.

All the preparations were made and the gifts were on their way to Esau as that night arrived. Now Jacob made one last preparation. He put another watercourse between his family and Esau placing them all north of the Jabbok, which was a tributary to the Jordan. It was just one last barrier for Esau to get across if he arrived in a belligerent manner. Now Jacob was alone with nothing else to do except to wait for Esau's arrival the next day. He would carry out that task alone. His camps were north of the Jabbok and his gifts were west of the Jordan that night.

As the night wore on, Jacob found himself in a wrestling match with a supernatural being (Gen. 32:24-32), a messenger from GOD. Nothing is stated concerning why their meeting became a wrestling match, so we must assume the contest was sent by GOD. Certainly the outcome suggests that conclusion. We may infer that the messenger was sent to encounter Jacob and to start the fight with him. The struggle was therefore symbolic of Jacob's struggles throughout his life. Certainly, he had faced—and overcome—numerous real and major obstacles. He had been persistent in some of his contests but certainly not in all of them. One suspects that GOD's purpose that night was to show Jacob that he was to persevere in the future. After all, he was the *son of promise* of Isaac and the possessor of the **birthright**, with all its heritage. He had been sent away like a fugitive with little more than the clothes on his back and had returned a very successful man. Now, the purpose of his life was to come to flower. He was to enter the land with the nation in tow.

The contest was arranged in such a way that Jacob would neither prevail nor lose the fight. Its purpose was perseverance. It went on for the rest of the night. As day was approaching, the messenger struck

Jacob with an injury to end the fight. It is not entirely clear what the injury was, but some scholars suggest the term used was a euphemism for a strong blow to his genital region. Others suggest it was his hip joint. Whatever it was, it was a wound that affected Jacob for the rest of his life. The mark of GOD was found in his life as a reminder of that encounter. Despite his injury, however, Jacob persisted, and the messenger demanded that he be released. Jacob refused to release the messenger without a blessing. He received the blessing of a new name. From that time forward Jacob had the name Israel, which means "he struggled." This was the name by which he would be known in the spiritual. It was the name he was to pass on to his sons. From that time to this time, they would be known as the *b'nai Israel*. That title for the Hebrews means the "sons of Israel." Jacob (now Israel) couldn't find out the name of the messenger with whom he had struggled all night, but he knew this was very important. In fact, he concluded that he had seen the face of GOD Himself, and therefore named the place "the face of GOD." When he crossed the river later that morning, he was a *new* man, a man who had struggled with men and with GOD and had prevailed. And he limped.

He limped across Jabbok and fetched his family for the meeting with Esau. There he was, across the Jordan. It was time. Jacob arranged the family for the meeting with his wives and sons in a particular order, Rachel and Joseph last (Gen. 33:1-2). He then led them across the river and adopted an obsequious manner as he approached Esau, but his brother alighted and came to him and embraced him in friendship. Jacob then introduced his family to his older brother. When Esau inquired about the gifts, Jacob explained them, but Esau told him to keep his property. He went on to say that he was happy to see his brother and that he was quite well to do and in need of nothing. Jacob then implored Esau to receive his gifts, which he finally did. This sealed the homecoming as a time of peace and rejoicing between them. There would be no killing.

Esau proposed they continue on together, but Jacob demurred, (Gen. 33:12-15) pleading the slow pace he would have to keep while

Esau could travel much more quickly. Jacob also turned down an escort that Esau offered, arguing that he did not need the escort. Finally, Esau parted company with Jacob and headed south to his home country in Seir. To our knowledge, except for Isaac's funeral, this was the last meeting of the brothers. Jacob's greatest fear was put to rest. He had finally overcome all impediments to his installation as **patriarch** in Canaan in his generation.

So far as he knew, there was nothing in the land of Canaan that would impede his success any longer. He had left the land a fugitive and returned a wealthy man with a **birthright** in that land. The **birthright** was GOD-given in its contents. He had wives and children qualified to be citizens in the coming Kingdom. His father would now have to receive him as his heir.

After a short journey, Jacob halted the people of the camp and built temporary dwelling structures. It is likely that his purpose was to allow the animals to recover from the more or less forced-march of the last few weeks and to permit things to be repaired. It is also likely that he sent out scouts to determine the location of safe pasturage as well as to generally have a look around. This area was not well known to him and he had been away a long time. The respite would be good all the way around. This area came to be called *Succoth* (tabernacles), which is the Hebrew word for "temporary dwellings." That word gives its name to one of the key Jewish holidays down to today (Lev. 23:33-36).

After a sufficient rest break, Jacob moved the camp on to the well-established city of Shechem. This was the first named stop of Abram when he had first come to Canaan some one hundred seventy-five years earlier.[28] Just as Abram had done, Jacob built an altar on the property he purchased outside Shechem. He called that altar *El Elohe Israel*, which might mean, "GOD is the GOD of Israel." Of course, Israel referred to his new name. This was a declaration, in a sense, of his intent to be monotheistic thereafter. He had promised that GOD would be his GOD if he ever got back home. It also marked the beginning of his new life as the heir of this land.

Please scan the QR code or go to the web address to view Corbett's video introduction to the book.

Chapter 4

THE PATRIARCH ISRAEL

http://bit.ly/1N3GxmQ

Please go to ravensfood.everykindred.com for access to additional supplements to the book. Content will be added from time to time as desirable to support this book.

CHAPTER 4

THE PATRIARCH ISRAEL

In another place we established that there were three patriarchs of the nation called the people of Israel. It is the third of these patriarchs, Jacob/Israel, who was to give his name to the nation. The nation had been *in* Abraham. Then, the nation had been *in* Isaac. Now the nation was *in the earth* in Canaan in the persons of the sons of Jacob. These sons, of whom there would be twelve, were the issue of Abraham through Isaac through Jacob and would take their places as leaders of *tribes in the nation* of Israel.[29] They would be patriarchs of the tribes, but not of the nation. That transition is important, but is not within the scope of this book. Jacob had produced sons who would become known as the "sons of Israel," *b'nai Israel*, as the story of the coming forth of the nation was lived out. While all except one were born to him before he became Israel, they were not called the sons of Jacob. Israel was the name GOD had given to the father of the nation, the last **patriarch** of the nation. In some sense Israel was a different person from Jacob. Israel was he of undisputed promise, and his sons would be called by that name – Israel.

For the moment, though, eleven of the twelve sons had been born and were with Jacob near Shechem. Joseph was the youngest of the sons and Benjamin was not yet born. Some of Leah's sons were approaching their adult years and no doubt were fully engaged in the labors of their father. Israel's (Jacob's) purchase of the land at Shechem for one hundred shekels of silver marked the beginning of their physical possession of the land. The altar built at that place marked the spiritual beginning. Remember that Abram had also built an altar at Shechem when he first arrived in Canaan about 180 years earlier (Gen. 12:6-7).

So here was Jacob/Israel, settling in the land, raising his animals, engaging in commerce with the local Canaanites, and caring for his family and his retinue of servants. We do not know how long he remained there. We do not know how soon he sent messengers to his father Isaac or when he went to visit Isaac. But in all likelihood some time passed while he was there. Jacob was responsible for those in his charge. He was not employed as he had been in Padan Aram; he was now the chief man in his own right. All was well.

Jacob was now engaged in twelve **father-son** relationships that we know of, including the one with Dinah. This was accompanied by 132 **fraternal** relationships when viewed from the sons' points of view. Not to mention four spousal relationships for Jacob. He also would have had a wide variety of relationships with those in his employ. This was a very rich matrix of human interaction. From this body of relationships we can learn quite a bit about how a family becoming the Kingdom of GOD can operate.

For example, when Jacob and Esau were lads there were only the two of them for folks to keep up with and tend to. Now there were many more sons and four mothers to take into consideration from the domestic perspective. There was no real model for the demands this would place on the camp. A lot of that had been worked out in Padan Aram, but this was a whole new set of circumstances. This is where we take up the story of the life of the last *national* **patriarch**.

In later chapters we will observe the various sons of Jacob with an interest in the character of their relationships. This will be seen in the way they dealt with one another and with their father. For example, the **firstborn** with **birthright** was a fellow named Reuben, whose very name speaks to the struggle between his mother Leah and her sister Rachel. Then there was Joseph, who was the eleventh son but the first son of the beloved wife. The sons of Bilhah and Zilpah simply did not have the status of the sons of the "true" wives. Relationships and events in the lives of these sons mark the character of their descendants and the course of the history of the "great nation."

AT SHECHEM

The decision to settle down, at least for a while, was probably a matter of convenience. Jacob's father and the family home were still quite some distance away. But he was in "the" land, and it looks like Jacob and his folks were just fine being in Shechem for the time being. He was no longer a servant. The city would benefit from mutually beneficial trade and from the rural peace that would come with the presence of this great encampment. After all, the herdsmen would be scattered out quite a bit to meet the needs of the herds and flocks.

Into this peaceful arrangement came the first crisis since the return to Canaan. Apparently Dinah, the daughter of Leah, was attracted to the culture of the young women of the city (Gen. 34:1). She had spent her entire life in the camps without the attractions and excitement of the city. If nothing else, she became curious about the glamour of the lives of the Shechemite women. Her own culture may have begun to seem inadequate in her mind. We know, of course, that this led to serious trouble. The young prince of Shechem saw her and was attracted to her. In his zeal for her attention, he violated her (Gen. 34:2). We cannot comment on the conditions of sexual morality among the Shechemites, but this was unacceptable for the culture of the nation of the sons of Jacob. After Shechem, the young prince of Shechem, violated Dinah, he concluded that he was in love with her, and asked his father to secure her as his wife.

This young woman had six brothers who were born to Jacob by the same mother, Leah. In addition, she had five other half-brothers. Apparently, at the time of the rape the brothers were not at home (Gen. 34:7). They were in the fields tending to the family business. Jacob was home, and when he heard the news he remained silent on the matter as the king of Shechem, Hamor, sought to make a marriage contract with Jacob so that his son could take Dinah as his wife.

In the meantime, though, the brothers heard about the event and returned to the encampment full of rage. Perhaps (probably) in Canaanite culture this was an acceptable thing, but it was not acceptable in the culture of the new nation. While Hamor and Shechem were trying to arrange the marriage with Jacob, his sons arrived back at the camp. Immediately Hamor and Shechem engaged them in an effort to promote the marriage. Shechem pledged to pay any price to bring that about. To be fair about it, the proposition of a closer alliance was in some ways attractive. However, this would create real problems if implemented. The nation would be mixing itself up with the Canaanites. The promise would be diluted by the curse.

The Canaanites ran into an old family tradition at that point—deception. Perhaps it was initially intended only as a cruel joke,[30] perhaps not. In any event, the brothers presented a culturally specific requirement in order for the agreement to go forward. The Canaanite royal family accepted the proposal and presented it to the Shechemites. The proposal was that they could all become allied through the mechanism of circumcision. Hamor presented the idea to the men of the city based on economics. Jacob was a wealthy man and by bringing him and his camp into their own sphere of influence, they could exercise considerable sway on the fortunes of Jacob and share in them. It worked. Hamor knew just how to appeal to the leaders of the city.

One of the reasons circumcision is best practiced on very young children is the very unpleasantness of the event and its aftermath. In effect, the men of the city immobilized themselves by agreeing to, and then carrying out, the circumcision pledge. As a result, they became incapacitated for a time. While they were in that state, two of Dinah's brothers, Simeon and Levi, took it upon themselves to slaughter the men of the city (Gen. 34:25-26) while they were unable to adequately defend themselves. Simeon and Levi were the second- and third-born sons of Leah and Jacob. After the slaughter they found their sister Dinah and took her home. Others of the brothers might have aided them, but these two were responsible.

We are not told how Jacob handled, or intended to handle, the matter of Dinah's rape. Surely, as the father of a girl in her teens, this was a very painful experience for him. All we know is that he remained silent on the matter while his sons took things into their own hands. Whatever his feelings on the matter, he was now the chief man of a significant band of nomadic people who depended on his decisions to maintain their very lives. They would obey him, but they knew they had to depend on him as well. Had he decided to attack the city to exact revenge for Dinah's injury, they would have carried out his request. However, Jacob had matured into the man who was qualified to lead the people. He knew he could not carry out such a plan because of the repercussions that would follow such an event. He was a stranger among a fairly large collection of Canaanite cities. If he worked his wrath in one of them, the others would become alarmed and might form a coalition to destroy him and take his wealth for themselves. Jacob had to weigh that possibility against his desire to avenge his daughter. In a way, there was really nothing he could do. Hamor was the king of the city and his son was its prince. To attack them would not be the same as to exact revenge on an individual, errant Canaanite. It would have been a national act and would have repercussions for his entire camp and probably mean its end. He placed the welfare of the people above his own feelings.

Perhaps his sons knew this when they entered into their deliberations. Perhaps they did not. In any event, Simeon and Levi plotted and carried out the revenge without their father's knowledge or approval. By doing so, they placed Jacob in a very awkward spot. The other Canaanites might well interpret Simeon's and Levi's acts to be his acts, as though he himself had ordered the revenge attack (Gen. 34:30). Jacob understood that this might well bring about some sort of organized retribution against him and his people. Hence, he scolded his sons severely. Their response was that they had to do something to defend their sister's honor. Jacob thought of the people, as a true father would. His sons had the luxury to consider only what they wanted to do without regard to such considerations.

Scripture does not indicate how much longer Jacob and his family and camp remained in the vicinity of Shechem after the slaughter. It is likely Jacob made ready to leave pretty quickly in order to get away from the scene that held so much pain for him. Soon, though, the LORD spoke to him and instructed him to move on to Bethel. Perhaps Shechem, in GOD's economy, was just not a suitable location for the matters of the nation. We just don't know. What we do know is that He sent Jacob to Bethel (Gen. 35:1).

BETHEL

Bethel, as we have already seen, was a very significant place for Jacob as it had been for his grandfather Abraham. Abraham had built an altar at Bethel to which he returned (Gen 12:8, Gen 13:3-4), the second time marking his return from Egypt. Jacob, too, was now to travel to Bethel for a second time. His first visit, you will remember, was marked by the wonderful dream and his visitation from GOD. It was at Bethel that Jacob had taken vows before GOD. If GOD would return him safely to the land, he would make GOD his GOD and he would tithe. Now he was to return to that place by the command of GOD Himself.

Jacob was finally back in the land of his birth, and now faced the need to fulfill the vows that he had made to GOD when he had had first departed the land over twenty years earlier. It was now time for him to take up full responsibility for who he was and the destiny GOD had for him.

His response to GOD's command was to instruct his entire camp in three matters (Gen. 35:2-5). First, they were to rid themselves of any foreign god figures they had in their possession. Second, they were to purify themselves, although we do not know exactly what this entailed. It was probably a matter of a ritual bath, which figures so prominently in the culture of both Jews and Muslims down to our day. Third, they were to change clothes. For many people in the camp, this may well have meant making some new clothes. These things marked the beginning of a new era, a new life. Taken together, these three instructions, in some sense, was the last event marking Jacob's transformation into Israel.

Before leaving the camp at Shechem, Jacob buried the foreign god figures the people had surrendered to him. Now there was only God Himself. In that mode they left for Bethel. It turns out that the slaughter at Shechem had no known effect on the Canaanites. They did not come together and attack Jacob and his camp. Unmolested, he and his camp made the journey that God required of him.

When he came to the already sacred place at Bethel, he built the altar the Lord had demanded of him. Here also the nurse of his mother Rebekah died and was buried,[31] marking another step of closure to his previous life. After the death and funeral of the nurse Deborah, Jacob had another encounter with God. In this event God confirmed the name change from Jacob to Israel and reaffirmed the promises He had made to Abraham and Isaac concerning the land and his descendants. Jacob/Israel was now the full custodian of all that had been promised in the two generations that preceded him. Inherent in this investiture was the expectation that he would fully take up the labor of patriarchal **primacy**. All obstacles were now gone. All the vestiges of his old identity had been dealt with. He was now the full representative of God in the earth. His grandfather Abraham was dead. His father Isaac was retired. His brother had moved to another land. His uncle Laban had sworn to remain in Padan Aram. It was simply up to Jacob, and his sons after him, to become the great nation in the land that God had promised.

After the Lord spoke to Israel to confirm these things, Israel set up another pillar and anointed it with oil, just as he had done when first leaving the land decades earlier (Gen. 35:14-15). This setting up of pillars at Bethel was uniquely related to Jacob/Israel. Abraham built altars. Isaac dug wells. Jacob set up altars as well, but he also set up pillars of memorial. It appears that the sojourn at Bethel did not last long. Soon the camp was on its way again. Now Jacob was qualified to rejoin his father Isaac at *Kirjath Arba*, or Hebron.

COMING HOME

On the way to Hebron, Rachel died in childbirth. It was near Bethlehem that she gave live birth to the last of the sons of Jacob. Jacob named his newest son Benjamin. Sometime after burying his wife near *Bethlehem Ephratha*, Jacob moved on. In his next encampment his son Reuben betrayed him by having a sexual relationship with Bilhah, Rachel's maid (Gen. 35:22). While Jacob knew of the event, it seems to have never been mentioned between the two of them until the final blessings of Israel given in Egypt many years later.[32]

Finally, after all the years and all the adventures Jacob had endured, he was reunited with his father Isaac in Hebron. Israel was now the main character in the continuing work of GOD to produce the great nation. Everything else we know about Isaac is that he lived to be 180 years old, which was nearly thirty years after Jacob returned to the land. Scripture points out that Esau joined Israel there at Hebron to put their father in the tomb of Abraham (Gen. 35:27-29). Now the first two generations of the "great nation" rested together in that place.

Esau was well established in his southern location by this time and was forming his own nation. He did not live among the Canaanites, but rather in more sparsely settled country among various small groups of nomads. It is probably true that he became instrumental in bringing together some sort of integration of these peoples. It also seems that he lived in close proximity to the descendants of Ishmael. Over time, the distinctions between the Edomites, which the descendants of Esau came to be called, and the Ishmaelites, probably became minor. Scholars credit both as being progenitors of the Arab people. As best we can tell from scripture, there was never any further conflict between Jacob/Israel and Esau. However, the descendants of Esau (Edomites) were problematic neighbors through much of the history of the nation of Israel later on.

Abraham had settled extensive lands south of the Canaanites in Beersheba and Beer Lehairoi. He had purchased property near Hebron for the family tomb. Jacob had purchased property near Shechem.

These were the holdings of Isaac and Jacob, which, as far as we know, were managed from Hebron for the rest of Isaac's life. Of course, many agreements had been developed regarding the use of open rangeland among the various cities of Canaan as well. These things needed management, of which Jacob was quite capable. He became the operational **patriarch**.

Much of the rest of what we know about Jacob/Israel has to do with the histories of his various sons. The sons themselves are the subject of later treatment in this book. However, it is worth our while to examine the rest of the Jacob's life from our **father-son** perspective.

JACOB AND HIS SONS

In the early years after the return to Canaan, Jacob's three oldest sons (all of whom were sons of Leah) disappointed Jacob very significantly. Simeon and Levi, sons numbers two and three, had instigated the slaughter of the Shechemites after the rape of Dinah. Reuben had had an affair with Bilhah shortly before the migration back to Hebron. Jacob had scolded Simeon and Levi after the events at Shechem because they had endangered the "nation" they were becoming. Scripture is silent concerning whether there were words between Jacob and Reuben over the Bilhah's seduction.

Reuben was the **firstborn** of Jacob with the assumed **birthright**. The **birthright** included the double portion of the wealth of the nation and the patriarchal **primacy**. Rightfully, the father had distinct expectations of the **firstborn**. The man who was to carry the essential identity of his father into the next generation needed to be a good quality representation of his father. Now, however, this matter of the violation of their relationship stood between them. While it was probably not intended as such, it was a humiliation for Jacob. Reuben's careless handling of his side of the **father-son** relationship between them was a grievous matter.

Neither Simeon nor Levi, of course, bore the distinction of **firstborn** or the assumption of **birthright**. Their individual **father-son** relationships with Jacob were of a different kind than that of Reuben. Still, their father undoubtedly loved them. When they deceived and killed the men of Shechem, the offense was not just a personal affront to Jacob. This offense involved the safety of the entire camp. It too was a serious matter, but not of the same kind as Reuben's offense. It is clear that Jacob was upset with these two sons of his, because he said so. It is of note that Simeon was second born, and in the event of something happening to Reuben, he would step into the place of the **firstborn** with the **birthright**. Levi, of course, would follow Simeon in the line behind **firstborn** because he was born third.

The Genesis narrative relates the first ten years or so of Jacob and his family living with Isaac in Hebron, then begins to shift focus onto various ones of Jacob's sons. This shift of focus informs us regarding the intergenerational relationships that matter to us in this book. The sons presented Jacob with quite an array of complexities in their relationships with him. We can observe quite a bit of human behavior in the related events. This, of course, is our stated purpose.

The narrative takes up again with several events in the life of Joseph that are full of all kinds of relational information. These instances, four of which are very brief in written content, are nevertheless full of important stuff.

You will recall that back in Padan Aram, Jacob's beloved wife Rachel was unable to conceive children for him. Leah's success in the baby war caused Rachel considerable frustration. If she could not bear sons for her husband, she would despise herself and would feel despised by the people. Furthermore, in the event that Jacob preceded her in death, there would be no heir to guarantee her the protection she wanted. This fear of "being turned out" would be magnified because of her poor relationship with her sister. She finally conceived of the idea of having her maidservant Bilhah become pregnant by Jacob. Such a child would likely be friendlier to her than would one of the sons of Leah. This plan was acceptable to Jacob and was successfully executed twice. Bilhah bore two sons to Jacob: Dan and Naphtali. This would not reduce Rachel's self-reproach but would take away some of Leah's social power over her.

At about the same time, Leah ceased conceiving, having borne four sons to Jacob. Taking a cue from her sister, she sent her maidservant Zilpah to Jacob also. Soon Zilpah produced two sons as well, named Gad and Asher. It is important to note that the sons of Bilhah and Zilpah were named by Rachel and Leah, and not by their birth mothers. This automatically tells us something. These two women were servants (slaves, actually), not members of the family. Hence, their rights were fairly limited. Their status was nowhere near the status of Leah and Rachel. Their sons, then, would suffer somewhat in terms of their status as well, even though they were reckoned among Jacob's sons.

The situation just described is a large part of the setting for the first Joseph adventure. It was these four men: Dan, Naphtali, Gad, and Asher, who were in the field with Joseph and some of the flocks (Gen. 37:2). For whatever reason, Joseph, who was their junior in age and experience, found their behavior unacceptable. We do not have any information as to what they were doing or not doing, but whatever it was, Joseph gave a negative report to Jacob about it. Now Jacob had relationships with each of his sons, but some were closer than others. It is highly likely that the four sons of Bilhah and Zilpah were not among those who were closest to their father. We know, of course, that Joseph was the closest because of who his mother was. Logically, these four would be among those most alienated in their **fraternal** relationships with Joseph. Therefore, Joseph tattling on them understandably upset them. Hence, each of their **fraternal** relationships with him was strained even further. We cannot say whether Joseph's tattling endeared him more to Jacob but it probably did no harm to their relationship.

On the other hand, the relationships between the four sons of the concubines and their father did likely suffer as a result. There is no reason to believe that the four brothers did not esteem their father. Almost certainly they did. However, their feeling of having been diminished in his eyes would have been a powerful one. We do not know exactly how they felt about Joseph before this event, but it was definitely worse afterwards. Whether or not the four shared their feelings with their half-brothers, the sons of Leah, is something we don't know either, but it is likely they did. This would add to the distance between Joseph and all the other brothers except Benjamin, who would have been perhaps ten years old at the time these things were going on.

The next event, quickly recorded, was Jacob's gift of the famous coat to Joseph (Gen. 37:3). Much speculation surrounds the language used to describe this coat, but it is safe to say that it was quite distinctive. Jacob must have kept all his sons well-clothed. They were the sons of the chief man, after all, and the wealth of the whole camp was at their father's disposal. So, certainly they had good quality clothing. Apparently, though, this new coat of Joseph's was a cut above the **typical** clothing of the family. This further enhanced the alienation between Joseph and his brothers. It was a special sign of **paternal** affection for him on the part of his father, but it was an irritant to his **fraternal** relations. Scripture says the irritation was so profound that the brothers shunned Joseph. Surely Jacob was aware that these pressures were building up inside his family. How could he not be? It is safe to reiterate that **father-son** relationships are different than **fraternal** relationships. There is more love and more power in the **father-son** kind than there ever is in the **brother-brother** kind.

The next two events come as a pair with interesting components (Gen. 37:5-10). First, we find that Joseph was a dreamer. By this we mean that a prominent feature of his walk with GOD was that the LORD informed him through the medium of dreams. These two quite prophetic dreams were very profound in their content.

In the first of the two dreams, Joseph saw sheaves of grain, representing his eleven brothers, bowing down to a sheaf of *grain* that represented him. When Joseph shared his dream with his brothers, it only intensified the disdain in which his brothers held him. Already they had shunned him. Now they were outright hostile toward him. It is interesting to note the motif of the dream in light of the fact that when the brothers did come and bow down to him, it was in the event in which they had to go to Egypt to get *grain* from him. GOD clearly made the motif fit the exact nature of the events to come. That lay years in the future, however. At this point, the brothers were livid.

Jacob may or may not have known of Joseph's first dream, but he certainly knew about the second one. In this dream, eleven stars and the sun and the moon bowed down to Joseph. This dream even irritated Jacob to some extent, and he took Joseph to task. As for the brothers, they were even more irritated and hostile than before. Again, the motif of the dream was itself prophetic. By the time Jacob and his family moved to Egypt about twenty years later, Joseph was the second luminary in Egypt. Virtually all Egypt was in thralldom to Pharaoh by Joseph's doing, but Jacob and his family came as honored guests of the throne. They were luminaries, but Joseph was, at least politically, their superior and sponsor, even to his father. It was by his grace they were able to come and live in the best that Egypt had to offer. But that was some years off in the future, and no one yet knew of it except GOD Himself.

Joseph had become *persona non grata* as far as his brothers were concerned, with the possible exception of Benjamin, who was still too young to fully understand the dynamics involved. Their enmity had built to a dangerously high level by the time the next Joseph event occurred. At a certain time, Jacob sent the ten sons of Leah and the two concubines to Shechem with the animals for grazing purposes.[33] Remember, Jacob owned some land there. Thinking the ten sons were at Shechem, he sent Joseph, after a little while, to fetch word on how things were going with the brothers and the animals. The father's heart in Jacob apparently did not understand that the brotherly affections were not positive. Surely, he had no idea the ten brothers would do harm to Joseph when he sent him on his errand. The beautiful innocence of the father's love in light of the hostility of the brothers is astounding to us. The love of the brothers was not innocent because it was conditional, and Joseph did not measure up to the conditions.

When Joseph arrived at Jacob's fields near Shechem, his ten brothers were not there (Gen. 37:17). They had gone to better pastures. Hopefully it is not melodramatic to state that the brothers were out of place both physically and spiritually when Joseph found them. We all know the story of Joseph's treatment at his brothers' hands. When the dreamer arrived, they took action against him. Much of that will be examined in later chapters.

There are a couple of things that deserve special attention at this point, however. First, the fact that the brothers were not where they were supposed to be emboldened them in their plotting. Had they been at Shechem, it is possible they would have feared being seen by local people who knew their father. Word might have gotten back to Jacob about what his sons had done to Joseph, which would not have been a desirable outcome for them. But being elsewhere, they had a greater chance of success because Jacob would not even know where they had been. He would think they were where they were supposed to be. Their being out of place made their plot seem more feasible to them. Jacob would simply never find out.

Second, at least two of the brothers didn't go along with the plan to murder their younger sibling. Reuben suggested they put Joseph in a well rather than kill him themselves (Gen. 37:21-22). Scripture indicates that he intended to sneak back later and get Joseph out of the situation and return him to Jacob. This desire probably had more to do with the love Reuben had for Jacob than with a brotherly concern for Joseph, but it would save Joseph's life. It would also improve Reuben's standing with his father after the Bilhah incident. For whatever reason, Reuben then left the immediate area, intending to return later.

But it was Judah who found the way out (Gen. 37:26-28). When the Ishmaelite caravan happened by, Judah saved Joseph's life by suggesting the brothers sell him into slavery rather than killing him or leaving him to die. Reuben's plan depended on the brothers leaving Joseph alone long enough for him to be rescued. In the final analysis, Reuben's plan might not have worked anyway because rescuing Joseph would have been difficult to pull off, especially trying to keep it secret from the other brothers. Judah's alternative, however, made good sense, at least in the minds of the treacherous brothers. There was no reason to believe Joseph would live very long time under the scourge of the Ishmaelites, much less ever make it home to his father. Their problem was solved. Joseph was disposed of, almost certainly to die as a slave.

Their hands were innocent of actually shedding his blood or even directly causing his death. And even better, they received a profit from selling their brother.

When Reuben discovered what the others had done, he was distraught (Gen. 37:29-30) because he could not now rescue Joseph for his father. His plan had failed. Regardless of his motivation, even if it was only to regain some favor with Jacob, his plan had failed and Joseph was lost to his family. They all believed that he had gone to an eventual, unhappy death in another land. The brothers' plot now took on the necessary dimension of deceiving their father regarding Joseph's disappearance. Fortunately for their plans, the very distinctive coat Jacob had given to Joseph in his gesture of love to him was in their possession. It became the vehicle of their unspoken message to Jacob.

Jacob's heart broke when he saw the bloodied coat. He filled in the blanks for himself as to what had happened so that the brothers did not have to stand about and lie to him and give false alibis. Jacob's beloved Rachel was dead, and now his beloved son by her was dead. Jacob's grief must have been very deep – even life threatening. The now mute brothers guiltily extricated themselves to go to their own dwellings. There was no way to console their father. Their brotherly malice had all but killed Joseph and all believed he was now dead.

Over some time, Jacob, believing Joseph was dead, moved his **paternal** affection from Joseph to Benjamin.[34] Benjamin was his youngest son and the second son of his beloved wife Rachel. He was also considerably younger than any of the other brothers. At the time of Joseph's supposed death, Benjamin was about ten years old and all the other brothers were grown men. It is likely that the subject of Joseph was not often heard in the camp. The brothers certainly wouldn't have wanted to talk about him, and Jacob grieved for a long time in the belief that Joseph was dead.

About thirteen years later, Joseph was released from prison by Pharaoh after a rather interesting set of events to be examined later. It is my belief that Joseph's release from prison in Egypt occurred at about the same time as Isaac's death in Hebron. The unofficial ban on Isaac's travel to foreign places would have been voided after his death. Joseph, therefore, could begin to prepare things for Jacob and his family to come to Egypt. There is no indication, by the way, that any of the players in this story were aware of these things at the time.

The seven years of bumper crops in Egypt go by before we again pick up the story of Jacob and the rest of the family. Twenty years after Joseph became a slave, a great famine came in Egypt and in Canaan. In the first or second year of that famine, Jacob and his sons heard there was a supply of grain to be had in Egypt.[35] Jacob sent the ten sons of Leah and the concubines to Egypt to purchase some of the grain that was available there. None of them had the slightest inkling that Joseph was alive in Egypt, much less that he was the *de facto* ruler of that country. So the brothers, less Benjamin, made the journey.

We know the story. The brothers went and Joseph (still unknown to them) chose Simeon to remain in the Egyptian prison as a guarantee that the rest would return to Egypt with Benjamin (Gen. 42:24). Simeon was an interesting choice. First, Joseph did not choose the **firstborn**, Reuben. Perhaps he knew of Reuben's plan at Dothan to rescue him, but more likely he passed over Reuben out of consideration for Jacob. Simeon was the second son, but he was also in some disfavor with Jacob over the slaughter at Shechem. Some propose that Simeon was likely a leader in the plot to eliminate Joseph and some payback was in order. However the decision was made, it was not likely a random choice. When Joseph arrested Simeon, he instructed the other brothers to return with Benjamin. If they did so, he would release Simeon to them and all would be well.

When the now nine brothers returned to Hebron, they were a sad lot (Gen. 42:27-28). They came back without one of their own. They were also under orders to return to Egypt with Benjamin. They knew that would not work because Jacob would never permit it. Then they discovered they still had the money they had taken to purchase the grain. Thereupon, they concluded they would be considered criminals back in Egypt. Upon learning of the imprisonment of Simeon, Jacob again went into mourning. The condition for returning to Egypt was unacceptable, and his reputation would now include the belief that his sons were thieves. He would not rescue Simeon.

At this point Reuben, as their leader by virtue of being **firstborn**, decided to try to strike a bargain with his father (Gen. 42:37-38). He would return and rescue Simeon by including Benjamin in the entourage. He would guarantee the life of Benjamin with the lives of his own sons. Surely, this was a serious effort on the part of Reuben. The stakes were very high for him. As he presented the bargain, his own sons' lives would be forfeit if anything happened to Benjamin. Still Jacob refused, deciding instead to accept the loss of Simeon rather than risk adding yet another son to the list of those lost, particularly the only remaining son of his beloved wife Rachel. His father's heart was broken and he would not risk more when it came to his sons.

The LORD arranged it so that the family had some time to remain in this broken state.[36] They probably assumed that the famine would soon pass and things would return to their typical state in Canaan. Joseph was gone, and the brothers continued to bear that burden of memory. Simeon was in prison and there was no reason to believe he would ever be seen again. It seemed as though this uneasy set of conditions would prevail into the foreseeable future for the family. Jacob was just about in a permanent state of mourning by now.

Finally, the LORD arranged the different outcome that He desired. The famine continued until it became apparent no relief was in sight. The time came when the family realized they would have to return to Egypt or their flocks would perish (Gen. 43:1-2). There was no other choice available. So Jacob instructed his sons to return to purchase more grain. At this point a real shift occurred in the family dynamic. Judah became the spokesman (Gen. 43:3) in Reuben's place. It was Judah who reminded his father they could not return without Benjamin or the trip would be of no avail. It was Judah who proposed the acceptable bargain for the family. His proposal involved his own person.

The bargain that Judah made was of striking importance. He reminded Jacob that they were forbidden to return to Egypt without Benjamin. In essence, he promised that if he did not return Benjamin safely to his father, that he would give up his position as a son in the house of Jacob, become a slave,[37] and serve his father for as long as they both lived. The essence of Judah's bargain was that he guaranteed Benjamin's safety with his own identity. In a way, that was more than his life. In such a status, his progeny would have no real future. This was an offer of self-sacrifice in the most humiliating manner imaginable. Not only would he give up his identity, but he would serve in perpetuity the man to whom he surrendered it.

We have no information as to why Jacob capitulated to the wishes of his sons expressed by Judah at this point, but he did. The bargain was sufficient. He approved the venture even with dread at the possibility of losing Benjamin. Not only did he send Benjamin, but he sent reparations to the Egyptians lest they still thought of his sons as thieves.

When Judah and the other brothers arrived in Egypt they were reunited with Joseph. It was at this time that Joseph finally revealed himself. Then his first dream from years before in Canaan came true. All eleven brothers were in his presence in the matter of grain (Gen. 37:5-8). This was the precise motif of his first Canaan dream. Later we shall look at the merits of Judah in his rescue of Benjamin from what he thought was certain punishment.

JACOB GOES TO EGYPT

After the events in which Joseph was reunited with his brothers, Pharaoh encouraged Joseph to send for his father and ask the entire family to move down to Egypt (Gen. 45:16-20). They were to be royally treated and settled in the best of the land. This launched the fulfillment of Joseph's second dream. Figurative heavenly luminaries, including the sun and moon and eleven stars, were to bow down to him. The family of Jacob was to come down to Egypt as celebrity guests of Pharaoh and the kingdom. They were to come as "luminaries" (celebrities, VIP's) with a higher status than most Egyptians.

When the brothers returned to Jacob in Hebron (Gen. 45:25-28) in Canaan, they came with gifts and the invitations of Pharaoh and

Joseph. Simeon and Benjamin were restored to him. Then they told him the good news that Joseph was alive and wanted him to move the family to Egypt. In joy Jacob made the preparations. As he left the land of Canaan at Beersheba, he stopped to offer sacrifices. His grandfather and father before him had made sacrifices there in the past. It seemed fitting that he do so now. The LORD again spoke to him in the night, assuring him that he should make the journey to Egypt.[38] In Egypt, the great nation to come from Abraham would become manifest. The LORD promised also to bring Jacob back to Canaan. When he died in Egypt, his sons brought his sarcophagus back for interment at the cave near Hebron, where his father and grandfather were buried (Gen. 50:12-13).

Every single person who could be considered a citizen of the nation went with Jacob to join Joseph and his sons there. As they journeyed to Egypt, Jacob gave to his son Judah the honor of leading the way for the family. Clearly, by the time of the brothers' second journey to Egypt, leadership had transferred from Reuben to Judah. Henceforth, Reuben would never again have any prominence due to his affair with Bilhah,[39] as we shall see later.

Jacob's joy must have been intense. Scripture indicates that he was overcome when he first got the news. Now he was actually going with GOD's blessing and command to be reunited with his son, whom he had presumed to be dead these twenty-plus years. This had to be very emotional for him and the rest of the family. Of course, the servants and all the animals went along as well. The whole camp was moving to a new encampment under the sponsorship of the Pharaoh of Egypt himself. Very soon after their arrival in Egypt, Jacob and Joseph were reunited (probably the day of their arrival) in what undoubtedly was the happiest day in either of their lives.

Joseph made final arrangements for their location in Egypt and then introduced his brothers to Pharaoh, who basically hired them to tend his own animals. That was quite an honor. Finally, Joseph introduced his father to Pharaoh to conclude the ceremonies. Jacob blessed Pharaoh—twice.[40] That may seem strange until you consider that Jacob now carried the full patriarchal **primacy**. This made him the highest priest on the earth of the Melchizedek priesthood. He simply trumped all the Egyptian priests, who had no such legitimacy before GOD. In that capacity he even outranked the Pharaoh himself. Hence, the priestly blessing was fully appropriate at such a time in GOD's eyes.

Finally, Joseph settled his family in the place he had prepared for them with the blessing of Pharaoh. Joseph had situated them in such a way as to keep for them the very high regard of the royal family, as one king would treat another.

The reunion lasted for seventeen years, in which time Joseph made virtually all the Egyptians into servants of Pharaoh and, after the famine ended, ruled in Egypt in Pharaoh's name. When Jacob's death was near, Joseph came to see him (Gen. 48:1-2) and Jacob required him to promise to take his remains back to the family tomb. Joseph readily agreed. In all things concerning the two of them, the great prime minister of Egypt was a son to his father and served him as well as he could, including this last wish. The wish was so sacred that Jacob required Joseph to take the oath on his father's genitalia.[41]

Subsequently, Jacob adopted Joseph's two sons, Ephraim and Manasseh, as his own sons (Gen. 48:5). The effect of this was to provide two shares of the **inheritance** to Joseph with his two sons as proxies. We shall see that this was a very deliberate act. In doing so, he also placed Ephraim, the younger, ahead of Manasseh, the **firstborn**. This was also a prophetic act. Further, he told Joseph why he was doing what he did that day.

Jacob then had all his sons appear before him to pronounce on them his patriarchal blessing. In the context of that patriarchal ceremony he determined many things about their offspring as the tribes of the great nation which they were becoming. We shall consider several aspects of these blessings in the pages to come when we examine the lives of various ones of the sons.

After the death of Jacob, he was accorded all the honors of Egyptian royalty. Afterward, his remains were taken up to the family tomb to be interred with Abraham and Isaac in Hebron (Gen. 50:12-14). Joseph fulfilled the solemn vow he had made to their father. Of the sons, he was the only one to have the authority to do so.

One by one the patriarchs of the great nation had finished their lives and their work. The time had come for the nation to grow greatly in number to be adequate to take possession of the land promised to Abram and to tend and govern the land. It would take some time for the full number of the tribes to be born into the earth. That time would be spent in Egypt, but that is another story.

Please scan the QR code or go to the web address to view Corbett's video introduction to the book.

CHAPTER 5

REUBEN, SIMEON, AND LEVI

http://bit.ly/1N3GuHz

Please go to ravensfood.everykindred.com for access to additional supplements to the book. Content will be added from time to time as desirable to support this book.

CHAPTER 5

REUBEN, SIMEON, AND LEVI

PREVIEW OF THE SONS

As we have already seen, Jacob/Israel had twelve sons. Only one of those sons was born to Israel; eleven to Jacob. Six of those sons were born to Leah in Padan Aram. This occurred in five phases of births. First, there were four sons born in fairly short order: Reuben, Simeon, Levi and Judah. Leah was apparently quite fecund at first. Later, Leah bore two other sons, Issachar and Zebulon. During her quiet phase, her maidservant Zilpah bore two sons to Jacob: Gad and Asher. In the meantime, Rachel's maidservant Bilhah also bore two sons to Jacob: Dan and Naphtali. Later, Rachel herself bore the last two sons: Joseph and Benjamin. The first eleven sons were all born before the family's migration back to Canaan. Only the last, Benjamin, was born in the land of promise.

Earlier we saw that there was a great contest between Leah and Rachel for the affection, or at least the loyalty, of Jacob.[42] In fact, the reason that Bilhah and Zilpah were involved and became mothers is that they were caught up as pawns in the great struggle between the two wives.

THE "BABY WAR"

Phase 1: Leah has *four* sons.

Phase 2: Bilhah has *two* sons for Rachel.

Phase 3: Zilpah has *two* sons for Leah.

Phase 4: Leah has *two* sons and a daughter after the mandrakes.

Phase 5: Rachel has *two* sons, one in Syria and one in Canaan.

In this and the following chapters, we shall examine the **father-son** relationships Jacob had with each of these twelve sons. In particular, we will consider Judah and Joseph because they became the more "important" sons in terms of the development of the nation. Their lives simply deserve closer scrutiny. While the relationship with each of the other ten sons will receive some attention, they are not as well known, mainly because the information we have about them is limited mostly to who their mother was and what Jacob says about each of them in his patriarchal blessings shortly before his death. Finally, we shall preview the impact of the patriarchal blessing on the subsequent history of the individual tribes.

By setting the stage in this manner, we will make more sense of both the nation to come and of the impact on that nation of **father-son** relationships of various content and quality. Having accomplished that overview, we will turn our attention to the first three of the sons of Jacob in terms of their birth order.

The "baby war" referred to earlier was the manner in which the two wives of Jacob sought to work out their rivalry. Through the trickery of Laban, Jacob was first married to Leah, even though it was Rachel he wanted for a wife. In this manner, Laban was able to wed both of his named daughters at the same time, more or less; about a week apart. Leah was aware of the fact that Jacob preferred Rachel. On the surface of the matter, there was nothing Leah could do about that. However, given the importance of children in the culture of their times she soon found that she had an advantage relative to Rachel that she attempted to exploit (Gen. 29:32-33). On the other hand, Rachel soon discovered that she was barren. However, by virtue of the fact that Leah had a weeklong honeymoon before Rachel's wedding to their husband, Leah found that she was fecund.[43] Because she could bear sons and Rachel apparently could not, Leah hoped to take Jacob's favor from Rachel.

Apparently it was in fairly short order that Leah was able to conceive and bear sons to Jacob while Rachel remained unable to conceive. From Leah's point of view, each son was another measure of her husband's favor she hoped for because the sons were important to her husband. Even the names she gave to her sons were statements about this fertility war she had engaged in with her sister. Four sons soon found themselves living in her tent and being tended by servants assigned to that task while Rachel had none of this success. Much of the gravity of attention of the developing camp now attended Leah and her sons while Rachel grew increasingly desperate to bear sons for Jacob.

In desperation, Rachel asked Jacob to impregnate her handmaiden Bilhah (Gen. 30:3-8) to bring some of the status in her direction. The exact timing of this is unknown but it is likely that she resorted to this mechanism even before all the first four sons of Leah had been born. There is some indication that Jacob quit visiting Leah's tent after Judah was born. As the Bilhah plan bore some fruit, Leah also sent her handmaiden into the fray. Each of these two women bore two sons to Jacob in a short while. At that point there were eight sons of Jacob in the emerging community.

On one occasion, Reuben, the first son in the camp, found some mandrakes in the field and brought them home (Gen. 30:15). The mandrake was believed to promote conception. "Aunt" Rachel, hearing of this, made a bargain with her sister Leah. If Leah would let her have some of the mandrakes that Reuben had found, she would send Jacob to Leah's tent (Gen. 30:16). Apparently Rachel hoped that the mandrakes would enable her to conceive. The purchase for the price of a night with their shared husband resulted in a peculiar thing. It was Leah who conceived. For her the mandrakes seemed to work. Rachel did not conceive. So Leah's womb was again opened and she bore two more sons, Issachar and Zebulon, and a daughter in fairly short order before she ceased having children altogether.

GOD would open the womb of Rachel when He chose to do so and was not impressed with her efforts to speed things up.[44] Whatever the reason, the LORD finally blessed Rachel's womb and she bore a son, Joseph. It is likely that this son was still an infant when the family left for Canaan. A few years later, maybe six or seven, in Canaan, Rachel conceived again and bore Benjamin, only to die in childbirth. While Rachel had been the preferred wife, and Joseph was the favored son, it was Leah who was now matriarch of the family in Canaan. The text is silent on the matter, but it is very likely that Leah even accompanied Jacob when he moved to Egypt.[45] Unfortunately, we cannot be certain but we may infer from Joseph's second Canaan dream that this was the case. Leah would be the moon in that dream.

Insofar as we can tell, there was no need for a son of promise in this generation. These were to be the tribal patriarchs, not the national patriarchs. It is interesting, though, that Joseph was born from a womb long barren, as had been the case with Isaac and Jacob. Whatever the reason, Rachel's wait was long. Of course, Joseph's destiny was rather remarkable in terms of the formation of the nation.

The baby war probably took in the range of eleven to thirteen years. In that time frame, eleven sons and at least one daughter were born to Jacob by four women in Padan Aram. One additional son was to born later in Canaan.

In this chapter we will spend some time with each of the first three sons of Jacob. All three came by way of the womb of Leah. After the migration to Canaan, each of these first three sons alienated himself in a significant way from his father Jacob. Jacob never disowned his sons. He did, however, strongly admonish Simeon and Levi for the role they played in the murder of the men of Shechem (Gen. 34:30). We do not know whether he ever spoke directly to Reuben about the situation involving Bilhah, but he did know about the affair, and it is fair to suppose that he did speak to Reuben about it.

Each of the three was significantly diminished in the patriarchal blessings enunciated by Jacob shortly before his death (Gen. 49). And, in fact, the tribes descended from these sons met fates suggested by the pronouncements of the **patriarch**. Not only did Reuben lose his **birthright** as **firstborn**, the tribe composed of his descendants was geographically isolated from the other tribes and eventually disappeared from existence as a separate political entity, the first of all the tribes to meet that fate. Simeon, as a tribal phenomenon, was essentially absorbed into the tribe of Judah. Finally, Levi was given over to the service of the tabernacle, and then the temple, without a landed **inheritance**.

In the next chapter we will examine what we can concerning the virtually invisible sons. They were viable, and became the fathers of tribes in the nation of Israel, but we know virtually nothing of their relationships with Jacob except who their mothers were.

After that we will take a look into the lives and relationships of Benjamin, Judah and Joseph. These three significantly impacted the nation in their own day and in terms of the dynamics of their descendants after the return and conquest of Canaan. Of course, we cannot speak of the history of Joseph without including his two sons, Ephraim and Manasseh, who were adopted as sons by their grandfather Jacob.

REUBEN, THE FIRSTBORN (the *b'cʰor*)

The first son[46] to be born to Jacob was Reuben (Gen. 29:32), whom Leah bore. Leah, knowing that she was not the favorite wife of Jacob, named this first son of hers Reuben, which means, "See, a son." It seems to have been her hope that bearing the **firstborn** for Jacob would cause his affections to switch from Rachel to herself. She stressed that this child was a son because he would be the possessor of the **birthright** to come down from Jacob. Regardless of whether Jacob shifted in his relative affections between the two women, Leah now had the upper hand in terms of future security. Should Jacob die untimely, this son of her womb would be the chief man in the camp. Thus she would be well cared for in her later years. Leah probably hoped that if Jacob would only pay attention he would see that she was able to secure the future for him by the bearing of sons.

It was not to be. On the other hand, we can be sure that Jacob loved his son Reuben and began to make all the arrangements necessary to be sure he grew up with all the training required to make of him a proper leader for the people. The nation had entered its fourth generation and leadership was important. But Rachel was still the woman he loved more.

Soon, though, Leah again became pregnant. Then again—and again. The nation was growing. The promise of large numbers of progeny began to come into view. In short order, there were four sons in Jacob's camp outside Canaan. Somewhere during this timeframe it is probably true that Rachel began to conceive her plan to have Bilhah bear children (hopefully sons) for Jacob. If that could be accomplished, the camp would no longer be so focused on what was happening in Leah's tent. Some balance would be restored, and a son of Bilhah would likely care more for Rachel than for Leah. In some sense, however, such a son would be the "property" of Rachel. As we know, a similar plan did not work out for Sarai.[47]

Imagine what Jacob must have been going through during this time. There had been very few births to Abraham and Isaac, but now in his time things really began to gain momentum in terms of the progeny component of the promise from GOD. Even though he was geographically dislocated, the prophetic promise was going forward.

Reuben began to grow up into his **birthright**. He was carefully trained in all the skills and customs that his father had grown up in. He also had the advantage of being exposed to the culture and ways of his grandfather Laban. Surely, he was a highly favored lad.

At a certain time, after the Bilhah plan went into effect, Reuben happened to find some mandrake plants (Gen. 30:14-16) when he was out in the fields during wheat harvest. We can't know whether he knew what they were, but his mother and aunt did. With those plants his mother was able to borrow her husband from her rival and to become pregnant again after Bilhah and Zilpah had borne sons. Perhaps it is no simple coincidence that Reuben, whose discovery permitted this phase of the baby war, was Leah's son.

Reuben, the heir apparent, grew up with the full expectation that when the time came he would be the chief man. Perhaps he thought that would be in Padan Aram near grandfather Laban. More likely, though, Jacob shared with him that a return to Canaan would occur. Jacob knew about the Lord's promises to Abraham and Isaac, and his own experiences at Bethel certainly made him even more aware of the import of these things. God had appeared to him in a dream at Bethel and promised to return him to all that was his in Canaan (Gen. 28:13-15).

Conversely, Jacob had no **birthright** in Padan Aram. Uncle Laban had his own sons and one of them was the **firstborn** and had virtual possession of the **birthright**. In fact, Jacob would have no **inheritance** at all in Padan Aram. The inheritances would go to the sons of Laban. It might be that Laban would be good to Jacob, but there was no customary guarantee. In Canaan, though, Jacob had a **birthright**. Sooner or later that **birthright** would pass into Jacob's hands. Reuben must have known this. It was perfectly reasonable that there was a much better future-in-waiting for Reuben in Canaan than in the land of his grandfather Laban. It is likely that Reuben loved his father deeply and had that additional motivation to be attendant to what his father spoke to him concerning his future and that of his family. By the time of the mandrake event, there were already at least eight sons[48] in the camp. Dividing up a much larger **inheritance** would look really good for all the sons, but particularly for Reuben, who would receive twice as much as anyone else when the time came. In Padan Aram the sons would get their shares from what Jacob was able to earn and retain. In Canaan, they would inherit all that, and whatever came down from Isaac, which was quite substantial.

JACOB-REUBEN DYAD

The **father-son** relationship between Jacob and Reuben contained all these expectations. Jacob would greatly desire that Reuben in particular would be successful in his ventures. This had nothing to do with the wives. This was about the future of the whole people and of the manifestation of the promises to Abraham and Isaac. None of the other **father-son** relationships in which Jacob was the father (first party) had these components. Surely, given the promises he received at Bethel, these things occupied a place in Jacob's mind and heart and affected his relationship with Reuben in a prominent way. The need to return to Canaan would never be forgotten. Jacob had fulfilled his father's commission to him and could eventually return home with "generation four" in his company. That would be a great and triumphal return. Of course, there were still the matters of Esau's grudge and Jacob's debt to Laban. Reuben would have to wait.

While we know quite a bit about the sons of Jacob with regard to their mothers, we know virtually nothing about their relationships with their father before the migration back to Canaan. At the time of the migration and for several years thereafter, there is nothing that points to Reuben in a specific way until the events that surround Joseph begin to come into focus.

It was shortly after Rachel's death that Reuben had his sexual affair with Bilhah. There is no evidence in scripture that explains how that came to be. However it came about, Jacob heard about it. (In this instance the name Israel is used for Jacob.) It appears that Jacob did nothing about the matter. Surely, though, the behavior was also noticed in the camp and informal corrections took place. It may even be that Jacob scolded his son in the matter. Two major conclusions emerge from these events. First, it must have been of short duration, perhaps only one event. Secondly, the Jacob-Reuben relationship was negatively impacted, probably significantly. This insult to Jacob could not have been simply ignored. This was a very serious betrayal. As a result, the future of Reuben's progeny was seriously impacted, as we shall see.

Our next encounter with Reuben takes place a few years after his affair with Bilhah. Jacob's strong attachment to Rachel carried over into his relationship with Joseph, who was son number eleven. Reuben was the **firstborn**, but Jacob's heart was with Joseph. At the time, Benjamin was still a small child, probably less than ten years old. Because of who Joseph was, events recorded in scripture conjoined in such a way as to cause very hard feelings between him and the ten older brothers. Suffice it to say, the stage was set for the hard times Joseph was to endure at the hands of his brothers and in Egypt. Quickly, the four events were:

Joseph gave a negative report on the sons of Bilhah and Zilpah.

Jacob gave Joseph the fancy coat.

Joseph shared the dream of the grain sheaves.

Joseph shared the dream of the heavenly luminaries.

A short time after these four events, all the brothers except Joseph and Benjamin were away at Shechem with the flocks. At least, that is where Jacob thought they were. Joseph, now seventeen years old (Gen. 37:13-14), apparently traveled alone on a mission from his father to find his older brothers. When he came to Jacob's property in the region, he could not find his brothers. Finding out from an inhabitant of the area that they had moved the herds to another place, Joseph followed them to that location. That's where the trouble began.

Seeing Joseph coming to their location, some of the brothers began to vent their hostility towards him by suggesting to one another that he be killed (Gen. 37:18-20). It seems there was no one else in the area, at least no one who knew them, and they might well get away with the murder. Their **brother-brother** relationships with Joseph were not very good, to say the least. The scriptural account of these events leave little room for doubt on this score.

Reuben, however, suggested to his brothers that they not kill Joseph themselves. Instead, they could put him in a nearby cistern and leave him there. The cistern was apparently so deep and difficult to climb that Joseph would not be able to get out of it once he was put into it. According to Reuben's argument, the brothers would not kill Joseph but he would be left to die in the pit. It was unlikely that anyone would find him. In that manner Joseph would be disposed of, but the brothers would not have killed him. They could rightly profess innocence and consternation to their father without having to lie to him. The other brothers agreed with Reuben's plan. So into the cistern Joseph went.

Reuben planned on returning when none of the other brothers were around so that he could rescue Joseph from the cistern (Gen. 37:21-22). His plan from the beginning was to return Joseph to their father. Based on the information we have, Reuben was less interested in the welfare of Joseph than he was in the welfare of his father. Reuben was still the **firstborn**, and Jacob had invested much in his training and preparation. He was probably secure in that position. There was the matter of his affair with Bilhah, but at this time it does not seem he expected any further consequences from that. His consideration for his father outweighed any disgust he might have felt for Joseph. In fact, he may even have figured that restoring Joseph to Jacob would result in forgiveness for the Bilhah matter. We cannot be sure of these things, but the text is clear that he saved Joseph's life in the moment, and that he intended to return him to their father.

One wonders how Reuben planned to explain these events to the other brothers. They would be pretty upset with him. Also they would worry that Joseph would expose them and their plot to their father. This undoubtedly would have increased the hostility in the camp and likely have led to other attempts on Joseph's life before very long. The brothers might even have tried to bring harm to Reuben as well. Regardless, Reuben intended to save Joseph.

There is no explanation as to why Reuben was absent from the scene when the caravan of Ishmaelites came along, but he was gone and missed the event. Judah (Gen. 37:26-28) came up with a plan for the brothers that resulted in Joseph being sold into slavery at that point. His motives are not clear, but Judah's plan saved Joseph's life and got rid of him at the same time. In fact, there was some money in it for the brothers. In any event, when Reuben returned to the cistern to rescue Joseph, he was gone. Reuben became distraught at that point, and took up a real lament. He even revealed to his brothers off-handedly that he was not in agreement with harming Joseph. Again, it appears he was very concerned with what the news would do to their father. Perhaps he had also learned from their father more consideration for his brothers than they had for one another. Being fairly close to his father's heart might well have caused him to exhibit a measure of **fraternal** concern above that of the other brothers, more like **paternal**.

Shortly after this event, the biblical narrative shifts to the events in the life of Joseph down in Egypt. Judah is the only other son who appears in the text for quite some number of years as the LORD's plan for Joseph's destiny played out. In fact, about twenty two years pass in Joseph's life with no word about the state of affairs in Jacob's camp. All we know is that Jacob mourned greatly over the loss of Joseph.

About a year[49] after the great famine began in Egypt and in Canaan, Jacob determined to send his sons to Egypt because they had heard that grain could be purchased there. The mission was undertaken by the ten older brothers—the same brothers who originally planned to murder Joseph but sold him into slavery instead. Benjamin was required to remain at home although he was a grown man, being in the neighborhood of thirty years old. It seems that Jacob took consolation in the company of this particular son. After all, he was the only other son of the favored wife, Rachel, and a brother to the lost son, Joseph. In addition to the consolation he took in Benjamin, Jacob had become very protective of him. Rachel was dead, and he thought Joseph was also. These things had struck very near to Jacob's heart.

The brothers were basically successful in their mission. They located the source of grain and made their purchase. However, Joseph then required them to give an account of themselves and used that as pretext to force their hand so that he could cause them to bring Benjamin to him. He kept the brothers in jail for *three days*,[50] probably to make them more compliant, and then kept a hostage from among them. The hostage was Simeon, who was the second son. It was Reuben who reminded the others at this point that they were guilty in the matter of Joseph and regarded their current situation as some form of retribution for that sin.

Upon the return of the remaining nine brothers to Hebron in Canaan and the discovery of the returned money, Jacob was almost in shock. Joseph was presumed dead; Simeon was in jail in a foreign country; the cost to get Simeon back was too high for him; and his sons would have a reputation down in Egypt as thieves. Not a lot more could go wrong.

It was Reuben who told their father that the brothers should return to Egypt with Benjamin to secure the release of Simeon (Gen. 42:36-39). That way, at least, only one son would remain lost to Jacob. Reuben even offered the lives of his two sons as the surety that he would make it back with Benjamin and Simeon. The possible cost was just too high for Jacob. He did not agree.

This was a remarkable proposition that Reuben made that day. His own sons' lives were to be forfeit if he was unsuccessful. He was the elder brother, the **firstborn**, who had quite significant responsibility and seems to have taken it quite seriously. To place one's sons on the line in that manner would be very hard on any father. However, Reuben seems to have been so heartbroken over his father's condition that he was willing to go that far to accomplish the proposed mission. Jacob rejected the proposition out of hand. There was no more to be done. The nine had to live with the loss of Joseph, and now of Simeon, and the great sorrow of their father into an indefinite future. One can sense a kind of gloom pervading the camp from that time.

This unsuccessful attempt on Reuben's part to lead a rescue mission for Simeon, and to repay the Egyptian official for the grain to restore their reputation, seems to mark the end of leadership for Reuben. He does not again enter the narrative except at the time when Jacob provided patriarchal blessings for his sons in Egypt. He was still **firstborn** and was still associated with the **birthright**, but he does not appear again as the leader, as we will see.

Actually, there was one other event in which Reuben played a role, but he is not named in the narrative. However, his position as **firstborn** was to be respected by Joseph when he held the banquet for the brothers after their return to Egypt and the release of Simeon (Gen. 43:33). Again, the real observation is that Joseph knew the birth order and his brothers were not yet aware of his identity.

Just before his death in Egypt, Jacob sent for his sons so that he could pronounce patriarchal blessings on them (Gen. 49). This was an important event for, as we have seen, the patriarchal blessing was also a priestly blessing. It was prophetic in nature. It was also binding once pronounced. It could not be repealed.

There are two parts to the blessing Jacob bestowed on Reuben (Gen. 49:3-4). First is a statement of praise couched in his being the **firstborn**. It was quite complimentary of Reuben as the **firstborn** and the son who had held the hopes of Jacob for the future. However, in the second part, his treachery and betrayal of his father in the affair with Bilhah essentially disqualified him. He would "no longer excel." We must assume that Reuben knew in advance that he was not to emerge as a chieftain over his brothers. His is the only truly mixed blessing among the twelve brothers. Later in scripture, it is made clear that the blessing did, in effect, take from him his rights as **firstborn** and transfer them to Joseph and Judah. He was still **firstborn** according to Jacob, but he had lost the **birthright** benefits of said position (1 Chron. 5:1).

TRIBAL DESTINY

Three generations after these things, the descendants of Jacob and his sons, now known as Israelites, left Egypt, where the blessings had been pronounced. One generation after that, the Israelites, including the descendants of Reuben, were ready to enter the land of Canaan. However, in the last critical months before the crossing of the Jordan River, two and one-half of the twelve tribes petitioned Joshua to allow them to stay on the east side of the river (Num. 32:1-33, Josh. 1:12-18). After some discussion and bargaining, the decision was made for them to remain in that place, which was not really in Canaan. The bargain was that the army units from these tribes would assist in the securing of Canaan proper, and then be allowed to return to the other side of Jordan. All agreed and it was done. One of those tribes was the tribe of Reuben.

When the conquest was essentially complete, Joshua and the other elders permitted the armies of the eastern tribes to cross back over Jordan and take up their inheritances. It is interesting to note that the territory allotted to Reuben in this situation was the least protected. The territory of Reuben was actually east of the Dead Sea. It was south of the point at which the Jordan River flowed into the Dead Sea. Its location made it the most difficult tribal portion to receive help from the others. It is not clear how and in what stages the territory of Reuben was gobbled up by Edomites, Ammonites, and Ishmaelites, but it basically disappeared from the narrative fairly early in the history of the Israelites. When Jacob took the **birthright** from Reuben, the tribe was forever weakened. In later history, it played no real role.

SIMEON, SECOND SON

Jacob's second son also came through the womb of Leah (Gen. 29:33). This son's name was Simeon, which may mean "one who hears," referring to the fact that GOD had heard her continuing lament because of Rachel and had answered prayers with a second son. In her thinking, this increased her hope that Jacob would switch his favor over to her. That didn't happen, as we know.

As was true for all the sons, there is basically no discussion of Simeon's early life while the family was still in Padan Aram. Once back in Canaan, however, Simeon, with his brother Levi, was the first of the sons of Jacob to begin to matter. Sometime after the return to Canaan, specifically when the camp was at Shechem, the rape of Dinah occurred (Gen. 34:1-3). Dinah was the full sister of Simeon and Levi. In fact, she was also the full sister of Reuben, Judah, Issachar and Zebulon as well.

Jacob was the first to learn of the event, but the sons soon heard somewhere out in the pasturage and returned to camp even before the discussion between King Hamor and Jacob was ended. The text tells us that unspecified sons of Jacob set up the tragedy for Hamor and Shechem by placing the requirement of circumcision on the whole city. For economic and political reasons, the men of Shechem agreed to the bargain.

JACOB-SIMEON DYAD

We don't know why these two brothers, Simeon and Levi, were more incensed than the others, but they were. On the third day after the men of the city were circumcised and were virtually defenseless, Simeon and Levi conducted a campaign of mass murder in the city. Then, apparently, all the sons joined them in looting the place. Jacob, learning of this, complained to his sons that they might well have started a war between him and any number of Canaanite cities. Simeon and Levi defended their actions by claiming it was retribution for the rape of their sister Dinah by Shechem, saying he had treated her like a prostitute. They offered no remorse for the potential harm done to their father and the "nation."

The narrative does not speak of Simeon again until the brothers went to Egypt quite some number of years later (thirty or so) to buy grain (Gen. 42:1-3). When Joseph decided on his plan to require the ten brothers to return with Benjamin, it was Simeon whom he imprisoned as a hostage to insure their return (Gen. 42:24). It was Simeon whom Jacob decided to leave in the Egyptian prison (Gen. 42:36) rather than to allow Benjamin to go to Egypt with his brothers. Of course, Jacob loved his son Simeon, but their relationship had suffered greatly about thirty five years earlier in the camp near Shechem. His love for Simeon, however, was greatly tempered by his attachment to Benjamin.

Some have speculated that the reason Joseph placed Simeon in prison is that Simeon might well have been the henchman in the attempted murder of Joseph. Simeon was at least the oldest of the brothers in the attempt, since Reuben was looking for another way to get things done. It might also be that Joseph kept Simeon out of some residual respect for the fact that Reuben was the **firstborn** and, at the time, the leader of the brothers. Joseph, of course, knew the birth order and could easily select the number two son for his hostage. However Joseph made the selection, it was Simeon who was imprisoned, for maybe a year or so. By that time we can be sure he doubted his rescue because he knew it was supposed to happen in a matter of weeks. Reuben and the others would return home, rest a bit, and return with Benjamin to rescue him from jail. As the weeks wore on into months and his brothers did not return for him, he surely began to despair in the Egyptian prison. He likely concluded, among other possibilities, that his father had abandoned him. In that event he would die there in that Egyptian prison. We can only imagine his relief when the time of his release suddenly arrived. In a short time after his release, he was reunited with his brothers, including Benjamin.

Simeon's release was soon followed with the brothers' reunion with Joseph and the migration of Jacob's camp to Egypt. As far as the biblical text is concerned, Simeon played no particular role in these events after his release from prison. Of course, his father welcomed him home, but that was lost in the news of Joseph and preparation for the move to Egypt.

We next hear of Simeon in the patriarchal blessings of Jacob (Gen. 49:5-7). There was nothing positive in Jacob's prophecy for Simeon. He was combined with Levi, just as he had been at Shechem. Their anger was cursed with respect to that matter. Jacob disavowed they should have any influence over him. Finally, he declared they would be scattered and dispersed in Israel.

We cannot know exactly what Jacob meant by the prophecy of scattering and dispersing. What we do know is that when the Israelites arrived in Canaan, the portion taken for Simeon was totally surrounded by the territory of Judah (Josh. 19:1). The tribe of Simeon shared no borders with any other tribe in the nation. Simeon is virtually never mentioned again and basically disappeared by absorption into Judah. By the time of the split Kingdom, there was no territory of Simeon. His descendants were dispersed so as to be absorbed out of awareness.

LEVI, THIRD SON

Jacob's third son, Levi, also arrived by way of the womb of Leah (Gen. 29:34). Leah continued to hope to switch Jacob's emotional attachment from Rachel to herself. When her third son was born, she thought that might do the trick. She was, after all, way too far ahead in the son-bearing for Rachel to ever hope to catch up. So she named the boy Levi, which may mean "attached." His early life is as obscure as the lives of the other brothers.

JACOB-LEVI DYAD

After his birth, the first named appearance of Levi in scripture is at the Shechem massacre (Gen. 34:25-27). He was the one who, with Simeon, slaughtered the helpless men of the city.

As we saw above, at the time of the patriarchal blessings (Gen. 49:5-7), Levi was paired with Simeon in the not-so-pleasant prophecy concerning their violent anger. He too, was to be scattered and dispersed in Israel.

As we know, the tribe of Levi was the tribe into which Moses was born (Ex 6:16-20). When the Israelites were at Sinai, this tribe of Levi was separated out for the service of the tabernacle (Num. 18:20-21) and the system of sacrifices. In the distribution of the tribes, Levi's tribe received cities but not territory (Num. 35:1). Their cities were scattered throughout the other tribes. In addition, Levi's descendants became the servants of the tabernacle and the future temple. There was some status associated with that. However, there was no possession of land and the means to build an **inheritance** for their sons. There was only the Aaronic/Levitical service for this tribe, which was permanently dispersed in Israel.

The Levites accompanied the northern tribes into Assyrian captivity and they accompanied the southern tribes into Babylonian captivity. They simply had no other vestiges of individual political identity besides the temple service. Many became quite wealthy, and over time they gained considerable status, but they were scattered and dispersed.

Please scan the QR code or go to the web address to view Corbett's video introduction to the book.

CHAPTER 6

THE "UNSEEN" SONS OF JACOB

http://bit.ly/1JGoGHH

Please go to ravensfood.everykindred.com for access to additional supplements to the book. Content will be added from time to time as desirable to support this book.

THE "UNSEEN" SONS OF JACOB

Having examined briefly the lives of the first three sons of Jacob, each of whom was somewhat discredited, we will now turn our attention to six of the sons about whom we actually know very little. Each received an **inheritance**. Each was the father of a viable tribe. Each tribe had a place in Israel. However, for the most part, the roles they played were fairly minor and we know almost nothing about how they related to their father as individuals.

What we do have regarding these sons of Jacob is some basic information:

- Birth order
- Birth mother
- Meaning of the name and the reason for the naming
- Content of the patriarchal blessing
- Disposition in the land of the descendants
- Minor aspects of tribal history

In this brief chapter we will examine these **father-son** dyads:

- Jacob-Issachar
- Jacob-Zebulun
- Jacob-Dan
- Jacob-Naphtali
- Jacob-Gad
- Jacob-Asher

It is important to understand going in that we have virtually no information concerning the personal lives of these six sons.

ISSACHAR

The ninth son of Jacob in terms of supposed birth order was Issachar (Gen. 30:17). He was the fifth son of Leah, and was born in her second phase of son-bearing. His conception might well have been related to the mandrakes Reuben brought home to his mother. We say his birth order was "supposed" because the narrative takes the sons in groups by birth mother. It is not necessarily so, then, that both of the sons of Bilhah and/or Zilpah were born before Issachar (Gen. 30:3-13), but they probably were.

Issachar's name means "reward." When he was born, his mother felt that the LORD had rewarded her for giving Zilpah to Jacob to bear sons and build up the family. Her declaration to this effect is the only evidence that GOD, in fact, did so.

Jacob's blessing for Issachar is a bit perplexing. He seems to suggest that Issachar, as a tribe, would consent to domination just for the sake of staying put in the place of its possession. That place was in the north near Galilee. It contained Mount Tabor, which we call the Mount of Transfiguration.

It is indeed a beautiful country even today. Its agricultural richness was of note. However, that country was somewhat difficult to defend insofar as the Kingdoms were concerned, and was often contested by foreign invaders.

Scripture provides no information concerning the JACOB-ISSACHAR **dyad**.

ZEBULUN

Zebulun was the tenth son of Jacob. At least, he was born after Issachar and was the sixth and last son borne by Leah (Gen. 30:20). Scholars believe his name is associated with "honor." His mother felt that his birth would cause her husband to honor her. In the naming of her sons, she was consistent in her hope of becoming the favored wife of her husband.

The blessing Jacob pronounced for Zebulun is an interesting one. It suggests that the tribe would be very successful commercially. The tribe of the descendants of Zebulun received its tribal allotment west of the area given to Issachar. It extended toward the coast. To the north were descendants of the Canaanites. Mostly it appears that relations were fairly good between them, and it was not until the time of the Assyrians that the tribal area of Zebulun was seriously disturbed.

As with Issachar, there is no scriptural information concerning the JACOB-ZEBULUN dyadic relationship.

These two sons of Leah were simply eclipsed by their brothers from the first phase, as well as by the sons of Rachel. They probably had more status than the sons of Bilhah or Zilpah, but were still very minor in the national dynamics.

DAN

Dan is the fifth son in birth order insofar as the Genesis account goes (Gen. 30:5-6). He was the first of two sons born to Bilhah, who was Rachel's handmaiden. It was Rachel who decided that Bilhah should bear sons on her behalf after it was clear that Rachel was barren. It was Rachel, not Bilhah, who gave Dan his name. Dan may mean "judge" or "vindication." Rachel said she had been vindicated, and claimed Dan to be her own son.

Jacob validated the name in his patriarchal blessing for Dan, declaring that he would be an instrument of justice for the people (Gen. 49:16-18). There is an interesting second part to the Dan prophecy that indicates he would be a kind of undetected guardian for the nation, like a serpent by a path.

During the times of the tribal disbursement in the land after the exodus from Egypt, the tribe of Dan had a hard time taking territory. They eventually settled in two areas. One area was on the coast just north of Philistia, and the other was in the northeast, east of the Sea of Galilee. In these locations, Dan was first to feel any restlessness from Philistia or from Syria. Both these areas were troublesome for the tribe, as significant invading armies came through them. Jacob's prophetic dictum regarding Dan was born out in that history. It is of interest to note that Samson was a Danite from the area near the Philistines (Judges 13:24).

Scripture provides no information concerning the JACOB-DAN dyadic relationship.

NAPHTALI

Naphtali was the sixth son born to Jacob, and the second son to come from the womb of Bilhah (Gen. 30:7-8). Again, it was Rachel rather than Bilhah who gave him his name. At the time, Rachel referred directly to the baby war with Leah and gave this son of Bilhah a name that means "my struggle" to mark the contest.

Jacob had very little to say concerning Naphtali in his patriarchal blessings. Basically poetic in its nature, the blessing has a pleasant softness to it that speaks little to the future of the tribe. The possession of Naphtali was in the northern part of Galilee on the west side of the upper Jordan River.

As was true for the tribe of Dan, this was a rather remote location from the centers of the Kingdoms. It was bordered on the north by

Canaanites, and on the northeast by Syrians. As such, it was in an area that was troubled when nations north of Israel were in the mood to make trouble for the Israelites. It is likely, for example, that when the Assyrians came, the people of Naphtali were among the first to feel that wrath.

Once again, there is no scriptural information concerning the JACOB-NAPHTALI dyadic relationship.

GAD

Gad was Jacob's seventh son, and the first to be born to Zilpah, Leah's handmaiden (Gen. 30:10-11). After Leah's first four sons were born and she finished bearing, she noticed that Rachel's handmaiden Bilhah had begun to bear sons who were claimed by Rachel. Leah decided that she would do the same thing, and sent Zilpah to Jacob for that purpose. When the son was born, Leah named him Gad. There are multiple suggested meanings for Gad. The name might mean "good fortune" or "a troop." Either would seem to suit Leah's mood at the time. She could now claim the score was five-to-two in her contest with her younger sister.

The patriarchal blessing Jacob provided for Gad (Gen. 49:20) was also a bit obscure. It suggested turmoil in the form of attacks on the tribe. It also suggested something like guerilla warfare in response to such troubles. Gad was one of the tribes that chose to locate east of the Jordan River. It was a small tribe that was situated along the lower Jordan River between Reuben to the south and Manasseh to the north and east. Not far away were the troublesome Ammonites, who were descendants of Lot.

There is no scriptural information concerning the JACOB-GAD dyadic relationship.

ASHER

Asher was the eighth son born to Jacob, and the second born to Zilpah (Gen. 30:12-13). Leah claimed Asher and gave him his name, which means "happy." She was happy that the score was now six-to-two in her contest with her sister.

Jacob pronounced a blessing of prosperity on this, the last son of his concubines. He suggested that the tribe of Asher would produce rich things for kings. The tribe's territory was located on the coast in the northwest, just south of the Phoenicians, who were a trading people. It is probably true that Asher, as a tribe of people, benefited greatly from this proximity. Of course, this very northern position placed the tribe in the path of the Assyrians when they came, and therefore was among the first of the tribes to disappear. By that time, there had been significant intermarriage with the residual Canaanites and Phoenicians.

As with all the others, no scriptural information is provided concerning the JACOB-ASHER dyadic relationship.

SONS OF THE CONCUBINES

The last four sons reviewed above were born to Jacob's two concubines, Bilhah and Zilpah. These women were the handmaidens of Rachel and Leah respectively. Their mistresses each claimed the sons born by them as their own. However, it is also true that these sons were not as fully accepted as the others. Once each of them had been claimed as a son by the respective mistress, they were not particularly associated with the sons born by that woman. They were somewhat apart. It is almost as though they were claimed by Rachel and Leah only as components of the contest between the two of them.

Bilhah and Zilpah are typically called by their names in the narrative. However, in one particular passage that does not seem to be the case. Jacob is known to have had sons by only the four women. He had no other wives or concubines, as far as we can tell. On one occasion, though, we are told that Joseph was out in the fields with the "sons of the concubines" (Gen. 37:2). Those sons must have been Dan, Naphtali, Gad, and Asher. Joseph took back to Jacob a poor report on their activities. This certainly must have angered these sons, who already had a lower status than the sons of the "true" wives. In fact, one wonders why they were grouped together that day to begin with.

Perhaps these "sons of the concubines" were among the more vocal in the plot that led to the near-murder and enslavement of Joseph. This stands to reason. They already were of a lower status due to the birth womb, and now their father was told they were not carrying out their responsibilities correctly. This begs another question. Why, in that case, was not one of the "sons of the concubines" selected by Joseph for a hostage rather than Simeon? One may infer that the Simeon's status was more prominent as second-born son. Joseph went to the highest status short of the **firstborn** in his selection in order to provide Jacob the motivation to act positively. Joseph little knew the attachment Jacob had formed with Benjamin at the time. Benjamin had become the replacement for Joseph in Jacob's affection. This outranked Simeon. Reuben would have been a more effective selection, but Joseph would not take the **firstborn** from his father in even a temporary situation. Besides, Reuben had tried to save him (Gen. 37:21-22).

We cannot say that the tribes of the sons of the concubines were deliberately placed on the frontiers, but that is essentially where they were located at the time of the division of the land. In fact, the division was determined by some sort of drawing of lots that we cannot detail at all. In any event, that is where they were. During the period of the judges who "ruled" Israel, these tribes were often the points of contact with the various invaders such as the Ammonites, Midianites, Amalekites, Philistines, and so forth. As such, they would suffer proportionately more than the other tribes, at least in the early history. A full discussion of this is beyond our scope, but worthy of note. These four tribes were always relatively far away from the seats of power in Jerusalem and Samaria. Thus their impact on the course of the history of the Israelites was minor.

Please scan the QR code or go to the web address to view Corbett's video introduction to the book.

CHAPTER 7

BENJAMIN: THE SILENT SON

http://bit.ly/1PoylPY

Please go to ravensfood.everykindred.com for access to additional supplements to the book. Content will be added from time to time as desirable to support this book.

BENJAMIN: THE SILENT SON

The story of Benjamin is a unique one among the sons of Jacob. Benjamin comes on the scene quite late in their collective history. He was born in Canaan (Gen. 35:16-19), which distinguishes him from all his brothers. His birth was preceded by the name change from Jacob to Israel.[51] Even in the Canaan portions of the narrative, he is removed from the other sons of Jacob. He was there, but almost invisible. When his presence in Egypt was demanded by "the great man" of Egypt (Joseph), Benjamin was spoken of as though he were not present (Gen. 42:29-36; 43:8-10). By then he was a grown man of about thirty years, and had several children of his own. He remains a man of mystery even today. Although not as obscure as the so-called "sons of the concubines," Benjamin still is not directly in the mainstream of the story either, except by indirect reference. We know nothing negative about him. He came to be greatly beloved by Jacob, especially as a sort of replacement for Joseph in Jacob's heart. Benjamin also became a bargaining chip in a significant family drama. All this, and yet Benjamin never said a recorded word in scripture.

Benjamin was born last of the twelve sons of Jacob. As the second of the two sons to come forth from the womb of Rachel, the beloved

(Gen. 35:16-19), Benjamin was in a natural place to receive love from his father Jacob that was exceeded only by Jacob's love for Joseph. The time gap between Benjamin and Joseph was almost definitely greater than that between any other two sequential sons. When Benjamin was born, Rachel knew his birth was killing her. As a consequence, she spoke of her sorrow when she named him, calling him *ben-Oni*, which is usually thought to mean "son of my trouble." Upon her death, though, Jacob renamed him. He called him *ben-Jamin,* which seems to mean "son of (my) right hand," which would refer to Rachel in terms of her importance to him. And so the family was all present.

Benjamin's birth in Canaan seems to mark the end of Jacob's homecoming from exile. It places the family in the land to be inherited from the hand of GOD, thereby finally establishing and settling who Israel was. The tragedy of Rachel's death notwithstanding, the nation was in its place. From here the nation began to build its wealth, its size, and its reputation.

Isaac was still alive in those days[52] and would surely have been pleased to finally see things settling after all Jacob had endured up to that point. With Esau having removed himself from the picture, Isaac could now view things in a more settled way. His son of promise had gone to the country of his ancestors and fetched for himself proper wives (Gen. 29:18-28). In addition, sons had been born to those wives, and they were near him at his home in the Hebron area. His grandsons were surely delights to him. Jacob and the young men would continue to build the **inheritance** and reputation that had begun with his father Abraham.

I reckon Benjamin to be past twenty years of age by the time Isaac died. He saw the nation forming and probably had a vision of its future. The thing that would have troubled Isaac most was the apparent loss of Joseph. He never saw him again.[53] Jacob's other sons were there, though, and Isaac could take comfort in that. He probably also understood quite well the very strong bond Jacob had with his son Benjamin. In fact, it probably reminded Isaac of his own strong attachment to Esau in earlier years.

Jacob had lived in the shadows himself, until the time he left Canaan. He had been a "camp boy," as we observed earlier. This seems to have been replicated in the way Jacob raised Benjamin. We may assume that Jacob was okay with Benjamin being invisible because he had been largely invisible himself. He certainly would have seen to it that Benjamin had the basic training he would need to work among the herds and flocks, but Benjamin was not trained to be the chief man of the tribe. His role, as far as we can tell, was to keep his father company after the losses of Rachel and Joseph (Gen. 42:38). Benjamin was a kind of consolation for his father. The result of that positioning of Benjamin is that he would also be mostly invisible to his brothers, much as Joseph had been, with the exception that Jacob would accept virtually no risks when it came to the young man's welfare or safety. Jacob probably never sent Benjamin on a journey to seek his brothers, for example.

We cannot know whether Benjamin appreciated or resented the unusual affection Jacob extended to him. Probably, he felt some of both in his heart as time went on. His father required of him a somewhat passive role in the life of the camp. Did this cause him to become restive? That is unknown to us because scripture provides us with no operational view of Benjamin's life except as an object.

It is quite likely that there was a strong bond between Benjamin and his older brother Joseph, for several reasons. They shared the same mother. They were the last two sons born. They both tended to have very close relationships with their father. In some sense, by the actions of their father, the two brothers had little to do with all their older brothers.

Furthermore, Joseph demanded that his brother Benjamin be brought to him in Egypt (Gen. 42:18-20). There are two fairly apparent motivations for this. First, they might well have been quite close and Joseph naturally would have desired to see his younger brother. When he saw the brothers for the first time during their visit to Egypt, he likely looked for Benjamin among them. This is further evidenced in that when Benjamin did arrive on the second visit, Joseph singled him out for special attention relative to the other brothers. A second reason for insisting on Benjamin's appearance might have been that he needed all eleven brothers present at once to fully actualize the "eleven sheaves" dream (Gen. 37:5-8). If only ten brothers showed up, there could be no audience with eleven of them. Whatever the actual motivation, it is reasonable to assume the two brothers had a close relationship. Each of them was likely to be closer to the other than to any of the other brothers from other wombs.

We just don't know much about Benjamin as a man from direct observation. In fact, he was an active participant only in the Egypt saga that involved the family. Even as a participant, he was only passively involved. We learn most about him from the actions of the other players in these dramas.

Aside from the obvious fact of Benjamin's obscurity, we don't have much about him until the Egypt drama. When the older brothers returned from Egypt with the news of Simeon's imprisonment, Benjamin became a prominent factor in the life of Jacob for a different reason than before. Obviously, Joseph had moved Benjamin out of his obscurity with the demand he had placed on the older brothers. Benjamin now was the central subject of things for some time to come. Joseph had no way of knowing how attached Jacob had become to his younger brother. On the other hand, the sheaves dream (Gen. 37:5-8) required all eleven brothers, whether Joseph was thinking about the dream or not.

When the brothers returned to their home in Hebron, they were a bit depressed. Not only had they been reminded of their treatment of Joseph, they returned with yet one less brother. We may wonder what they thought would happen when their father was informed, but at any rate, they could not have been looking forward to that meeting. They dreaded mentioning the requirement of returning with Benjamin to effect Simeon's release.

Then there was the added matter of the returned money in one of their sacks. Upon unloading the goods from the trip they discovered the rest of the money — all of it they had taken to Egypt. With the discovery of the rest of the money, Jacob raised a lament concerning his sons Joseph and Simeon. He could not bring himself to agree to the return trip.

Jacob's reluctance prompted Reuben to bargain with his father concerning Benjamin's welfare. Reuben took it upon himself to become the guarantor of the return of all eleven sons. He made a very solemn promise on the lives of his own sons. A disconsolate Jacob refused. His patriarchal authority caused the conversation to end. Simeon would remain in an Egyptian prison. Benjamin would remain at home in Hebron with his father.

Throughout the conversation, Benjamin occurs only as an object, not a participant. He was being talked about with no apparent opportunity to enter the conversation himself. We can only wonder what he thought about these discussions of his life and welfare. He was, after all, a man of twenty-five to thirty years of age. He already had ten children of his own when all this was going on (Gen. 46:21).

We know, of course, of the journey to Egypt that involved all of Joseph's brothers and its outcome. The sheaves dream was fulfilled and Jacob was invited to come to Egypt as a permanent guest of Pharaoh under the care of his son. Benjamin was present, but not really an actor in the events.

On the other hand, we find a tribe of Benjamin's descendants with quite a history. In examining the lives of his brothers so far, we have found some correlation between the man Benjamin and the tribe that later descended from him. When Jacob pronounced the patriarchal blessings (Gen. 49:27) over his sons, the last of them was for Benjamin, who was the last born. It was a peculiarly short blessing, given the duration and intensity of their relationship. Every element of the prophecy speaks to a predatory and opportunistic nature. Did Jacob view Benjamin as predatory, or was this only about his descendants? It seems likely that the nature of the obscured man was at least partially reflected in the prophecy.

At the time the nation of Israel returned to Canaan to conquer it, the portion of the land given to the tribe of Benjamin was fairly small.

Furthermore, it was nestled up against the portions given to Judah and Ephraim. Ephraim, of course, was the dominant son of Joseph, so there was a kinship of sorts there. The small tribe of Benjamin was also notable for its war against all the rest of the Israelites well before there was a king in the land (Judg. 19-21). This is also the tribe from which came Israel's first king, Saul (1 Sam. 9:15-21). Prophetically, Saul should not have been the king because the Kingdom was clearly assigned to Judah. Perhaps the Lord gave Saul to the people to show them how to not be a Kingdom. Finally, when the Kingdom split under Rehoboam, Benjamin's tribe was the only other intact tribe to remain with the tribe of Judah in the southern Kingdom. Otherwise, the tribe of Benjamin was small and fairly unimportant in the larger matters of Israel. The apostle Paul was a Benjamite, by his own assertion (Rom. 11:1)

The JACOB-BENJAMIN **dyad** was obviously a very close one. However it appears it was only a substitutionary one for Jacob. Benjamin's comfort in the relationship is simply unknown.

Please scan the QR code or go to the web address to view Corbett's video introduction to the book.

CHAPTER 8

JOSEPH

http://bit.ly/1RiRnNm

Please go to ravensfood.everykindred.com for access to additional supplements to the book. Content will be added from time to time as desirable to support this book.

CHAPTER 8

JOSEPH

Joseph was the eleventh son of Jacob and the first son from the womb of Rachel (Gen. 30:22-24). Rachel named him Joseph at birth because in so doing she asked the LORD to add another son to her tent. Joseph means "may he add," or something very like that. Rachel, we know, was the beloved wife of Jacob, and it appears he transferred much of that affection to his son Joseph. This is completely understandable, considering how deeply Jacob loved Rachel despite her many years of barrenness. Now, however, after "giving" Jacob two sons through her handmaiden Bilhah, she had now given him a son who came forth from her own womb. Thus, at a very early age—probably even from birth—Joseph became the darling of his father.

Some time passed after the family moved back to Canaan before the birth of Benjamin. Joseph was probably in the neighborhood of seven to ten years old at that time. Before that, he was surely the darling of the camp because of who his mother was. Leah had won the baby war but had never gained her husband's preference. Because Rachel held Jacob's heart, so also did Joseph, the son of her womb. Reuben may have been in training to be the chief man, but Joseph was the little prince of the camp. It appears he simply spent more time at home than the other brothers.

As we have already mentioned, an occasion came up in which Joseph gave a negative report to his father concerning the labor of four of his brothers, the sons of Bilhah and Zilpah (Gen. 37:2). This event, of course, angered his four brothers, and might not have set well with his father either; we simply don't know. These brothers already had a lower status than the sons of Leah and Rachel, which made the event even more uncomfortable for them.

At some later point in time, Jacob had a coat made for Joseph (Gen. 37:3-4); a particularly splendid coat. Its very existence made the older brothers jealous, especially Joseph's possession of it. After all, none of them had received such a garment from their father. By this time, Rachel was already dead and Benjamin was just a youngster, so Joseph, displaying his unique status in his fancy coat with all its accoutrements, must have cut quite a figure in the camp.

These two events, which occurred when Joseph was about seventeen years old, caused tremendous friction between Joseph and his older brothers, particularly the sons of the concubines. Joseph seems not to have noticed his brothers' anger, or perhaps he just did not care. The next events recorded of Joseph are his dreams, first, of the sheaves of grain, and second, of the heavenly luminaries (Gen. 37:5-11). When Joseph shared the sheaves dream with his brothers, they were incensed at the plain meaning of the dream. His father was present when he shared the second dream. This luminary dream even upset Jacob to some extent because of its obvious implications. He remonstrated with Joseph on that occasion, but there is no indication their relationship actually suffered any real damage.

Sometime later, Jacob decided to send Joseph to find his older brothers, who supposedly were tending the flocks at the family property near Shechem (Gen. 37:12-14). This is the occasion in which we see the full effect of the poor **brother-brother** relationships Joseph had with his brothers. They set out to kill him, or at least some of them did. Reuben attempted to save Joseph from the wrath of the other brothers, and was able to at least postpone matters. Judah finally found a way to actually save Joseph's life, perhaps as a side-effect.

Joseph's disappearance and presumed death was a serious blow to Jacob. Scriptural evidence strongly suggests that Joseph was Jacob's favorite son, probably as an extension of Jacob's deep love for Rachel. Rachel was dead, and now Joseph too was lost to Jacob.

From Joseph's perspective, he never desired, and certainly never expected, to journey to Egypt, much less live there.[54] While on the road to Egypt, his thoughts surely must have turned often to his father and younger brother, and how comforting it would have been to be with them. He hoped for life, but as things progressed, he surely came to realize that his life would never again be the same as it had once been. Whenever his thoughts turned to that awful day at Dothan where his whole world fell apart, Joseph's brothers could not have been his favorite people, to say the least. He probably wondered for hours on end why they had so turned against him. Although scripture never once mentions this about Joseph, it is only natural to imagine that he struggled many times with feelings of despair. This certainly must have been the case at the beginning of his ordeal, the moment he realized what his brothers were doing to him.

As Joseph's new life in Egypt unfolded, his natural aptitudes came into play and he began to rule his master's house, though still a slave (Gen. 39:6). After the treachery of his master's wife reduced him again, despair no doubt arose again. After all, the Egyptian prison could not have been a happy place. Prisons of despots, especially in those days, were dark dens of frequent abuse and arbitrary punishment. This was a dark time in Joseph's life, yet there was no blame in him. His natural aptitudes once again came into play and he began to "rule" in the Egyptian prison (Gen. 39: 21-23).

It is reasonable to assume that those dark times of despair continued to arise unbidden from time to time, but over the years began to diminish in frequency and intensity, especially after he became the "prime minister" of Egypt.[55] How often, even in those later years, must he have thought of his father and Benjamin with familiar longing! He might even have begun to think of his other brothers with more acceptance of what they had done. His bitterness related to those events probably began to melt away as he exercised his authority among the foreigners. At any rate, it seems clear that Joseph had made peace with his circumstances as well as his brothers' treachery by the time he saw them upon their first trip to Egypt to buy grain. In time, Joseph essentially became an Egyptian. He even married the daughter of an Egyptian priest and had sons there.

Scripture contains quite a bit of material on the life of Joseph in his years in Egypt. During this phase of his life, which was over twenty years in duration,[56] he was mostly alone. Neither his father nor his brothers had any current knowledge of him. His father and brother Benjamin assumed he had been killed by a wild animal and mourned for him. His brothers knew he had left Canaan as a slave and had no further knowledge of him. They probably all assumed that he had died in his captivity. It is likely that the brothers felt varying degrees of guilt over what they had done to Joseph. Most probably, they had long since given up all thought or hope that he was still alive, or if he was, that any of them would ever hear of or see him again. Certainly none among them expected to meet Joseph again as the great man in Egypt. Except in bitter memory, Joseph had ceased to exist. Apparently, not one of the family members remembered Joseph's two dreams.[57] Why should they? At the time Joseph had originally recounted his dreams, the family had largely discounted them anyway. Joseph's assumed death would make them null and void to the family members. Only after their fulfillment would they return to remembrance.

The story of Joseph in Egypt is very important to us in terms of understanding how he could be who he was when his brothers arrived there. The domestic slave rose to the top quite soon. The innocent prisoner soon became the manager of the prison. It was his capacity with dreams that freed him from prison. All these things caught the attention of the Pharaoh, who made him the virtual ruler of Egypt. Joseph's rise was entirely unprecedented. His transition from slave to prisoner was necessary so that he would be in position to attend and assist the Pharaoh at the appropriate time. Many important lessons beyond our current scope can be learned from his life.

By the time of the famine, Joseph had become so powerful that his relationship with Egypt was that of an essentially absolute ruler.

Formality attended his relations with the Pharaoh, but he had proved himself so thoroughly that the confidence placed in him was absolute. About a year into the famine, the ten older brothers were commissioned by their father to fetch grain from the Egyptians. This commission set up the inevitable events that followed. It was no accident that they would encounter the despised one on their journey. The LORD had so changed and empowered Joseph that their encounter with him would begin their salvation. It would also put into motion the events that would lead to the eventual enslavement of their descendants, even as Joseph himself had been enslaved. GOD Himself had prophesied this enslavement to Abram many years earlier. Now it was set in motion. Of course, neither Joseph nor his Hebrew family understood these connections. In fact, the opposite appeared to be the case; they were to be among the most fortunate people in Egypt.

However, Joseph's reunion with his father and with his brothers affords us the opportunity to examine the **brother-brother** relationships in close relief. Much of the complexity of those relationships had altered significantly during the twenty years Joseph had been in Egypt. The older brothers had cruelly used their younger brother and had carried that guilt for years in secrecy from their father. The relationship repairs they needed were between them and Joseph, and did not involve their father. This encounter was necessary for the brothers, as we can see in Reuben's address to the rest of them. It was also the final proving of Joseph's character.

Keep in mind that Joseph recognized his brothers immediately, but they did not recognize him (Gen. 42:6-8). They had not changed much, while he had changed significantly. They were still shepherds, but he was virtually a king. They had been grown men and he a teenager when they were parted. He would not be surprised they were alive and still in the same status as when he had last seen them. They had no reason to believe he still lived. They still spoke the language of their birth, while he spoke Egyptian, a tongue unknown to them. They dressed as they always had. He dressed as a nobleman of Egypt. The encounter was entirely under Joseph's control and the brothers were at the mercy of a ruler in a land not their own. The events at that cistern so long ago were now turned on their head.

We may wonder at the way Joseph handled things. Why did he not immediately reveal himself to them as their brother? Why did he maintain a kind of deception? These things are not clear. On the other hand, he might well have remembered the dream of the sheaves, and the others would have no idea of the context that dream provided for the present situation. In terms of the dream of the sheaves, though, things were not fully aligned. When they bowed down to him, while seeking grain from him, there were only ten sheaves bowing, not eleven. Their appearance before him was short of what the dream called for. GOD can count. If there were to be eleven, there were to be eleven, not ten. Whatever Joseph was thinking, whether of the dream or not, things were not all in place at the time. Another event was needed in which all eleven of the brothers would be present to bow down to him, knowing who he was. That event had to precede the coming of Jacob and Leah. Otherwise, the dream of the luminaries could not be fulfilled, at least in its proper order.

While both dreams contained family bowing before Joseph, they were of different character. The dream of the sheaves dealt with a kind of supplication, the brothers coming to get something. The dream of luminaries dealt really with a homecoming. A sheaf of grain was not a heavenly luminary after all. The whole family was not to come to "get something"; they were coming to an unprecedented reunion. These dreams had been given to Joseph over twenty years earlier in that particular order. The fulfillment of the first would lead to the fulfillment of the second. The order was ordained by GOD. As were the dreams, so were the events, both in order and in content.

So when Joseph's ten brothers came and bowed before him, it was not enough. The eleventh brother needed to be present and he was not. When Joseph inquired about the family of the brothers, he knew who they were. He knew who Jacob was, and he knew who Benjamin was. That Benjamin was not present might have been a bit of a mystery to him, but that soon became clear. Perhaps it was only his human nature, but he needed to assure that the next trip would produce Benjamin. After all, he knew the duration of the famine, but his brothers had no way of knowing (Gen. 41:27). One suspects they thought it was a one-time visit. Joseph knew they would have to return. However, they would return as the ten if there was not a reason for Benjamin to accompany them. Therefore, the hostage would change the nature of the next visit and likely produce the situation in which all eleven brothers were before him in supplication. The taking of Simeon set all that in motion.

As it now turned out, one of the brothers who had wanted to harm Joseph was totally in Joseph's power. The others returned home with the warning not to return without Benjamin. Perhaps it took longer than he expected, but eventually the brothers returned with Benjamin in their company. Joseph's closest brother was now in the room with him. When Simeon was released into the company of his brothers, all eleven were there in his presence in the status of supplicants. The dream of the sheaves was virtually complete.

However, the second chapter of that story involved the framing of Benjamin to discover the hearts of his brothers. When they were all forced to return to Joseph, the eleven bowed down together, totally in his power. In response to the mock anger of Joseph, Judah, who had convinced their father to permit Benjamin to go with them, took the lead yet again (Gen. 44:18-34). He did so by volunteering to stay in Benjamin's stead and be a slave rather than to fail to return with Benjamin. Judah had now offered his life as a surety to his father and to Joseph. When Joseph witnessed this self-sacrifice of Judah, he was overcome and revealed himself to his brothers. Judah, as a father would, had rescued Joseph. Judah, as a father would, had now rescued Benjamin. To have been a slave before a father was to be preferred to being a slave-prisoner before the great man in Egypt, but Judah would endure even that to keep his word and rescue his brother. No greater thing could have been garnered from the brothers. All was in place, and the first dream was so fully manifest that no other element of fulfillment could be found. It was done.

The immediate reunion with his brothers was a thing of great joy to Joseph and Benjamin, and more a thing of great surprise to the other brothers (Gen. 45:14-15). We may imagine that Benjamin was delighted beyond any of the others. But certainly Judah was quite pleased at the outcome. Not only had he actually saved Joseph over twenty years earlier, he had also saved his youngest brother. Not only that, he now would not have to be a slave. Rather, he would be a savior as far as their father was concerned. Reuben, although undoubtedly satisfied with this outcome, was no longer a power in these matters. The rest of the brothers, especially the sons of Bilhah and Zilpah, who of all the others had felt they had the greatest cause to hate Joseph, were probably happy too, not to mention relieved, but also probably a bit worried. But it was a happy occasion overall. The twelve brothers were together again. There was little if any jealousy. Joseph had learned how to relate to his brothers, not as the brat in camp, but as a mature leader and savior in his own right.

In the euphoria of the reunion, Joseph formally approached the Pharaoh and gained an invitation from the king for his entire family to join him as honored guests in the very best land in Egypt (Gen. 45:16-20). It is easy for us to overlook the fact that Joseph would soon consign virtually all the native Egyptians to a lower political status than his own family. In the moment, things could not be better for the "great nation" that had sprung from Abraham in Canaan. Things were better than ever between Joseph and his brothers, as good as they ever could be.

Now it was time for Joseph's second dream to come into fulfillment. In that dream, the sun and moon and eleven stars, the luminaries, had bowed down to Joseph (Gen. 37:9-11). Of course, this would not be an act of supplication, but rather an acknowledgement of who he was and what he had done for them. In order for this to occur, the brothers needed to fetch Jacob and Leah and their own wives and children from Canaan. That is what occurred next.

Imagine Jacob's joyful, unbelieving wonder when he was told of the invitation! But his eyes verified that Simeon and Benjamin stood before him. He saw the carts and other artifacts that were sent from Egypt for his use. It remained but for him to make the arrangements necessary to take the family, the servants, and the animals down to Egypt for the reunion. His old heart must have nearly broken with excitement at the prospect of that marvelous event. His great sorrow over losing Joseph was now turned to the greatest joy. He had received his son back from the dead, as it were.

Finally, the day came for their departure. In their excitement, they likely set the quickest pace possible with consideration of the weakest members of the party such as small children or young herd animals. That would have been too slow for Jacob and Benjamin, but they would have to endure it. The gloom that must have often pervaded the camp was gone, replaced by wonder. Back in Egypt, we can imagine that Joseph was counting the hours as well. This would be the greatest reunion imaginable.

When Jacob and the family left Hebron, they soon came to Beersheba (Gen. 46:1). Because of the importance of the place to his grandfather and his father, Jacob stopped there to make offerings. Keep in mind that once he passed out of the area of Beersheba he would be leaving Canaan. The LORD renewed the national covenant with him (Gen. 46:3-4) and instructed him to make the journey, because it was in Egypt where the great nation would finally be made. It would no longer be in the person of the national **patriarch**, but would be installed in the people themselves. Jacob's numerous descendants would come forth down there and GOD Himself would see to it that they came up out of Egypt ready to dispossess the Canaanites. Finally, GOD promised him of the longed-for reunion with his beloved son Joseph.

At the appropriate time in the journey, Judah was sent ahead (Gen. 46:28) to meet with Joseph and make the final arrangements for the arrival of the family. This task assigned to Judah was a high honor, and further marked his emergence as the ruling brother within the household. This is in distinction to the role Joseph had played in preparing the place. Joseph had made the place ready, and now Judah led into the provision.

In conjunction with describing the beginning of the journey, which consisted of leaving the holdings in Canaan, traversing the wilderness and arriving in Goshen, we have a cataloging of the persons with Jacob who were his kin. This is important because it is the "starter kit" for the actual populating of the great nation. From those who went down to Egypt with Jacob came the tribes that left Egypt for Canaan in the fourth generation.[58]

At some point in time, Joseph and Judah sent out watchmen to discover the progress of Jacob and the camp. These watchmen had the responsibility of notifying the brothers in a timely manner of the imminent arrival of Jacob's camp. They could also carry messages back and forth if there were any matters that needed attention. And as the journey came to its conclusion these watchmen would add a layer of safety to the journey. Their presence would insure that no random events would have an impact.

As the very last days of the journey were winding down, last minute preparations were made at what was probably a ceremonial site for the camp. It is likely that such a site was put in place to mark the end of the migration before the formal receptions put on by the Egyptian government. The well-guarded and provisioned campsite would be as comfortable as could be managed. It would be a place where some rest could be had. It would be near the final destination, and from it was probably a quick journey into the presence of the Pharaoh. Of course, Joseph would go as soon as possible to the long-awaited reunion with Jacob (Gen. 46:28-30). That would need no more formality than Joseph would allow. Very soon, probably in a matter of a few days, the formal audiences with the Pharaoh would begin. We know that at least two, and probably three, phases of the ceremonies occurred. These were scripted and well-rehearsed. The formality was important to all parties. As far as Jacob and Joseph were concerned, this was a meeting of two equal governments and would need to be impressive to all concerned. After this, no Egyptian would dare "randomly" do harm to the Hebrews.

The likely scenario is that at some point Joseph took up a stationary position in the path of his father. As Jacob and the camp arrived at that position, Joseph probably ran ahead of his bodyguards to embrace his father. The great separation of more than two decades was ended. Surely there was great weeping of joy between them there in the most unlikely of places and situations. Joseph's work was ended. He had made the place for the Hebrews. What remained was the ceremonial affair with the Pharaoh. With full hearts the camp could then be reunited with Joseph, the great man of Egypt. The nation was in its nursery.

Joseph oversaw the various events surrounding the official welcome of Pharaoh that was extended to Jacob and his sons (Gen. 47:2-10). The first meeting was between Joseph and the relevant part of his court, to include scribes to record the events. Phase one was an announcement that the family had arrived. In phase two, Joseph presented five of the brothers who had been coached on the questions they would be asked and how to answer them. At that point the grant of the best of the land was made, and Pharaoh gave to the family the status of keepers of his food animals. The final phase was the introduction of the two "heads of state." This was the most formal of all the events that day. Jacob and Pharaoh met to fully finalize their new relationship. At that time, Jacob blessed Pharaoh.

From our perspective, the blessing that Jacob provided to the Pharaoh was quite appropriate. At that time, Jacob was the senior living representative of the eternal priesthood of Melchizedek. The greater blessed the lesser, even though things did not really look that way at the time. Jacob's blessing would mean much to the Egyptian Kingdom, even if they were unaware of it. It must have been strange to some of the courtiers who witnessed the blessing and the following discussion, but GOD was in charge and this priestly blessing was surely prophetic in some ways. We have no record of its contents but we can be sure it was full of promise concerning the prosperity of the Kingdom as a return for its generosity.

In a more informal way the Pharaoh inquired as to Jacob's age. Jacob's response was a bit strange, as it spoke to the hardships of his life (Gen. 47:7-10). After that, probably on the basis of some prearrangement, the ceremony ended with Jacob blessing the Pharaoh yet again as he left. The formalities having ended, the change from the moving camp to the fixed place of settlement took place. Joseph had not only made a place, he had become the guarantor of possession of the place. For a while after that, Joseph turned his attention to the well-being of Egypt. In the following five years (Gen. 45:11), Joseph took over the entire economy of the nation, except for his family and the class of priests from which his wife came (Gen. 47:26). While he and Jacob lived, the family of Jacob lived at his expense.

At the end of seventeen years, Jacob realized the time of his death was very near. He sent messengers to ask Joseph to come see him, which Joseph did. At that time, Jacob asked for the repatriation of his remains, to which Joseph agreed (Gen. 47:28-31).

A bit later when Jacob's death was truly imminent, Joseph took his sons to a meeting (Gen. 48:1-2) with their grandfather. He presented them to his father in a very particular way with very particular intention.[59] He positioned Manasseh, the older of his two sons, in such a way that his father's right hand would be placed on Manasseh's head during the granting of blessing. At the same time, he positioned Ephraim, the second son, so that Jacob's left hand would be on his head. This would result in both sons receiving a grandfather's blessing, and would preserve their relative seniority. The right hand was considered to be the more honorable for these purposes. Jacob did it his way. Once again, he went against the expected and conventional. He crossed his arms and placed his right hand on the younger son. The blessing he pronounced at that time essentially adopted the two sons of Joseph, making them his own. He also reinforced the order of that blessing in spite of Joseph's objection. He clearly stated that in his family, Ephraim had **primacy** over Manasseh.

Jacob then had all his sons brought to him for the purpose of announcing the patriarchal blessings that passed the great nation into their care (Gen. 49). Particular emphasis was placed on Judah and on Joseph. Of course, we know that Joseph's blessing was actually distributed to his two sons as far as tribal destiny is concerned. But on that day in Egypt, Jacob was blessing his twelve sons.

Jacob's death followed soon after (Gen. 49:33). Joseph honored his request for the repatriation of his remains to Hebron where his father and grandfather, their wives, and Leah were already buried. However, a full royal funerary cycle was carried out in Egypt before the remains were carried to Hebron, where there was undoubtedly great ceremony yet again. The first seventeen years of Joseph's life, and the last seventeen years of Jacob's life, they had spent in one another's company. The struggles of the man Jacob were ended. The struggles of the people Israel would run on for generations.

Jacob saved the patriarchal blessings of the sons of Rachel until the end. The blessing of Joseph was extended and profound. It spoke to fruitfulness, of overcoming great adversity, of great power, of the particular attention of GOD in the life of this son, of sheer scope in the creation as a context for the blessing, and of his position of importance among his brethren. Indeed, in scope and grandeur, it was very powerful and spoke of the love between the two as well as the greatness of Joseph's labors.

JACOB-JOSEPH Dyad

This particular **dyad** was a very interesting one. The destiny of the man Joseph diverged of necessity from the destiny of the man Jacob. Jacob's destiny was to finish the era of the national patriarchs by bringing into the world those who would give it shape. Joseph's destiny was to place the seed of that nation into the crucible which would refine it to give it its character. A **father-son dyad** was necessary to bring about such a transition. This was that **dyad**.

This was a particularly close **dyad**. Jacob was drawn to Joseph in the context of his great love for Rachel. The tragedy of her death and the assumed death of Joseph several years later deepened in Jacob the place of that affection. Upon the restoration of their fellowship after some two decades spent apart in great grief, the bond certainly deepened.

One very important aspect of this **dyad** was Jacob's adoption of Ephraim and Manasseh.[60] These two Egypt-born sons of Joseph were taken from that time as Ephraim *ben* Jacob and Manasseh *ben* Jacob. In the eyes of Jacob, they were his sons thereafter. In doing this thing, he assured that there would be two portions of **inheritance** that went to the family of Joseph upon his death. When Jacob pronounced the blessings, he took the **primacy** from Reuben. In the two sons of Joseph he simply moved the **primacy** to that house. We know that he placed the future rule of the nation into the hands of Judah as well, but the portion of the **firstborn** now went to Joseph by way of his two sons.

In some ways we may view this particular **dyad** as a continuation of the very important ones that preceded it, ABRAHAM-ISAAC and ISAAC-JACOB, because of the patriarchal weight they bore. Each of these four men was a part of defining the future of the great nation, and each lived out much of that greatness in isolation. Great trials came to each of them.

After the period of slavery in Egypt, when the Israelites left that land, there was no mention of a tribe of Joseph. Instead, there were the two tribes of Ephraim and Manasseh (Num. 1:5-15), who had inheritances in the new land. There was no territorial **inheritance** of Joseph. Conversely, the tribe of Joseph is listed in description of the "sealed ones" found in the Book of Revelation. In that context, the names of the tribes of Ephraim and Manasseh do not appear, only the actual sons of Jacob's own flesh.

After Jacob's death, the eleven brothers of Joseph considered that he might resurrect his old grudge with them related to his mistreatment at their hands. Even though there had been a great reunion with them upon his revelation of himself to them, and another great reunion when they returned to Egypt, they still feared his wrath. Their relationship with him was **fraternal**. Joseph, however, had matured beyond that. He had borne for them the burden of a father, whether he had intended to do so or not. GOD had required of Joseph that he become a kind of firstfruit of the exile that was to come. In order to accomplish this, the LORD had removed Joseph from all he had known and thrust him into thirteen years of hardship. Even after he became the virtual ruler of Egypt, that past was still with him, as we can deduce from the naming of his first son, Manasseh.

The man Joseph had become could no longer harbor ill will towards his brothers. His response to their entreaties gave them comfort out of the place of their anguish (Gen. 50:19-21). He was now bearing the mantle, if you will, of the love of Jacob for his sons, as expressed in the splendid coat Jacob had provided for Joseph all those years before.

Joseph did exact a price from his brothers, however. He requested of them that they or their descendants carry his sarcophagus out of Egypt and into Canaan when they departed. This is a prophetic acknowledgement of the future occupation of that land. This request was quite gracious in its nature. The brothers were happy to agree. And it was carried out. Exodus 13:19 says that when the Israelites departed Egypt, "Moses took the bones of Joseph with him," just as Joseph had made his brothers promise to do.

EPHRAIM

Our examination of the twelve sons of Jacob is incomplete if we omit the two he adopted (Gen. 48:5). It is worthy of great note that these two men were the sons of Jacob's favorite son, Joseph. Considering Joseph's position, there can be no doubt that he acquired great wealth from the Egyptians. He was in need of no practical thing. Nor would his sons be wanting. They were actually half-Egyptian and descended from priests, who alone among all Egyptians were free in the realm. But their adoption by Jacob gave Joseph even more status among his Hebrew brothers, *bnai-Israel*.

Scholars propose that the name Ephraim speaks to the fact that Joseph had now been fruitful twice with the birth of this, his second son. Note this is a Hebrew name and not an Egyptian one. Joseph knew who he was, even though he had been in Egypt half his life.

When Jacob adopted Joseph's sons, it is not clear that Joseph knew it ahead of time. However, the precision with which Joseph arranged the blessing suggests he might well have known. In any event, he arranged the two young men exactly as he intended. It was Jacob who reversed their order. And he did so deliberately. In explicit prophecy, Jacob placed Ephraim ahead of his older brother.

The prominence of the descendants of Ephraim over the descendants of Manasseh is well attested in scripture. In fact, the great servant of Moses, Joshua, was an Ephraimite.[61] In him, Ephraim was one of the two tribes who wanted to take on the giants in Canaan (Num. 14:6-9) before the forty years of wandering was imposed on Israel. In later years, it was the territory of Ephraim that became the home of the various capital cities of the northern Kingdom, beginning with Jeroboam. In some cases, the name Ephraim is used synonymously with the northern Kingdom. This was indeed an important tribe, not always in a positive sense.

JACOB-EPHRAIM Dyad

Apart from his adoption, in which he received **primacy** over his brother Manasseh, there is no mention in scripture of any content of the JACOB-EPHRAIM **dyad**. There can be no doubt that in the seventeen years in which Jacob lived in Egypt, he saw his grandsons, the sons of Joseph often. They lived in close proximity and we can be sure when the affairs of state permitted such visits, Joseph brought his sons to visit their grandfather. They were not strangers at the time of the adoption. Rather, Jacob's language was of a formal sort. Jacob and Ephraim must have gotten to know one another as grandfather and grandson. That **dyad** was replaced, though, at the adoption. After that, we know nothing, and the time was very short, maybe even only hours or days, in which Ephraim occupied that position.

MANASSEH

The first son of Joseph (Gen. 41:50), whose name means forgetfulness, was born during the years of plenty, as was his brother Ephraim. They were young lads when their grandfather, uncles, and cousins came into Egypt from Canaan. The two boys had the same Egyptian mother, who was a peer of the realm. They were in the class of Egyptians who did not go into servitude when all the rest of Egypt did. So these two sons of Joseph grew up as "royalty" on both sides of their relations.

Being the **firstborn** of the two sons of Joseph, Manasseh possessed the **birthright** insofar as his father was concerned. We know nothing of the laws of Egypt and how they might have affected such things as **inheritance**. But we do know that Joseph thought of such things the way a Hebrew would. Manasseh was the **firstborn** with **birthright**.

This was the reason Joseph was a bit upset with his father Jacob placed his right hand on top of Ephraim's head at the time of the adoption and blessings. In Joseph's mind, the person rightfully at Jacob's right hand was his **firstborn**. As had been true in his own lineage, though, Jacob changed that. It appears he changed it to suit what he saw prophetically for the two men.

The descendants of Manasseh had a peculiar heritage in the land of promise. They, for whatever reason, asked Joshua that their land portion be split (Num. 32:1-33), part of it on each side of the river. For that reason, the eastern branch suffered considerably more depredations at the hands of such people as the Ammonites and Moabites. After a while, they were even divided among themselves in their language. Their very choices in their land of **inheritance** weakened them significantly relative to the descendants of Ephraim.

JACOB-MANASSEH Dyad

Apart from his adoption, in which he was reversed with his brother Ephraim in terms of **primacy**, there is no mention in scripture of any content of the JACOB-MANASSEH **dyad**. As I said before, there can be no doubt that Jacob saw his grandsons, Joseph's sons, often in the seventeen years in which Jacob lived in Egypt But as with Ephraim, there is no mention in scripture of the content of Manasseh's relationship either as grandson or as adopted "son" of Jacob.

Please scan the QR code or go to the web address to view Corbett's video introduction to the book.

CHAPTER 9

JUDAH: KEEPER OF THE SCEPTER

http://bit.ly/1PoymDv

Please go to ravensfood.everykindred.com for access to additional supplements to the book. Content will be added from time to time as desirable to support this book.

JUDAH: KEEPER OF THE SCEPTER

Jacob's fourth son by his wife Leah was named Judah at his birth (Gen. 29:35). Leah gave him this name as a statement of praise that GOD had made her so fruitful in the baby war. As was true of all the sons born in Padan Aram, there is no particular mention of Judah, other than his birth, before the migration to Canaan.

He was not a middle son; there were eight after him. But he also was by no means the **firstborn**. No **birthright** inhered to him. He certainly outranked the sons of the concubines and was older than the later sons of Leah, but beyond this he had no special preeminence.

In fact, even in Canaan, Judah was invisible until the events surrounding the attempted murder of Joseph (Gen. 37:26-30). In that event, he emerged as the brother with the plan that ultimately saved Joseph's life, regardless of his motives. Was he trying to save Joseph or was he only trying to save his brothers from becoming murderers? We cannot know the answer, but the ultimate outcome was quite good for all concerned.

As was true of all the sons born before the Canaan migration, Judah was raised to be a herdsman. We can be sure all the sons received excellent training. However, Reuben got the special attention given to the future chief man. When they left for Canaan, Judah was of equal rank with all the other brothers except Reuben and Joseph. Reuben was **firstborn**, and had the **birthright**. Joseph was first from the womb of Rachel, and had his father's adoration. The other nine were well off, but almost interchangeable insofar as Jacob was concerned.

Of course, we know that Judah and his descendants eventually excelled,[62] but in his early life he was just one of the sons.

When the terrible events happened at Shechem (Gen. 34:25-26, the murder of the Shechemites), scripture makes no mention of Judah's role. As far as we know he played no part in the plot of Simeon and Levi, and did not earn his father's anger at that time. Surely he was influenced by his older brothers, as boys nearly always are, but the extent of that influence is simply unknown.

As the years passed and the ostracism of Joseph and the plot against his life developed, Judah played no discernible role. His father gave him no special coat. He ran no special errands for his father. He was simply there in the background as far as we know. Rule was out of his reach and we see no effort on his part to distinguish himself from his brothers. At least, no such things are recorded in scripture for us.

At Dothan, where the brothers set out to kill Joseph, Judah's behavior among the brothers was unique. In essence the brothers became a mob filled with bloodlust (Gen. 37:17-19). Their anger at Joseph's special treatment had turned into a deep hatred for him. His two prophetic dreams had pushed them over the edge. This was their chance. It is the nature of a mob that its members begin to take on a single mind. Independent thought is typically obliterated once the mob begins to take action. Intuitively, Reuben and Judah both knew that to simply go against the mob to save Joseph was not going to work. Reuben's quick thinking, however well intentioned, really only postponed the inevitable.[63] The ring leaders, whoever they were, had intended to kill Joseph, and Reuben knew it. After their intentions became known, they could not permit Reuben to take the boy home to his father. Reuben's intent to save his father from that grief would not be enough, because Joseph would surely tell their father what had happened, and that could not be permitted under any circumstances. It was Judah, then, who actually saved Joseph's life by suggesting that he be sold as a slave.

Earlier, we examined the idea that Judah might not have been that interested in saving Joseph's life (see the previous chapter). His statement to his brothers was about avoiding guilt (Gen. 37:26-27). If they did the killing themselves, they would bear that guilt and knowledge forever. Sooner or later, one of the ten of them would let the matter slip in a setting that would do damage to their cause, exposing their treachery to their father. However, letting someone take Joseph into an unknown future would remove him from their presence and likely result in his death anyway. The secret of his enslavement would simply be much easier to keep. It was not nearly as heinous in its nature as the murder would have been. The goal of removing him from their lives would be met. He would no longer be there to irritate them. There would be some feelings of guilt, but at least they would not be guilty of murder. Judah somehow arrived at the solution in a timely manner before the brothers' anger boiled over again, as it certainly would have done.

This is the first distinct sign in scripture of Judah's character.[64] He had saved the life of his brother, at some risk to himself. All the brothers had agreed to Reuben's plan temporarily because he was the **firstborn**. Judah was just one of the other sons. His risk was that they would not agree with him, in which case he would become a problem for them. That would likely have ended badly for him had they concluded he would inform Jacob.

TAMAR AND HER SONS

For whatever reason, Judah separated himself from the rest of Jacob's camp (Gen. 38:1) a short time after the enslavement of Joseph. In so doing, he went to live among the Canaanites, probably as a city dweller.[65] He married a Canaanite woman and three sons were soon born into the family. As soon as his sons began to reach marriageable age, he found a wife for the oldest of them, Er. The woman was another Canaanite. Soon, though, Er himself died and left his wife, Tamar, a widow.

It is at this point that we get an interesting look into the culture of the time. It was typical for the childless widow to marry one of the brothers of her dead husband. Assuming a son were to be born to that marriage, that son would inherit the property of his dead father. In this particular case, Er was the **firstborn** of Judah and had the **birthright** in virtual possession. Er, had he lived, would have received a double portion of Judah's wealth upon his death. Therefore, Er would have received twice as much of Judah's wealth as would Onan or Shelah. Er's death passed on the expectation of the **birthright** to Onan, but only if Er died childless himself, before his father Judah died. If Er had a son of his own, he would receive the **birthright**. If he had only one son, the **birthright** would eventually pass on to the one son in the form of the full wealth of Er, which was at least the double portion from Judah's wealth.

Er's son would become the heir in his father's place if said son survived his father, and if said son was born before the distribution of **inheritance** upon Judah's death. Because Er died without a child, Tamar, as his widow, was left with no **inheritance** in which to live. She was entirely dependent on the mercies of her father or her father-in-law. Judah took the solution in hand. In order to preserve the order of things and to keep the inheritances intact, Tamar would wed Onan. If Onan produced a son with Tamar, that son would be reckoned to be the son of Er and would receive the **birthright inheritance** of Er in his father's place. If Onan and Tamar produced no son before Judah died, Onan would receive the **birthright inheritance** of a double portion relative to his brother Shelah. Onan's response to the dilemma was to refuse to impregnate Tamar, thus depriving her of a son and a place in the world (Gen. 38:9). In so doing, Onan assured himself of the portion of the **firstborn**. The LORD did not respond favorably to this plan, however, and struck Onan dead. He had despised his older brother and denied him any progeny when it was his duty to produce progeny for him. Thus, the name of Er would be lost in the tribes-to-be of Israel. It was as though Onan had murdered his older brother. **Fraternal** love was weak in the face of these matters of wealth.

Judah and his family owed Tamar her place in the camp because she had married Er to begin with. However, Judah sent her home to her father, lest Shelah also die and he lose all his sons (Gen. 38:6-11). He pledged to wed Tamar to his son Shelah when the boy came of age. In the meantime, sending Tamar home would keep her barren until Shelah was old enough. Without such an arrangement, Tamar faced a bleak future. She would be comfortable enough in her father's house, but once he died, she would once more be a desolate widow, a woman with no place unless some other kinsman had pity on her. Moreover, the Canaanites were not as interested in land as were the Hebrews. This simply was not as good an outcome for her as being a child-bearing wife of Shelah. Judah, however, failed to follow through on his pledge. It appears that Judah would have allowed these things to remain unresolved permanently, but that was not to be. GOD had other plans for the family.

Sometime later, Judah's wife, the Canaanite mother of Er, Onan, and Shelah, died (Gen. 38:12). Soon after the time of his mourning, Judah was tricked by Tamar, who pretended to be a harlot. In that time and culture a harlot would cover her face, so Judah did not recognize her. Part of her deceit was to take pledges from Judah for some payment to be sent later. When Judah sent the payment for the harlot, she was not to be found. She had taken Judah's personal pledges and kept them in lieu of the normal payment. Judah let the matter go until he was told that his daughter-in-law was pregnant. How could it be that a Canaanite child would now be permitted to take that which should have belonged to Er out of the family? The insult was more than Judah could bear.

Judah was within his rights when he demanded Tamar's execution. He believed she was pregnant outside what was permitted, not knowing she was bearing his offspring. Her death was the only solution he could see to the dilemma now presented to him. Adultery was already

151

frowned upon. Of course, we know that upon her arrest she embarrassed him by publically presenting his personal pledges as belonging to the father of the child she was carrying (Gen. 38:25-26). This public embarrassment caused Judah to confess his unrighteousness. Tamar was released.

She would now bear a son into the family, not to some Canaanite. The logic was that this son would now be somehow reckoned an heir and receive the **birthright** that was rightfully the property of the **firstborn** of Er. The calculus of this was acceptable and the son was born. Of course, "he" turned out to be twins, who were named Zerah and Perez (Gen. 38:27-30). We know the story of the scarlet thread attached to Zerah's hand because he was expected to arrive first. But true to his name, Perez (breaker) displaced at the moment of birth. Thus, Perez came to be reckoned as the son of Judah with the **birthright**, which left uncle Shelah with the regular portion that had always been his to begin with. Because Tamar had now borne a son to Judah, it was no longer appropriate for her to be married to Shelah. At the same time, as the widow of his son, Judah could not marry her either. She was then kept in the full status of the mother of the **firstborn** in the camp, but was never married again (Gen. 38:26). But she was the mother of the **firstborn**, and her future was secured.

It appears that this amazing side story was preserved just to let us see even more into the lives of these almost mythical men. The failure of the **brother-brother** relationship to bring forth proper behavior in Onan stands in stark contrast to the care that Judah showed his sons out of his **paternal** love for them. Everything was preserved in an orderly manner once it was over. Furthermore, Tamar, this Canaanite woman, was the mother of the son of Judah who was in the direct lineage of King David and JESUS (Ruth 4:13-22; Mt. 1:2-16).

THE FAMINE—FIRST YEAR

During these years, Joseph was busy preparing a place for Jacob's family in Egypt.[66] We do not know the timing of these events, but eventually Judah returned to live with his father Jacob and his brothers. It was in that setting that we next encounter him in scripture.

We know that when the famine started, the Egyptians had just had seven years of bumper crops to prepare for it. Joseph, under the authority of the Pharaoh, had taken a portion of the excess grain of the Egyptians each year, and stored it up against the time of the famine to come (Gen. 41:46-49). In Canaan, knowing nothing about this, Jacob and his other sons had made no provisions for the coming famine. When it arrived, they were afflicted by it just as were the Canaanites. But the Egyptians were just fine, living off of the grain Joseph had stored up for them. Somehow, Jacob learned that the Egyptians had enough grain that they could sell to others. Only the Egyptian government knew that the famine would last for seven years. As far as the folks in Canaan knew, it would be over by the next growing season. But the family was running short of the grain necessary to keep man and beast alive.

As the famine continued, Jacob finally decided (Gen. 42:1-3) to send his sons as a delegation to Egypt to see whether they could buy grain for the rest of the year. This probably occurred before even the first year of the famine had passed. The famine would have become apparent when there was no harvest in that first year. So the sons were off, but not all the sons. Jacob did not send Benjamin with the older sons. Benjamin was his consolation for the deaths of Rachel and Joseph, and probably remained with him virtually all the time.

So the ten older sons went. This was as prestigious a delegation as Jacob could send. Anything more prestigious would have required his own participation, which he was disinclined to do. So the ten, including Judah but led by Reuben,[67] went to conduct family business in Egypt. Reuben served as their spokesperson in dealing with the Egyptians, which was perfectly appropriate. As we know, the delegation was required to meet with the "great man" before the grain purchase could be secured. We know also how Joseph manipulated the meeting to acquire news concerning Jacob and Benjamin, and that Reuben innocently provided the information (Gen. 42:8-13). Then Joseph executed the scheme that resulted in Simeon's arrest. Judah was a witness to all this, but Reuben was the spokesman.

When the nine brothers finally returned home without Simeon, and discovered their money, everyone was alarmed (Gen. 42:35-36). Even more difficult was the matter of the requirement the great man in Egypt had made for Simeon's release. It is not likely that the brothers expected Jacob to refuse the bargain, but refuse he did. Reuben then made what he felt was a reasonable offer of the lives of his own sons in exchange for any loss of Benjamin. To Jacob, the lives of Reuben's two sons would be insufficient consolation for the potential loss of Benjamin, and he would have none of it (Gen. 42:38). Meanwhile, Simeon languished in prison in Egypt. Joseph probably saw to it that he was okay, but we may assume that Simeon was not a happy man.

THE FAMINE—YEAR TWO

Time dragged on. The next round of grain crops was planted, but probably without much hope for the harvest. The naturally occurring grasses were not doing well either, as is the nature of famines. About the normal harvest time, likely early spring, it became apparent that a second year on short rations was in store for the family and their animals. Once it was apparent the grain harvests would fail again, the family had to reckon with their survival. The news was probably still out there that Egypt still had grain to sell.

It is at this point that Judah's destiny began to come into view (Gen. 43:1-10). Jacob had refused Reuben's proposal the previous year, but now it was time to get serious as far as the sons were concerned. We do not know why, but Judah now became the spokesman (at least the only recorded speaker). He was the one to address their needs to Jacob this time around. All of them knew what had to be done, but it appears that the brothers were very reluctant to breach the subject with their father. For some reason, Judah decided to do so.

Judah went to Jacob with a bargain of his own. He proposed to bear the risk himself, not to have his sons do so. He reminded his father that they could not return to Egypt to buy more grain unless Benjamin accompanied them. Therefore, if they went down without Benjamin, the trip would be wasted, and Simeon would remain in jail. His proposition of surety for the safe return of Benjamin was his own identity and **inheritance**,[68] or any other punishment Jacob might decide to mete out. Even his own death was a possibility. If he was permitted to take Benjamin and failed to return with him, he would be as a slave to his father upon his return and for the rest of his life. Neither he nor his sons would have anything of their own in that case, not even an **inheritance**. In terms of the stakes, this was a superior guarantee than the one Reuben had made a year earlier.[69] Whatever his reasoning, Jacob recognized there was no other way for the camp to survive the famine. He was still very worried, but there appeared to be no other options. In his worst fears, he would lose Benjamin in addition to Joseph and Simeon. He would be free to take whatever vengeance he wished on Judah, but what difference would that make? Three of his sons would be gone. He expressed his anguish to Judah and then permitted the journey (Gen. 43:1).

It is not likely that any of them thought about Joseph's dreams (Gen. 37:5-11) on the journey to Egypt. And it was probably not a very happy group that made that trip. What if Benjamin became a target in some way? How would that work with Jacob?

We know about the events that transpired with Joseph (Gen. 43:16 – 44:3). He welcomed his brothers again and showed special favor to Benjamin. He returned Simeon to the company of his brothers. He then released all eleven of them to return home, but arranged to frame Benjamin and have him arrested. The brothers returned to Egypt in a panic upon Benjamin's arrest (Gen. 44:11-13), and their spokesman, Judah, addressed Joseph and presented the narrative to him. This was the first time the eleven brothers had arrived together before Joseph. At this moment, Joseph's first dream was fulfilled exactly (Gen. 37:5-8).

With Benjamin supposedly in great jeopardy, Judah proposed yet another bargain. He offered to stay in Benjamin's place. He would serve whatever sentence Joseph meted out if only Benjamin could return home. To Judah, returning Benjamin to his father was worth any cost, even his own life.[70] Judah's substitutionary proposal broke Joseph's heart. The brothers, or at least Judah, had not repeated the sins of Dothan that day. Out of concern for their father and their youngest brother, Judah had made the highest-stakes bargain he could. This one was not a guarantee. It was a trade with immediate consequences for him. In this Joseph saw the quality of the man who now represented his brothers as though he were the **firstborn**. No higher price could have been extracted from the brothers.

We can imagine the tremendous relief of the brothers when Joseph revealed who he was (Gen. 45:1-15). Judah went from virtual death to life in an instant. The others, including Benjamin and Simeon, could return home and bring the good news to their father. The celebration was surely the greatest any of them had ever known.

From our perspective, Judah had done an unprecedented thing. He had shown the highest quality of the love of a brother, while also showing a very high quality of love for his father. It can be argued that the very high quality of the **fraternal** love was founded in the very high quality of his **filial** love. In other words, when he loved his father properly, he could love his brother(s) properly. Judah became a qualified "redeemer" that day (Gen. 44:33-34).[71]

After some days of celebrating with one another, it was time to return to Jacob with the good news. They were not reckoned to be thieves; Simeon had returned from an indefinite prison sentence; Benjamin had returned unharmed; Pharaoh had issued an invitation to the family to be his honored guests in Egypt; they had the grain and everything else they needed for such a journey; and Joseph was alive and was the "great man" in Egypt. It is useful to note Jacob's response (Gen. 45:25-28). At first, he could not believe what he was being told. His lost son was found. He would go, and then be content to die.

Almost surely there was an Egyptian honor guard that came along to escort the family along the way. Nonetheless, Jacob proceeded in his own manner. With due care for all things, and with great expectation for the reunion, he prepared the entire camp for the journey (Gen.

46:1). Beersheba was along the way, so stopping there added no difficulty. While at Beersheba, Jacob had an encounter with GOD (Gen. 46:3-4), who blessed the journey and prophesied to him in patriarchal terms.

Some days later, as they neared Egypt, Jacob sent Judah ahead to find Joseph and make the final preparations for their arrival (Gen. 46:28). This was no band of vagabonds coming to Egypt. This was the "great nation." To be selected as the pathfinder and herald was a very high honor for Judah. In this, Judah was finally installed in his place as chief among his brothers. Joseph had prepared a place, and Judah had the honor of bringing his father and family to that place. His would thereafter be the place of honor in the east (Num. 2:3). When the tribes moved in the desert, Judah led the way.

The formal disposition of the family got under way. It is certain that Judah was one of the five brothers whom Joseph presented to Pharaoh as representatives of the family (Gen. 47:1-2). Scripture does not say so, but it is likely that Judah was the brother who answered Pharaoh's questions as the chief spokesman for his brothers. Besides Jacob and Joseph, he was probably the only member of the family to ever speak with Pharaoh. But it was enough. The family was now officially installed, and with great honor.

PATRIARCHAL BLESSING

Earlier we saw that the patriarchal blessing pronounced for Joseph by Jacob was a kind of unrestrained song (Gen. 49:22-25). The blessing for Judah was also magnificent, if not as broad of scope. Its themes were rule and provision (Gen. 49:8-12). The promise of rule was quite specific and included a scepter, the symbol of royalty. Joseph had been called a prince, but the rule was placed in the care of Judah. We know that the figurative scepter was to be in Judah's keeping until Messiah should come. We also know that Messiah came from this tribe, the tribe of the descendants of Judah. We also know that David, who was the archetypal king to the Jewish people, was of the same tribe and in

157

the same bloodline from Judah to JESUS (Matt. 1:2-17). In some sense, this was the path of the spiritual seed that connected Abraham to JESUS in the promises GOD made to Abraham.

Judah was undoubtedly the leader of the brothers in matters that did not involve the direct presence of Joseph for the rest of their lives. Then, as time ripened, his descendants were those from whom the kings of the southern Kingdom came in continuous, direct lineage (1 Chron. 3:10-24).

The brother who placed the lives of his brothers above his own life twice was rewarded by becoming the steward of the earthly shadow of the heavenly Kingdom. No wonder his descendant David sang so many songs.

JACOB-JUDAH Dyad

Interestingly enough, despite Judah's obvious and recognized importance, scripture records very little interaction between Jacob and Judah. There can be little doubt, however, that in Jacob's old age the two developed quite a bond. In Egypt, Joseph was occupied with the affairs of state of Pharaoh, not the matters of Jacob's household.[72] He had made splendid arrangements for his father and brothers and all that was theirs, but he probably had little to do with carrying out the business of the family. It is quite likely that after the settlement in Egypt, Judah began to be the man upon whom Jacob leaned for the welfare of the camp from an operational perspective.

Judah had not been prepared for the rule by his father. However, his emergence during the famine insured that he would become the ruler. Therefore, for much of the rest of Jacob's life, Judah would be very present preparing for the rule that would be his after his father's death.

Jacob required Joseph to promise with the most solemn oath to return his remains to Canaan.[73] Joseph made the promise, and when the time came, Jacob received full, royal, funerary honors in Egypt before the journey to Canaan. Once the funeral party came to Canaan, it is likely that Judah became the primary officiant for the actual interment. This would have been a great honor, and it is quite likely that Joseph would have deferred to Judah as the chief among his brothers for its execution.

From that time on, the honor due to Jacob within the camp fell to Judah insofar as the people were concerned. Joseph was certainly held in awe, but Judah ruled in the camp. It was probably Judah who spoke on behalf of the brothers after Jacob's burial, when they went to gain reassurances they were safe (Gen. 50:15-21). Not only did Joseph reaffirm his forgiveness of them, he also placed them in his own economic care for the rest of their lives.

Concerning the subsequent history of the descendants of Judah, they included such luminaries as Caleb (Num. 13:30), who wanted to take on the giants to conquer Canaan soonest. They included Boaz, who redeemed Ruth (Ruth 4:11-22). They included David and Solomon. They included all the kings of the Kingdom named after their ancestor (Mt. 1:6-16). They included the Messiah (Mt. 1:16; Lk. 3:23-38), for whom the scepter had been kept. Those stories are beyond the scope of this book, so we will not enumerate them here.

These sons of Jacob were the men who carried the promise GOD had made to Abram concerning a great nation into the actual people of that great nation. From them were descended what we call the "tribes of Israel." To their descendants a few generations later belonged the conquest of the land, the building of the national land, the peculiarity of being GOD's own, and so forth, until He came whose it was. These men and their descendants were living entities who modeled the relationships of fathers and sons and brothers so that we can see in the flesh the way GOD means for spiritual men to live.

ONE DAY IN PHARAOH'S COURT

We have indirectly observed some things about the installment of the sons of Jacob in Egypt. It will prove useful to look more directly at the events that relate to that. This is useful for understanding the disposition of the "great nation" at a very critical time in its social and political history. The following story is drawn from the scriptural evidence, with an emphasis on protocol. The specifics presented are not provided in scripture, and the intent is to see what those events might well have looked like. While Abraham, Isaac, and Jacob had been quite successful in their ventures among the Canaanites, the whole family was about to move into a well-organized nation that was not under the curse on Canaan. That nation (Egypt) was also not particularly aware of GOD.

When the eleven brothers presented themselves before Joseph as an entire group, the first of Joseph's two dreams, the dream of sheaves, was particularly fulfilled. That fulfillment allowed for his second dream to begin its fulfillment. The dream of the luminaries, you will recall, specified that the sun, the moon, and eleven stars would bow together before Joseph (Gen. 37:9-11). Jacob immediately understood what the dream portended, and protested. However, Jacob's discomfort did not invalidate the dream. It remained for GOD to cause fulfillment in due season. And He did.

Joseph was a very important person in Egypt. When Pharaoh heard that Joseph's brothers had been reunited with him, it was a cause to be happy for his "prime minister." At the same time, he might also have worried a bit. What if Joseph simply decided to go home with his brothers? Pharaoh knew that would be bad for Egypt because Joseph ran things there. Whether or not he had such thoughts, he acted anyway to extend an invitation to the family of Jacob. It appears this was not done at Joseph's request; the invitation seems to have originated with Pharaoh himself. Of course, Joseph was delighted. He was one of the richest and most respected fellows around, and now he could have even more happiness in being reunited with his father and brothers.

Because Pharaoh issued the invitation and outlined the arrangements, Joseph was free to bring this thing about however he desired, sparing no expense. Everything was in his power in the matter once Pharaoh had started the ball rolling. This was to be a grand and formal event with significant involvement of the head of state so that all would be aware of what was taking place. With this beginning, we construct a reasonable scenario for the events that followed.

There were three key components, each with numerous details. First was the issuance of the invitation. Second was the solemn appearance of the family in the court of Pharaoh. Third was the actual situation of the family in its honored status. By the time these things were consummated, there would be no doubt in the minds of anyone in Egypt that these were really important people, these kinsmen of the prime minister.

The invitation was probably written down on papyrus, most likely employing language with great flourish. Two copies of the invitation were made, one to be kept by either Joseph or Jacob and the other to be placed in the royal archives in Egypt. It is possible that one of the brothers, specifically Judah, was given possession of the written invitation. He would be solemnly instructed as to its safeguards and so forth. Or, there might have been a party of fairly important Egyptians assigned to carry the document to Jacob. Either way, there was gravity in this element of the process.

The court appearance needed considerable preparation. Because of who Joseph was, it is likely that most high ranking personages in Egypt were invited—in fact, required—to be present on the day of the solemnities. This took time and careful coordination, which meant the date for the ceremonies had to be set well in advance. It is likely that the time was decided on even before the brothers departed from Egypt to bring the news to Jacob. Or, perhaps, a messenger was dispatched from Hebron once Jacob accepted the invitation. Either way, at Joseph's end preparations began immediately for a very important day to be held in Pharaoh's palace at such-and-such a time. Nobody would decline the invitation. After all, Joseph was a very important person.

Joseph probably carefully scripted the actual reception at the palace, working with other palace officials on all the details. He had such access to Pharaoh that he no doubt discussed the specifics with the king, and together they agreed on even the smallest detail. They discussed the three phases of the audience and arranged them in such a way as to have maximum impact in Egypt.

Finally, there was the matter of the physical disposition and location of the family upon their arrival. The original, informal invitation had spoken of a very positive location for the family. The day of their royal audience called for a specific location, as well as the establishment of some sort of official relationship with Pharaoh that would make sense in terms of the choice location to be provided. It is quite likely that some folks had to be moved to make this possible, so specification was absolutely essential.

Jacob and his sons would not immediately arrive in that location. The specification would be formally announced and arrangements for those who would have to move would be made. This was, after all, the best land in Egypt (Gen. 45:16-18, 47:5-6) and was unlikely to be empty.

The "move in date" would be after the family's day in Pharaoh's court. But the date of the royal audience depended upon the arrival of the family. So a temporary location for the family had to be found that was very near the final location. Upon arrival near the palace, Jacob's family would then settle into that temporary site in order to rest up from the trip. Then, after some number of days, the appearance in the palace took place. Joseph surely met his father and greeted the family at the temporary campsite and visited as much as he could with them. His second dream (luminaries) was now perfectly manifested. Affairs of state would intervene, but the formalities were not very far off. Once the formalities were ended, the move to the permanent location would occur fairly quickly. So, for maybe a few weeks, the family settled into a temporary location while the people in Goshen who would need to move did so. It is likely this all took place with some time to spare, but the formalities had to be attended to before the final settlement.

Finally, the day came. The court of Pharaoh gathered for the solemn events. In some ante-room in another part of the palace, Joseph waited with his father and a party of his brothers. After the solemnities of formally convening an assembly ended, Joseph appeared before the

Pharaoh where all eyes could see him. No doubt there were some formulaic utterances once Joseph had performed the required obeisance to the Pharaoh. Those things done, Joseph informed the Pharaoh that his father and brothers had come to Egypt and were ready to appear before Pharaoh to receive his instructions. Likely, Pharaoh said some things to further highlight the importance of the occasion. Court scribes scribbled away on their papyrus, busily capturing the details of the day's events in writing for the royal archives.

Prior to that day, Joseph had appointed a delegation of five of his brothers to appear in phase two of the audience. These brothers were then carefully coached regarding the customs of the court, how to address Pharaoh, what questions they would be asked, and how to answer them. They would also be properly clothed for the audience. Joseph surely must have selected his full brother Benjamin as a member of the delegation. He probably also selected Reuben because of his status as **firstborn**. Judah was likely a member of the delegation as well because he was now the spokesman for the brothers and could be trusted to represent Jacob's interests. The other two chosen by Joseph were probably one each from the two pairs of sons of Bilhah and Zilpah. Of course, we don't know if this is the way things actually went down, but based on the circumstances, these assumptions make good sense.

As Joseph brought the five brothers into the royal presence, he performed the formal introductions. Pharaoh then began the audience with the comments and questions he and Joseph had pre-arranged. The brothers answered the questions as they had been coached. The result was the land grant for Jacob and his family, as well as receiving the honor of becoming the herdsmen for Pharaoh. The entire court was witness to these things and they were recorded for the royal archives.

The last phase was the introduction of Jacob. Last was the position of honor. All the niceties of the grant and defining the relationship were over now. The sons of Jacob now owned a good portion of the best agricultural land in Egypt, and were on Pharaoh's payroll. Everybody knew it. Now it was time for the two heads of state to meet one another. No matter how unequal the Egyptians perceived this to be, it bore great weight with GOD. This would be ceremonial, but mostly a matter of pleasantries. Upon being introduced to Pharaoh, Jacob pronounced a blessing on him. This might have seemed of minor importance to the court, but the **patriarch** Israel carried a lot of weight with GOD. Whatever the blessing was, it would have impact in the days and years to come. We know little of the conversation between the two of them. The only item recorded was the Pharaoh's question regarding Jacob's age. At the end, Jacob blessed Pharaoh again. This might have been only a polite thank you, but the **patriarch** had pronounced it before Egypt and GOD.

All ceremonies end, as did this one. Joseph was now free to oversee the move of the camp of Israel into the granted land. What a grand procession it must have been from the temporary camp into the permanent grant in the presence of all Egypt!

Please scan the QR code or go to the web address to view Corbett's video introduction to the book.

Chapter 10

PROPHETIC PATRIARCHAL FRAMEWORK

http://bit.ly/1mRn7MO

Please go to ravensfood.everykindred.com for access to additional supplements to the book. Content will be added from time to time as desirable to support this book.

PROPHETIC PATRIARCHAL FRAMEWORK

Before we undertake an analysis of the "prophetic" framework of the patriarchal period, it will be worthwhile to examine the big picture of the timeline involved. Our tendency is to view these eras in some sort of undefined state insofar as time and space are concerned. We have handily handled the space aspects quite well. Now it is time to grasp the time considerations. Fortunately, scripture provides us with the information needed. Unfortunately, we have a significant bias when it comes to the period of slavery in Egypt, which we will examine below. After examining and clarifying the timeframe of the period, we will return to its "structure" as designed by GOD Himself.

THE FOUR HUNDRED YEARS OF SLAVERY PROBLEM[74]

There are two critical passages of scripture that need some sort of reconciliation in order for us to understand fully the impact of the "Egyptian period" of the patriarchal era. The Egyptian period transitions the descendants of Abraham into the "nation" of the sons of Israel. The mechanism for the transition was the "furnace of Egypt"

(Deut. 4:20, Jer. 11:4, 1 Ki. 8:51), which speaks of the time of enslavement that was experienced by the descendants of Abraham, Isaac, and Jacob that began at some point in time after Jacob migrated to Egypt.

The most common understanding of this time of slavery was that it covered a period of *400 years*. Indeed, most translations of Genesis 15 seem to imply this was the case. However, this approach to understanding the passage does not harmonize well with other biblical information about that timeframe.

First, the passage in Genesis 15 also states that *in the fourth generation*, the descendants of Israel would come out of Egypt. Even casual analysis of these two "understandings" should reveal the harmonization problem. If the sons of Israel were enslaved in Egypt for 400 years, yet came out of Egypt "in the fourth generation," this requires that a "generation" be more than 100 years in length. No use of the word "generation," either then or now, spans anything close to a century. Furthermore, information we have concerning the lifespans of the generations in the ancestry of Moses (Ex. 6:16-20) make a 400-year period virtually impossible given the other information on this period we glean from scripture.

Second, in Galatians 3 Paul describes a specific time frame of *430 years* between the time when Abram received the promise of GOD and the time when Moses and the sons of Israel received the law at Sinai. The two passages are not addressing exactly the same thing, but we need to seek some sort of harmony between them because they occur in essentially the same timeframe. They both speak of real time.

Fortunately, the two periods end at about the same time. The giving of the law at Sinai occurred within a matter of a few months (as few as two or three) after the day the Israelites left Egypt. We know for sure that all the subsequent activities that took place at Mt. Sinai were wrapped up before the end of the first year (Ex. 40:17). For purposes of understanding the two passages, we will say that the 400- and the 430-year periods ended at the same time. This leaves us with different start times for the two periods, but the two start times can now be evaluated against one another. When Paul spoke of the contrast of the promise to the law, he specified that the promise came before the law (predated the law) by 430 years. When GOD spoke to Abram, He stated that the descendants of Abram would leave their place of oppression four hundred years after some other start date, not the moment in which He spoke it.

Comparing the two passages for their content, we reach the conclusion that the promise came 30 years before the beginning of the 400 years spoken of in Genesis 15. For the sake of simplicity we will assume here that Abram was about 70 years old when he first received the promise. About 30 years later, something occurred that started the 400-year period before the descendants of Israel left the land of their oppression. If Abram was 70 years old at the time the LORD first instructed him to leave home and go to another land, the other event, whatever it was, occurred when he had reached the age of 100. In fact, Abraham was 100 years old when Isaac was born (Gen. 21:5).

Why would the birth of Isaac begin some sort of 400-year period? When Isaac was born, Abraham had the *reality of descendants* as defined by GOD. Until the birth of Isaac, Abram/Abraham had no descendants. In the absence of descendants, there could be no oppression of said descendants. When Isaac showed up in the world, the natural possibility of the descendants of Abram going to another land and being oppressed became real. It simply was not real before that. Using this reckoning, we should expect that the end of the time of oppression would be about 400 years after the birth of Isaac. This would coincide with the 430 years Paul spoke about. They would end at the same time.

This analysis yields three cogent observations. From the time GOD charged Abram to move with the promise of progeny to the release of that progeny from oppression was 430 years.[75] From the time of the promise to the realization of progeny as GOD reckoned the progeny was 30 years. From the time of the appearance of progeny for Abraham to the release from oppression and the giving of the law was 400 years.

Will 400 years of oppression work with these other facts? The simple answer is no. Let's see why not. As things stand, Isaac would have had to go to the land of oppression soon after his birth in order for this timing to work out. In that event, the departure from Egypt would have had to occur before the generation of Moses and Aaron, or the "fourth generation" part of the prophecy would not work.

We know that Isaac never went to Egypt. In fact, the LORD explicitly instructed him not to (Gen. 26:2). His appearance in the land of oppression simply did not occur. Let's subtract Isaac's lifespan from the 400 years and see what happens. We know from scripture that Isaac lived 180 years. Those years were not spent in oppression. This leave us with 220 years as the longest possible period in Egypt and, hence, of oppression.

Another thing we know from scripture is that Isaac's grandson Joseph was never oppressed in Egypt after he became "prime minister" of Egypt (Ex. 1:6-8). He was a slave early on and then a prisoner, but when his life ended he was not at all oppressed. Joseph was about 30 years old when he was released from prison and elevated to second-in-command in Egypt. This occurred at about the time of Isaac's death. Joseph lived to be 110 years old. This means he was a ruler in Egypt for about 80 years. Those 80 years saw no oppression for the sons of Jacob. In fact, they occupied a rather privileged position in Egypt, above that of the average Egyptian. When we subtract those 80 years from the 220 years left after Isaac's death, we are down to a period of 140 years before the exodus. To clarify, Joseph died about 140 years before the Israelites' departure from Egypt.

We do know also that Moses was born during the time of oppression (Ex. 1:22 – 2:4), and that he was 80 years old when he led the descendants of Abraham out of Egypt. Subtracting that 80 years from the 140 years after the death of Joseph leaves us with a period of 60 years in doubt. In other words, the oppression lasted at least 80 years, but no more than 140 years.

We know that Levi lived 137 years. He was about ten years older than Joseph. Thus, he would have been about 120 years old when Joseph died. His remaining 17 years need to be subtracted as well because none of the brothers of Joseph ever suffered from the oppression (Ex.1:6-7). This brings the unknown time down to a maximum of 123 years. If Levi was the longest-lived of the brothers, then the period of the oppression would have lasted a minimum of 80 years, and a maximum of 123 years.

It turns out that some time must have passed after the last of Joseph's brothers died, because the Pharaoh who began the oppression "did not know about Joseph" (Ex. 1:8-10). If that is true, he was in no way a contemporary of the generation of Joseph and his brothers. Some years would have needed to pass before that condition would occur. From Levi's death to Moses' birth was only about 47 years (discussed below). The changes in conditions in Egypt that led to the oppression of the Israelites would have to have occurred during that 47-year timeframe. We can then conclude that the Israelites' time of oppression lasted only from 80-100 years. Nobody wants to be a slave for even one day. However, scripture does not require a 400-year period of abject misery. In fact, it only allows a period of a little over 100 years.

The last fact we want to examine is the fact that GOD had told Abram that his descendants would come out of the land of oppression *in the fourth generation* after they entered that land (Gen. 15:16). As we observed earlier, four generations doesn't line up very well with 400 years either. The following genealogy occurs in Exodus (Ex. 6:16-20). Levi had a son named Kohath who was born in Canaan and accompanied his father to Egypt as a child (Gen. 46:11). Remember that Levi lived to be 137. He was about 45-50 years old at the time of the migration to Egypt, and his son Kohath was already born. Kohath was, in fact, the second of the three sons of Levi, so he was at least several years old at the time of the migration. He would then have been about 80-85 years old when his father died.

In Egypt, at some point in time, Kohath had a son named Amram (Ex. 6:18). Kohath lived a total of 133 years. Amram was the oldest of his four sons. So even if Kohath was old when Amram was old, which is very doubtful, the birth of Amram was not at the time of the death of Kohath.

This Amram was the father of Aaron and Moses (Ex. 6:20). He lived to be 137 years old. By the time of his death it is likely that his sons Aaron and Moses were grown men.

All these lives can fit quite comfortably into our 140-year time-frame during which the oppression took place. These data suggest this shorter estimate for the time of the oppression.

Joseph and Levi were brothers. Their generation was the generation that first went down into Egypt (Joseph was the first to go live in Egypt after the prophecy in Gen. 15:13-16). Their father Jacob was a part of that migration, but he was the last of all of them to enter Egypt. If we count Joseph and Levi as the first generation in Egypt, then the generation of Aaron and Moses was the fourth generation in Egypt. It was the fourth generation that was to leave the land of oppression, according to the word of the LORD spoken to Abram many years earlier.

There are very few assumptions built into the preceding analysis. It harmonizes several scriptural facts quite well. Given some rounding error, it matches quite well with the scriptural passages taken as a whole. Our Father can really manage details. A more detailed analysis with a proposed timeline can be found using the endnote at the beginning of this section.

PROPHETIC "STRUCTURE"

Jacob lived some 17 years after the move to Egypt (Gen. 47:28). In that time, the family was able to settle into the way of life they would always have there as far as they knew. Relations with the Egyptians, both formal and informal, would have developed in mostly positive ways. The new neighbors would adjust to one another and life would assume its rhythms. New approaches to pasturage and water sources would have been developed. Other commercial and civil relationships also would have been developed.

As Jacob's death approached, he needed to accomplish two things: first, the adoption of Joseph's sons as his own sons (Gen. 48:5, 12-22) and, second, the prophetic disposition regarding his sons in the flesh (Gen. 49).

With regard to the first matter, there is no place in scripture where Ephraim and Manasseh are called sons of Jacob. But by the time of the exodus they were enumerated among the sons of Israel (Num. 1:4-15). In fact, they came to be designated as tribal patriarchs, giving their names to the tribes composed of their descendants. Their adoption by Jacob and the manner of it have already been discussed.

In the preceding discussions we have also briefly disclosed key elements of the blessings of each of the sons of Jacob. Ephraim and Manasseh were not included in those blessings, but Joseph was (Gen. 49:22-25). We may assume that the basic ideas of Jacob's blessing of Joseph came to inhere in the consciousness of the Ephraimites and Manassehites. In turn, all of the Israelites would come to view them in terms of the prophetic blessings Jacob enunciated in regards to Joseph.

We are then left with a distinction between the sons of *Jacob* (Joseph plus the eleven who came from Canaan) and the sons of *Israel* (the twelve born to Jacob, minus Joseph, plus Ephraim and Manasseh). The "substitution" of Ephraim and Manasseh for Joseph causes the distinction. Furthermore, the eventual exclusion of Levi from a tribal territorial **inheritance** (Num. 18:20-24) produces even more of a separation. GOD is no idiot. Therefore, the distinction between "sons of Jacob" and "sons of Israel" has some purpose. Earlier we suggested that Jacob was a man who lived his life in the flesh. At the time of his re-entry into Canaan, after his time in the east, he was renamed Israel by GOD Himself (Gen. 32:28-30). That had the purpose of distinguishing the man of flesh from the spiritual phenomenon. Jacob was a man, but in him GOD worked out a spiritual purpose for Israel.

Israel was his new name, but it was not frequently used in scripture in his lifetime, even after it was bestowed. On the other hand, in the history of the descendants of Jacob the name used was generally Israel rather than Jacob.[76] That is why one might say that Jacob was a man and Israel was a spiritual phenomenon. Jacob continued to live out his life in the flesh and to exhibit primarily human characteristics, while Israel was not so constrained. This spiritual man who completed the work of founding a nation was not the same as the natural man who fathered twelve sons and whose life had involved so much deceit and struggle. It is to the spiritual phenomenon that we now need to turn our attention. The natural man was inadequate to get done what was necessary.

Paul the apostle showed us an important point of view in one of his letters to the specific churches (Gal. 3:16-18). He labored to distinguish the spirit and the law by pointing out that the spiritual context of "the promise" was provided before the law. Specifically, he stated that the promise was given 430 years before the law. The promise clearly has to do with Abram/Abraham and the law has to do with Mount Sinai. This distinguishes a "natural" man from the "spiritual" man living in the same flesh.

Let's then use this *promise* as our starting place. In fact, we have basically done that already, but a summary here will be helpful. At a particular point in time Abram received a promise from GOD. If we can specifically locate that point in time, we can rush ahead of that time some 430 years to the commandments at Sinai. The entire history that has been the subject of this book will then be located historically between these two points. In fact, that 430-year timeframe extends well beyond our era under analysis.

The promise was extended to Abram in what we may call a "prophetic context" (Gen. 12:1-3). In fact, GOD being who He is, any promise He makes is prophetic by definition. It will be manifested. Our goal here is to discover and analyze the actual impact of the prophetic promises and instructions of GOD on the history of these characters we call patriarchs. In order to do that we will start with the first manifestation of the promise GOD made to Abram in the context of requiring him to move to Canaan. In that statement of promise, the same as prophecy, given the source, the promise that GOD would make of Abram a "great nation" was given. We should interpret this as meaning that Abram would become a "great nation" if for no other reason than that GOD said so. In essence, there was no requirement on Abram except that he move to the location that GOD specified. At the time Abram actually moved, he was about 75 years old (Gen. 12:4).

A few years later, say five years, the incident of the smoking fire pot took place (Gen. 15:17-21). In this instance, the LORD extended the information relative to the promise to include the fact there would be a time when Abram's descendants would be mistreated in a foreign country. Their mistreatment would end after 400 years. Also, He told Abram they would come out of that country *in the fourth generation.* When you put the 430-year period in the same context with the 400-year period, you have an impossible situation. Both cannot be true. Abram/Abraham lived for most of another 100 years. Isaac died about 105 years after Abraham's death. Only then were things set in motion for the move to the foreign nation some seven or eight years later. At that, after Jacob moved to Egypt, it was still quite some time before the mistreatment began, because it was more than 70 years later that Joseph died, and he died a fair number of years before the mistreatment began.

Then there is the matter of the "fourth generation." Fourth generation can refer either to the fourth generation from that moment, or the fourth generation after the move to the foreign land, or the fourth generation after the mistreatment began. It turns out that the lineage of Moses from Levi contains two generations between Levi and Moses (Levi, Kohath, Amram, Moses). If we start the count to the fourth generation from when Levi went to Egypt with his father, Moses would be in the fourth. All three sons of Levi, by the way, were born before the migration. Only Amram and then Moses were born in Egypt, but Moses is in the fourth generation. Since Moses led the people in their exit from Egypt, we can see that this prophetic instruction to Abram falls quite well inside the 430-year timeframe Paul specified.

After Abraham died, the LORD spoke to Isaac while he was living among the Philistines (Gen. 26:2-6). At the time, GOD instructed Isaac to avoid going down into Egypt. This was a curious requirement, but it appears the LORD was honoring the wishes of Abraham in the matter. If Isaac never went to the land where the enslavement was to occur, he at least could not become the victim of the enslavement.

When Jacob was leaving Canaan to avoid the wrath of Esau and to get a non-Canaanite wife, the LORD appeared to him in a dream and told him that He would see to it that he came back to Canaan (Gen. 28:14-15). Twenty years later he came back a wealthy man.

Finally, there are the two dreams of Joseph to consider (Gen. 37:5-11). The twin dreams required that his eleven brothers appear before him as supplicants in some context. The context was grain. The other dream required that his father and mother and eleven brothers appear before him, not as supplicants but as important persons, luminaries. The luminaries would come and bow before him, not in supplication, but in a form of thanksgiving and rejoicing.

The scope of this book ends before the beginning of the Israelites' enslavement in Egypt. From the first giving of God's promise to Abram to Jacob's migration to Egypt took about 240 years. To fit another three generations in and keep everything to less than 430 years is quite feasible. Joseph lived about 70 years past the migration. Moses was born into slavery. These things we know. Those two facts tally to 150 years. That leaves about 40 years as the timeframe within which the slavery could have begun. Furthermore, it was some number of years after Joseph's death that the slavery began. It is possible that the period of slavery began between the birth of Aaron and the birth of Moses about three years later. This offends what we have generally believed about these things, but is consistent with what scripture tells us. The sole fly in the ointment is God's second message to Abram,[77] but there are textual variations that make that consistent as well.

The point is that we can consider the entire patriarchal period as not only managed by God, but announced by God as things moved along. He told the patriarchs what He was doing in regards to their lives along the way. Each preserved the knowledge in scripture and lived the manifestation in their lives, whether aware of it or not.

THE PROPHETIC PROGRESSION

To Abram the LORD promised a specific land, progeny, and the creation of a great nation with unusual characteristics (Gen. 12:1-4). He also told Abram that his progeny would go elsewhere for a while, be mistreated, and come back in the fourth generation (Gen. 15:16). He even stated that wickedness among the Amorites (Canaanites) would ripen by then, so that the judgment of those people would be completely suited to their wickedness. The land, of course, was Canaan, where GOD planted Abram. Abram despaired of ever producing progeny, but the LORD finally blessed Sarah's barren womb with Isaac (Gen. 18:10-11). Even though GOD later asked Abraham to sacrifice Isaac (Gen 22:2), He still intended to make the nation from the progeny. As we know, Isaac was spared by the LORD, who was the Prophet in this story. Abraham died before anything that looked like a nation could come forth. His two grandsons, Esau and Jacob, were about 15 years old at the time of his death. So Abraham had to accept the "nation" part in faith.

Abraham seems to have been predisposed to resist GOD on the matter of the mistreatment of his progeny. Specifically, he forbade his servant from taking Isaac out of the land in search of a wife (Gen. 24:6-7). The bargain he made was that if a wife could not be found for Isaac from Padan Aram and brought to him, then and only then, Isaac could marry a Canaanite woman. He was dead set against Isaac leaving Canaan. If he never left, he could never be a slave somewhere else. Abraham did not live to see that the LORD spoke true. In his lifetime half of what the LORD promised him became manifest. The rest was manifest after Abraham's death, but it was all made manifest.

The LORD spoke to Isaac to confirm the covenant He had made with Abraham (Gen. 26:1-6). He had instructed Abram that if his progeny would be true to Him, He would bless him inter-generationally. He was true to His word. In confirming the covenant with Isaac, He instructed him to not go to Egypt, even though eventually that would happen a generation later with Jacob. In this we find confirmation that the foreign land of mistreatment was Egypt, as was subsequently manifested.

When Jacob fled Canaan, GOD appeared to him at Bethel to inform him He would bring him back (Gen. 28:15). This happened absolutely. In the intervening twenty years, GOD even cleared up matters back home to make things work properly when Jacob did return. In the return, Jacob even got a new name, a spiritual name that spoke to the fact that the nation was now coming into manifestation. The promise to Abram was now visible, where there had been very few persons previously.

During Isaac's lifetime, Joseph was enslaved in Egypt (Gen. 39:1). This might well be considered a precursor to the fate of the family somewhat later. However, the enslavement and then imprisonment of Joseph in Egypt set in motion the events that would lead to Jacob taking his family to Egypt, little aware of the fate awaiting them a couple of generations later. But the LORD had instructed Isaac not to go to Egypt. Isaac couldn't go to Egypt, but Joseph was down there preparing a place for Jacob and his family. These matters seem to be at cross purposes in some way. As it turns out, though, Isaac died about thirteen years after Joseph was sold into slavery.[78] At the time, Joseph was 30 years old. That was the year in which he was released from prison and became the prime minister of Egypt. After that, the things that caused Jacob to move to Egypt were well under way. About the time Isaac died, Joseph became involved in the processes that got Israel into Egypt. Isaac couldn't go there, but there was no such instruction to Jacob or his sons.

Shortly before Joseph fell into such disfavor with his brothers that they eventually wanted to kill him, his dreams occurred (Gen. 37:5-11). Quickly, the dreams indicated the eleven brothers would bow before him in a context involving wheat. This would be followed by the event in which his parents and his brothers would bow before him in a context that spoke of some sort of glory for them. We know that both dreams were precisely fulfilled a little over 20 years later.

GOD informed the patriarchs of all these things in advance of their occurrence. They did not necessarily see or understand all of them, but they were meticulously fulfilled in the timing of GOD.

There are more to these prophecies of GOD than we have discussed here, but the other elements are beyond our scope. Suffice it to say that GOD announced the main events, and then GOD saw to it the events were scrupulously adhered to in their time.

THE BARREN WOMB

The barren womb has been mentioned several times in this book. For our purposes, we will describe a barren womb as one that was dormant so long after marriage that the wife and the husband feared no children would be born of it. Isaac was born to a barren womb (Gen. 18:11). Jacob (and Esau) were born to a barren womb (Gen. 25:21). Joseph was born to a womb feared to be barren (Gen. 30:1-2). This same phenomenon occurred in the generations of each of the three national patriarchs. The small number of sons relates to this. It appears the LORD was first permitting ambiguity (Ishmael and Esau) and then clarifying His election by removing the ambiguity to the desert country to the south and east of Canaan.

In the generation after Jacob, the sons were fairly fruitful.[79] It was time to grow the nation. The existence of the nation had been purified; now was the time of growth. For example, Benjamin had ten sons when he went into Egypt and he was still a pretty young man. In that time, it was no longer necessary for one man to bear the burden of the promise of the Kingdom. The Kingdom was moving from promise to realization, and it needed a large community to move it forward.

SOLITARY MEN

The generations of the national patriarchs were characterized by a single man bearing the burden, if you will, of moving things forward. It was as though no distractions of kinship could be allowed to get in the way. Both Isaac and Jacob had a natural brother each, but it was clear where the election was by the time it mattered. Ishmael had to leave when Isaac was a child (Gen. 21:8-10). Esau's mind was changed while Jacob was away from home so that Esau removed himself from the picture (Gen. 33:9). But even before that, it was clear that the **birthright** and the patriarchal blessing had gone to Jacob. There was nothing there for Esau, just as there had been nothing there for Ishmael.

179

In the transition from the national **patriarch** to the tribal patri-archs, there were still solitary figures. Joseph was sent to Egypt alone by the LORD. He was there beyond the knowledge, hopes, or expectations of his family for over 20 years. He spoke of forgetfulness with the birth of his first son (Gen. 41:51). However, he gave the babe a Hebrew name in a country where no one spoke Hebrew. He was required to be solitary while he unknowingly prepared a place for his father's family.

In that same generation, Judah was also solitary for quite a long time. He left Jacob and moved among the Canaanites (Gen. 38:1) for most of the 20 years before the move to Egypt. This seems to have been to prepare him for his role as the leader of the brothers as the nation moved. This phenomenon is similar to the isolation of Moses from his people for 80 years before he led them out of Egypt.[80] Judah and Moses were a kind of beginning and end for the Egyptian period in terms of leadership. Each was a solitary man for a major part of his life.

The amazing precision with which the LORD managed all these things, and the motifs He established for doing so, plead with us to pay attention to the mighty works of our GOD. He managed isolation, fertility, separation, generational distinctions, priestly functions, new names, and so forth, to bring these things about. As He did so, He also announced to the patriarchs how and when He would accomplish each component of the emergence of the "great nation." He did these things using His very own **father-son** paradigm as the human glue for fallible, mortal men.

Please scan the QR code or go to the web address to view Corbett's video introduction to the book.

Chapter 11

ETERNITY AND PATRIARCHY

http://bit.ly/1ZXnxzy

Please go to ravensfood.everykindred.com for access to additional supplements to the book. Content will be added from time to time as desirable to support this book.

CHAPTER 11

ETERNITY AND PATRIARCHY

To the human mind there exists an inherent paradox between patriarchy and a nation. On a very small scale of human endeavor, patriarchy can work as an effective governance device. As the scale of a nation grows, it is much more difficult to envision effective patriarchy. To find in the world examples of effective patriarchy on any large scale is essentially impossible. However, we have set to ourselves the task of relating patriarchs to the Kingdom of GOD. GOD presents Himself as a **patriarch**, or at least as a Father to those who want to argue the matter. We cannot imagine a father with higher authority than that of GOD, so He is a **Patriarch** by definition.

GOD is The **Patriarch** to any reasonable person who acknowledges His existence. Those who do not or cannot recognize His patriarchy cannot benefit fully from it. Many who believe cannot or do not actually recognize His patriarchy to any meaningful extent. Some cannot fully realize the patriarchy of GOD because their image of a father is so flawed, usually by sad experience. Some will not fully recognize the patriarchy of GOD because it is too personal, too fraught with accountability. Those who will, or wish to, recognize and live within the patriarchy of GOD will accept its intimacy and accountability.

The paradox of scale and intimacy is quite difficult to work out by oneself. In this two-volume work, we have examined the specific nature of **father-son** relationships, both in the abstract and in very particular examples. It is in the amazing capacity of GOD to be the Father of a man, and a man to be a son of GOD, that we have found the intimacy and accountability that are required by patriarchy. At the same time, we have witnessed the founding of a nation from the womb of that same intimate accountability. The nation was still in its infancy as we finished our analysis, but we know that it not only survived but became the womb, as it were, of the Messiah in due season. We have observed the eternal nature of the **father-son** relationship as it served as a vessel for the coming forth of the will of GOD for mankind in a shadow form.

As in the case of the Gordian knot, the resolution of the paradox of scale and intimacy in human activity is quite simple, even though most find it elusive. The resolution of the paradox lies in the potentially highest quality of all human relationship forms – the **father-son dyad**. That **dyad** has the highest potential for human beings because it is precisely the first form of dyadic relationship and it is given, at the highest temporal and authoritative **primacy**, in the **FATHER-SON** relationship. It is precisely the primal relationship. From it all other human relationships are derived. GOD the Father and JESUS the Son relate in eternity in precisely that form of **dyad**. All dyads are unique to some extent, but this one is given to us as the eternal standard. Its perfect form, replete with *perfect **paternal** love* and *perfect **filial** obedience*, is the goal of anyone who seeks to know and live in the phenomenon of the heart of GOD. There is no other way of life that is superior; no other way that even comes anywhere close to its equivalent. That is the reason our Father spent so much of Himself in it.

Filial obedience is not merely hypothetical; otherwise, Calvary would not have been necessary. Let us be clear, **filial** love is precisely the same thing as **filial** obedience. A theoretical **filial** obedience can only produce a **filial** love that is theoretical. It will not be real until it costs something in the son that is very precious to the father, no matter who the parties are in the **father-son dyad**. The standard, again, is the

FATHER-SON dyad. The intimacy required as the context for the giving of **paternal** love and the response of **filial** obedience is quite close. It is really co-extant.

The primary reason we mostly want to keep GOD at a distance is precisely the fear of intimacy in our relationship with Him. We seem to believe that if He will stay up on the mountain, be quiet, and let us perform rituals of various kinds, we can have what we want from Him and avoid intimacy with Him. Not so. Intimacy is required in order for the Son to be formed in us.

We have seen that when these phenomena occur in us, GOD can do great things, even establishing a "holy nation and a royal priesthood," which He has stated is His intent. This is the *raison d'etre* for the **father-son dyad** in the world of men of flesh—that we mortals might live in the same way the Father and the Son live together. He did not provide another model. The model of marriage, for example, is about Christ and His bride, which is His **inheritance** but is not the **father-son** relationship in which He has His being. The **brother-brother** relationship provides a context in which we must get along and show love and mutual respect for one another. It, however, does not require **paternal** sacrifice or **filial** obedience. It is not found to occur across generations per se. GOD is not the husband of JESUS. GOD is not the brother of JESUS. GOD is not a business partner of JESUS. GOD is not the employer of JESUS. GOD is the Father of JESUS. In that, and only that, can come forth the "nation" and "priesthood" GOD so desires. There is no other way.

How gracious of GOD to model these things for us and not leave them as abstract ideas. The first relationship involving a human was the **Father-son** relationship He established with Adam. The second was his **Father-son** relationship with Eve. He then introduced, in short order, the inter-human relationship of marriage, or the husband-wife **dyad**. In that, he established subsequent, human-based **father-son** relationships that we might carry on in the manner in which GOD and JESUS enjoy their relationship with one another. Humanity was commissioned to live in this manner, father and son, from that time on.

This was not intended to be a purely mystical "me and GOD" existence. It was designed to be very tangible insofar as the flesh is concerned, in order to provide context for the spiritual relationship we each have with GOD as Father. We were designed to live in both relationships as long as we wear the mantle of the flesh. When, and only when, we put off the mantle of the flesh do we leave behind the matters of the flesh entirely. This is by GOD's design. Abraham was required to experience the relationship with Isaac. Isaac was required to experience the relationship with Jacob. Jacob was required to experience the relationships he had with each of his sons. No matter how imperfectly these men lived these relationships, they were required of them.

Some maintain they can live without any **father-son** relationship; they only need a **Father-son** relationship. This implies they sprang forth into the life of the flesh in some spontaneous manner, or one that is not customary to man. Only three persons got here in other than the customary manner. Adam was created from inert matter. Eve was created from the living flesh of Adam. JESUS was created by the direct action of the Spirit of GOD on the womb of Mary.[81] The rest of us came in the customary manner. While we exhibit many different kinds and "levels" of intimacy with GOD, we all got here the same way. There was a **father-son** phenomenon of the customary manner. We are designed then, to live as fathers and sons. The idea that we can do away with that in this life is a form of arrogance and disrespect for the ways of GOD. Brotherhood cannot be used as a substitute for **father-son** relationships.

We saw earlier that GOD adopted Abram so that He could place Himself into the place of patriarchy in the life of Abram. He did not set aside the fact that Terah was Abram's father in the flesh. Rather, at the time GOD determined to begin the building of the nation, He adopted Abram so that He could require of him a greater obedience than Terah could have. Terah was not capable of making of Abram the man that GOD needed to father the nation of His intent. For one thing, Terah could not have been the origin of the nation, or the national idea, in this case. No matter the extent of his ego, he could not aspire to do such a thing. It was GOD who declared to Abram that He, GOD, would bring about the great nation, not some man. The "great nation" in its spiritual manifestation is the work of JESUS the Son. The great nation in its natural manifestation was the work of the man of GOD's selection. That man was Abraham, who would be made from the man Abram by the work of none other than GOD Himself. Someone who was not His own son would not be adequate to the task. Neither could such a one be assigned to it. Only a son of GOD would do.

GOD adopted Abram/Abraham to provide for Himself a son He could assign to be the birthplace of the great nation. When GOD adopted Abram, He established beyond legal reproach the device through which He would build the nation. In so doing, He placed beyond the reach of man the starting point for this great work, and He did it in such a way that nothing was violated. Furthermore, He used His own original context, that of father and son, as the operational mechanism for that work.

Having adopted Abram, GOD brought into being a particular **father-son** relationship. We can designate that relationship as GOD-Abram/Abraham, or more to the point, GOD-Abraham, as it was the spiritual phenomenon that He was interested in. Having established the necessary **dyad**, GOD could then begin to bring about the maturation of Abram/Abraham to the full stature of a mature son (*huios*), one worthy of carrying the required destiny.

In the economy of GOD, it was necessary that JESUS become an "exact representation" of GOD so that men could "see" GOD when they saw JESUS. In a similar way it was necessary that Abraham carry a unique destiny (culminating at Mt. Moriah) that would accurately portray who GOD was to the nation to be birthed through Isaac. That, in turn, required not only the **filial** obedience of Abraham to the will of GOD, but also the **filial** obedience of Isaac to the will of Abraham. That day, Abraham was at once both perfected in his **filial** love for GOD, and in the patriarchal burden of a father, which was focused in Isaac. At the same time, Isaac was required to step up to the place of a mature son who surrendered himself to the will of his father. Only in these actions could the nation be furthered. It had to be a nation different from all others. This set of relational phenomena is an important dimension of its particularity.

We stated very early on (in volume one) that the **father-son** relationship is the device, the vessel if you will, of eternity in the here and now. Having brought into the earth the touchstone of the nation (Kingdom) of GOD's desire, how was it to be maintained among mortal men? Would it be necessary in every generation to do again the work of Mt. Moriah? Such a thing would further nothing. We would always be only at the beginning. What was needed was something that would carry Mt. Moriah into the future. We know that in the spiritual realm that is the work of the cross, but in Canaan the cross was a long way off in human terms.

The answer lies in the paradox that the **father-son dyad** is at once very particular and found in the specific identities of the father and son in question, and is also eternal in its nature. The mortal father and son have in their possession an eternal phenomenon in the image of the GOD-JESUS **dyad**. This is so because each requires the other, and that humans are designed to be reproductive. In each generation, people are born as sons. They have a father. As they mature, they learn to become fathers themselves and to pass on the identity found in the relationship into which they were born. Because there cannot be a **father-son** relationship that is only one generation deep, the relationship carries in itself its own future through the inherent replicative characteristic it possesses. Thus it is never-ending, just as is the GOD-JESUS relationship.

Do all **father-son** dyads look like the eternal **dyad**? We know, of course, that they do not. Is GOD, then, eternally thwarted in His designs? Our immediate response is that GOD could not be deprived of that which He desires, a nation of His own design. But, humans are humans. Their fallibility, when measured against GOD's standards, is breathtaking. Most human men never gain the spiritual maturity required to produce sons who would seek such maturity for themselves. Observation indicates, in fact, that this is very rare in the world. Of course, we have already observed that Terah was not up to the task of preparing his son Abram to take his place as the first **patriarch** of the "great nation" of GOD in the earth. GOD adopted Abram in order to bring the necessary discipline into his life. That was the only way Abram could become who he was to become. On the other hand, GOD did not adopt Isaac or Jacob. He relied on their natural fathers to do that which was necessary to bring them into their own inheritances. The GOD-Abraham **dyad** was sufficient to produce a useful Abraham-Isaac **dyad**, and then a useful Isaac-Jacob **dyad** in time. Men continued to be fathers. In the context of the nation of GOD's choosing, they carried, and passed on, the destiny inherent in that national calling.

The Kingdom of GOD is already established in the relationship between GOD and JESUS, who is the Son of the eternal Father. How is it to be lived out in the world? We are often tempted to declare that all that is necessary in the world is "me and JESUS." Nothing else is needed in order for the Kingdom to be fully manifest. This arrogant boast is the product of a prideful heart that does not know "what spirit it is of." This is simply not the way GOD has set things up. If we are not careful with that logic, we may well claim as individuals that JESUS only "needs me" to have a perfect eternal bride. We know better.

GOD made the **father-son** relationship eternally unique in the heavens. He then used it to create the context in which men live. Each man is called to be a son so he can learn to become a father. This can only happen if he lives in a **father-son** relationship that has as its primary aim just such an outcome. We get back, though, to the fact that human **father-son** relationships are typically broken. These broken things cannot carry the weight of the Kingdom GOD desires.

Praise GOD! He has made it possible for us to be "born again" into a new reality! The spiritual entity that we are after we experience this other birth is different from the natural entity we were before. It calls for a new **father-son dyad**. If the flesh results in **father-son** dyads that are characterized by the flesh-nature of man, can there be **father-son** dyads that are characterized by the spiritual nature? Of course there can. Can the father of flesh be also a spiritual father? Of course he can. Is this likely? It is not our observation that men in this world are often qualified spiritual fathers. Is there a remedy for that? Can persons born in the flesh be brought into families with mature spiritual fathers? Yes, but if the father of the flesh is not up to the task, one must find another father who is. One can have both a natural and a spiritual father in this life in the earth.

In the emerging, but already present, Kingdom of GOD, we will expect to see that men are at once both natural and spiritual fathers to their natural children, who then become their spiritual sons. When that phenomenon is absent, GOD must provide fathers who can take on the spiritual tasks which most natural fathers abrogate, or at which they fail. In this way, all men (humans) can become the "sons of GOD" just as all Israelites are the "sons of Abraham."

CONCLUSION

Before the creation commenced, GOD was already present in the persons of the Father and the Son. When the creation cycle was undertaken, GOD created a natural, or created, son. This son was of the substance of creation and of the substance of the eternal. GOD created the natural son by placing a spirit sourced in GOD into the inert substance. This eternal spirit wrapped in the substance of creation appears to have been designed to increase the number of entities in the eternal. However, He designed things so that the created would need to attain to the full status of son through the process of obedience. To this we are called.

While GOD called the created sons to obedience, He provided the models required so that we can understand. He did so in such a way that no man can claim ignorance as a defense. The first model was the model of the relationship which is found in the **dyad** inherent in the Godhead as the **father-son** relationship composed of the eternal prime entity, GOD Himself, and the eternal Son, JESUS. Then, at the time of His own choosing, He sent the Son from that **dyad** to model perfect **filial** obedience. Mankind has then seen the perfected **dyad** and the perfected operational relationship for such a **dyad**. For mankind there is but emulation, no excuses.

When the creation cycle was undertaken, GOD created man to be naturally reproductive. At the same time, He gave to mankind the capacity to inhabit **father-son** relationships that were not only natural but were also spiritual in nature. These were also designed to be increasingly mature throughout lifetimes. We have examined how He used those very natural relationships to reveal His own government (Kingdom) in the creation. He did this in such a way that mankind was empowered to become a full participant in the works of GOD. Not bad work for a sheepherder from the mountains in northern Aramea and his descendants. Not bad examples for men in our times.

GLOSSARY

This book makes particular usage of three general types of words.

The first are certain English words that in common parlance often have vague, ambiguous, or even shifting meanings. One of our goals is to peer beyond the ambiguity of these words to see what the scripture means, rather than to play the games men typically play in the process of scriptural interpretation.

Second are words that are less-commonly used, and therefore need to be clearly defined so that we can accurately understand what is meant with their usage. Otherwise, our meaning remains muddy, which leaves understanding muddy.

Third are words that leave specific etymological trails that enable a greater degree of understanding.

Words included in this glossary are indicated in the text of the book by placing them in **boldface** font. For example, the appearance in the text of "**normal**" (without the quotation marks) indicates that the word "**normal**" appears in the glossary.

BIRTHRIGHT: The implicit rights associated with the first son of a father in biblical and Hebrew culture. These rights generally included a double inheritance and some measure of authority that was greater than the authority of any other sons of the same father.

DYAD: some phenomenon that occurs as a specific pair of something. Two persons are a dyad if there is some reason for considering them at the same time. For example, a married couple is a dyad by virtue of a specific definition as well as by a high degree of affiliation. For our purposes, dyads have origin (located on the left side of the pair symbolically) and object (located on the right side of the pair symbolically). This is a very important term in this book, particularly in the early chapters. A list of the specific dyadic relationships under examination in this book follows.

FATHER-SON: The dyad consisting of GOD the Father and JESUS the Son. Its mirror is **SON-FATHER**.

Father-son: A dyad consisting of GOD the Father and any human individual who may respond with a corresponding involvement through a **son-father** response.

father-son: A dyad consisting of two human individuals, one of whom occupies a relational posture that emulates the FATHER. The other occupies a relational posture that emulates the SON.

Brother-brother: A dyad consisting of JESUS and any human individual who may respond with a corresponding involvement through a **brother-brother** response.

brother-brother: A **dyad** consisting of any two human beings who have some fraternal relationship. In this book fraternal goes beyond biology to any relationship based on common interest, but does not contain any parent-child relationship.

For us, we are the *origin components* of the following four dyads:

son-Father: Person as origin and God as object.

brother-Brother: When I am the origin and Jesus is the Brother.

son-father: When speaking of our human fathers

brother-brother: When speaking of human brothers from our side of the relationship

FILIAL: having to do with a son. Although not as commonly used in English as "paternal," this word does occur on occasion. It is an adjective derived from the Latin word for son, *filius*. The corresponding Greek word is typically *(h)uios*.

FIRSTBORN: The meaning of this word may seem apparent, but because of its importance in the study of the Kingdom of GOD, we include it here. The first son of a father was his firstborn and was imbued with birthright. A mother's first son would also be called a firstborn, but might not be the firstborn of his father. Such a person had specific requirements of redemption associated with his birth.

FRATERNAL: having to do with a brother. This word and related words are somewhat more commonly used in English than is filial. It is derived from the Latin word *frater*, which means brother.

INHERITANCE: Some property passed from a parent to a child, normally at or near the time of death of the parent. In biblical times, the firstborn generally received twice as much as any of the other sons, who all received equal inheritances generally. For example, a man with two sons would leave two-thirds of his wealth to the firstborn and one-third to the younger son. In the case of the prodigal son, the younger son asked for his inheritance early, thus providing a major insult to his father.

NORMAL: according to some specific standard. It is nearly always the case in this book that the word refers to the way a thing should be understood using the scripture as the standard understanding. Usually, "normal" is well-defined and unchanging. It is not negotiable for the sake of common parlance.

NT: A simple abbreviation for the New Testament.

OT: The corresponding abbreviation for the Old Testament.

PATERNAL: having to do with a father. It is an adjective derived from the word for "father" in both the Greek and Latin languages. That word is *pater* (emphasis on the *pa*). A related word is "paternity."

PATRIARCH: Derived from two Greek words, *pater* for "father" and *arch* for "first" or "primary," this term is used in a formal sense to refer to the three men, Abraham, Isaac (his son) and Jacob (son of Isaac).

PRIMACY: Being first or most important; often, both meanings are used together. Preeminence is a commonly used synonym.

PRIMOGENITOR: Simply, the one who begets or causes the birth of the firstborn.

PRIMOGENITURE: Basically, this is the state of being the firstborn of some father. A firstborn exhibits the trait of primogeniture. It may also be a synonym for birthright.

INDEX

G

Gad, 83, 95, 114, 117-118

GOD, ix-xiii, xv-xix. 2-12, 15, 17, 18, 19, 22, 24, 25, 27, 30, 31, 33, 34, 35, 37, 38, 41, 48, 49, 50, 53, 54, 59-70, 73, 74, 78, 79, 80, 84, 85, 91, 92, 98, 100, 101, 108, 114, 122, 133, 134, 137, 139, 141, 142, 147, 151, 157-160, 164, 167, 168, 169, 171, 173-178, 180, 183-191, 194, 195

Kingdom of, x, xvi, xix, 7, 35, 183, 189, 190, 195

Spirit of, 37, 186

H

Ham, 42

holy nation, ix, x, 38, 185

Holy Nation, xi, xvii, xviii, xix

huios, 187

I

inheritance, 1, 2, 5, 8, 15, 16, 25, 26, 34, 92, 99, 101, 111, 113, 122, 142, 145, 150, 155, 173, 185, 193, 196

Isaac, xv, xvi, xix, 1-27, 29, 30-49, 54, 56, 64, 68, 70, 73, 74, 79, 80, 81, 82, 87, 92, 98, 100, 101, 102, 122, 160, 168, 169, 170, 175, 177, 178, 186, 187, 189, 197

Ishmael, xix, 1, 2, 4, 5, 6, 8, 9, 15, 33, 34, 39, 41, 47, 80, 179

Israel, xv, xvi, xix, 2, 50, 69, 70, 73, 74, 75, 77, 79, 80, 81, 95, 99,

T

Terah, 3, 66, 186, 188

Z

Zebulun, 114, 115

Zerah, 152

Zilpah, 58, 59, 61, 75, 83, 95, 96, 100, 103, 114, 115, 117, 118, 130, 136, 163

ENDNOTES

1   Genesis 13:5-12 describes the mutual decision that Abram and Lot made to separate their camps. This was a practical arrangement. However, the result was two very different lifestyles. Abram continued to be a shepherd in the high country, while Lot took up the life of the men of the cities of Sodom and Gomorrah. Later, when Abram rescued Lot from the Babylonian confederacy, there is no mention of a reunion between the two. Lot went back to the way of life of the city of Sodom and Abram went back to Hebron to continue his life as a herdsman. In the final analysis, Lot's decision finally separated him from Abram and disqualified him as a potential heir to Abram. How could Abram trust his estate to a man of the (wicked) city?

2   Genesis 21:8 implies that Isaac was weaned in some sort of official event. It was not simply a matter of noticing that he no longer was nursing. It seems that the event was decided in advance and a feast was arranged, probably to announce the change in life-status of the heir. It may well be that Isaac was several years old (probably his fifth birthday) when this event occurred. This would have been culturally determined and we have no information as to the exact timing.

3   Isaac would be thoroughly engrained in his father's business so he could take up the stewardship of his father's house in time. This reminds us of Jesus in the temple at age 12 (Lk. 2:49-50). This was the time of His bar Mitzvah, which was a transitional time in His life.

4   Sarah was 127 years old when she died (Gen. 23:1). Isaac was born to her when she was 90 years old. Hence, Isaac was 37 years old at the time of her death. Genesis 25:20 states that Isaac was 40 years old when he married Rebekah. His marriage to Rebekah marked an end to his period of mourning for the loss of his mother (Gen. 24:67).

5   Genesis 25:22-23 informs us that Rebekah sought the counsel of the LORD because of the atypical pregnancy she was experiencing. One may take the position that any first pregnancy in particular would be an experience with the unknown. Often there are aspects of pregnancy that are quite worrisome to the expectant mother regardless of her head knowledge on the subject. I contend herein that her situation did not fit the typical pattern; that, in fact, the twin sons were locked in a perpetual struggle that would carry forward many generations into the future. We must remember that in her previously barren womb was Jacob, the "son of promise" for generation 3 of the "great nation." The other son, Esau, was locked with him in a struggle of a spiritual origin to prevent that great nation from arriving. His life, for its first seventy years, was devoted to maintaining a kind of pre-eminence over his brother Jacob, the son of promise. This would be a logical design of the enemy of mankind. If the son of promise never achieved the measure of the promise, then the nation project would not go forward. There was much at stake in this struggle. I maintain that the struggle was so important that supernatural phenomena even accompanied the period of the pregnancy. It is likely that whatever Rebekah felt in her womb was not normal even for a mother of twins. It is my assertion that it was a one-time pregnancy that reflects the divine will of

GOD as contested by the flesh. Esau comes to represent the extreme nature of the flesh in the matter of the sale of the **birthright.**

6   Isaac was primarily a shepherd. In some instances, of course, where land was available to do so, shepherds planted grain crops for the benefit of their valuable animals. Farming was not their primary activity however, and might not occur at all due to the lack of availability of land. It is probably true that Abraham and Isaac did conduct some farming operations because of the long sojourn in the land and the goodwill they had developed with their Canaanite neighbors. When the famine forced Isaac to move to the area inhabited by the non-Canaanite Philistines, it was probably a matter of his normal pasturages failing to produce grain crops. Many years later, Jacob would send his ten older sons to Egypt because of the same kind of shortage (Gen. 41:56-42:2). The area inhabited by the Philistines was coastal, and thus less affected by a drought, which is probably what caused the famine. Farming, then, was a common profession among the Philistines. They were maritime traders, and one of the commodities they traded was agricultural produce. This man Isaac was so successful among them as a farmer and a herdsman that they became jealous of his success and took action against him (Gen. 26:12-16). First, they stopped up his father's nearby wells and then demanded that he leave. Previously, the LORD had told him he would be blessed in the land of the Philistines (Gen. 26:2-3).

7   Genesis 27:1-4 presents to us the narrative of Isaac's commission to Esau specifically relating to his desire for a specific feast. It is likely that we can accept straightforwardly the elements of Isaac's motivation. He specifically commissioned Esau to carry out this wish. Gen. 25:27-28 presents the reason for Isaac's preference for Esau in this matter. Later, however, Jacob presented Isaac with a goat stew (Gen. 27:25-26) that was indistinguishable from the desired stew. It was this lack of distinction in the stew and in the earthy smell of

the clothes Jacob was wearing that convinced Isaac that he was dealing with Esau rather than Jacob. We must believe that Isaac fully intended to give Esau the patriarchal blessing that day because when Jacob purloined that blessing, Isaac was upset, along with Esau (Gen. 27:33). The food was a thing of the flesh, while the blessing was a thing of spiritual significance. Isaac's intent was to pass on the spiritual in exchange for a desire of the flesh. In this, he, like his son Esau many years earlier, reduced the value of the spiritual thing in favor of the natural thing. When that failed, it was no longer possible for Esau to maintain any real **primacy** with respect to his brother. All that was left then was to work out the arrangements that propelled Jacob to his position of promise.

8   *Birth of The Holy Nation, volume 1*, by C. Gaulden, the predecessor to this volume, provides an extensive discussion of the concept of the "**firstborn**" in scripture. The discussion is the central concern of chapter 5 of that book.

9   See Endnote 25 of *Birth of The Holy Nation, volume 1*, p. 212. When Isaac was 40, Abraham was 140. Abraham lived to be 175. Hence, the last 35 years of his life are unexplored in scripture. Rebekah was barren for 20 years, at the end of which period she bore Esau and Jacob. At that time, Isaac was 60 years old, which made Abraham 160 years old when the twins were born. Hence, they were 15 years old when Abraham died.

10 After Isaac's birth, Ishmael's primary role was to oppose GOD's plans in Isaac's life. Scripture reveals that this was inevitable (Gen. 16:11-12). GOD did not "cause" Ishmael; he was the result of a plan for progeny that was created by Sarai and Abram (Gen. 16:1-4). GOD's plan for progeny was Isaac (Gen. 17:19-21). The inevitable conflict resulted eventually in the expulsion of Ishmael from Abraham's camp. Dismissal from the camp was the only reasonable resolution

to the conflict. It is interesting to note that Ishmael settled outside the area known as Canaan.

In the case of Esau, the same spiritual conflicts were in place. Because of who Esau was (Gen. 25:22-23), the ongoing conflict would have to be resolved in favor of the son of God's choice. This was done in four stages: moving the **birthright** to Jacob (Gen. 25:29-34); the patriarchal blessing given to Jacob (Gen. 27:27-29); the temporary removal of Jacob from Isaac's camp while things were resolved with Esau moving out of the territory of the Canaanites; and Jacob being trained to become the leader of the people under the tutelage of his maternal uncle.

11 Laban was a treacherous man. He required his kinsman to labor for his keep. The seven years' price for the hand of Rachel was reasonable, but the lack of hospitality was what put them on the track to the bride price. Substituting Leah for Rachel at the wedding is another example of Laban's treachery. Treacherous also was his requirement that Jacob labor seven additional years for Rachel's bride price, seeing that there had never been a bridal agreement regarding Leah. Then there was the virtual theft of Jacob's wages in the matter of the unusual sheep and goats (Gen. 30:31-36). Jacob specified for his wives that Laban was a cheater (Gen. 31:4-7). Laban's pursuit of Jacob was somewhat understandable, but his claims of ownership were not (Gen. 31:38-44).

12 Isaac was unequivocally the **firstborn** of Abraham. Even though Ishmael was still in the camp up until the time of Isaac's weaning ceremony, the LORD had made it clear to Abraham what His will was with respect to both the **birthright** and the **inheritance**. Abraham had fully acquiesced to God's will in the matter and it was settled. Ultimately, Ishmael had to be sent away, but that was not because of Abraham's heart. Ishmael would continue to make minor trouble in the camp as long as he remained. Hagar might even have ultimately motivated him to revolt against Isaac—or

even Abraham—had things not changed. Hence, from the time Isaac began his education, he was trained to be his father's full and uncontested heir. There would be no co-heirs, no one to challenge his position. He was raised to be who he was.

Jacob, on the other hand, was raised to be the second son. Of the twins, he was born second. The word of the LORD to Rebekah notwithstanding (Gen. 25:23), Jacob was not raised to be the full heir of his father. Esau was. The text makes it very clear this distinction was largely based on the affinities of the two sons (Gen. 25:27-28). As the **patriarch** of the camp, it was up to Isaac to determine how the two boys were trained. His preference for Esau makes it clear to us that Esau would have been trained to be the **patriarch**. But, what about Jacob? He too was a son of Isaac and that was quite important to the camp and to Isaac. Isaac needed to make the decisions concerning the roles Jacob would play in the future and to provide for that. It is unlikely he would train both of his sons in the same overall regimen because he did not need for Jacob to seek to usurp anything from Esau. He would have preferred peace to that kind of conflict. After all, he had seen with his own eyes the necessity of removing Ishmael from the camp when he was a young boy. He could not, however, cast Jacob out into the world. So, Isaac would do the best he could for Jacob to insure his success as long as he was not a contender for Esau's place. Hence, given Jacob's natural temperament and the education his father provided for him, he was just as well off remaining in the camp. In later years he would be a distant second to his older brother without disrupting anything.

Of course, Jacob was not to be the second son in terms of **primacy**. Notwithstanding the deliberate actions and plans of Isaac, Jacob was to be the ruler, according to GOD Himself. But by temperament, training, and (probably) everyday life, he was not a leader. His father Isaac was a leader in every way. They were different men.

13 Lot disqualified himself as a potential heir of Abram by his choice
of lifestyle. Eliezer was not truly qualified to be the heir because
he was a servant. When Abram grumbled to GOD about Eliezer,
he was only stating that while Eliezer was not qualified, he was the
most qualified of the unqualified in the event the estate had to go
to an unqualified person. Ishmael was the son of a slave woman.
Hence, he was as much property as he was a son. Abram loved
him but that was not adequate before the LORD. There would be
no cloud left to hang over the status of the true heir. Each was
"removed" in his own way so that Isaac alone would emerge as the
heir—the son of promise.

14 The covenant between GOD and Abraham was presented to Abram
in a number of stages, with each stage more complete and specific
than the previous one. It began with GOD's command to Abram to
move to another place and become a nation (Gen. 12:1-3). This
command was given before the migration was made. When Abram
arrived in the land at Shechem, the LORD added the specific element
of progeny (Gen. 12:7). Next, some specific information concerning the land was added (Gen. 13:14-17). I aver that the blessing of
Melchizedek added the element of triumph to the promise, which
was not yet specifically a covenant (Gen. 14:20). Soon another element was added in the form of protection (Gen. 15:1). Clarification that the servant Eliezer was not the heir came next (Gen.
15:4-5). After that, Abram received the prophetic dimensions of
the hardships in Egypt that his descendants would endure (Gen.
15:13-16). Then came the application of the term covenant to the
prophetic strain (Gen. 15:18-20) after Abram made the required
sacrifices. The addition of the covenantal requirement of circumcision was the next stage that God revealed (Gen. 17:1-14). The extension of the covenant to Isaac was added at about the same time
(Gen. 17:19-22). The final element was added at Moriah (Gen.
22:15-18), where GOD swore on His own being that the sacrifice
of Abraham brought the covenant to its fullness.

15 1) Isaac was selected in advance by GOD to be the heir of Abraham.

2) Jacob was selected in advance by GOD to be the heir of Isaac (in spite of Isaac).

3) Joseph and Judah were distributed the double portion and overall leadership, respectively, in the patriarchal, pre-funerary blessings of Jacob at the demotion of Reuben.

4) GOD directed Samuel to continue to inspect the sons of Jesse until he came to the seventh, David, even at some inconvenience, to become the king of GOD's choice.

5) David had various notables accompany him to anoint Solomon and declare him king because he was previously selected by David.

16 Esau despised his **birthright** and forfeited it (Gen. 25:29-34). Because of this, GOD turned His back on Esau (Mal. 1:2-3). The writer of Hebrews likened Esau to a person of no morals over the matter (Heb. 12:16).

17 Genesis 27:6-29 recounts the events by which Jacob gets the blessing from Isaac rather than Esau receiving it, which clearly was Isaac's intent (v. 1-4).

18 It seems strange to us that when Isaac sent Jacob away (Gen. 28:1-5) to fetch a bride from among his kindred, he did not provide a bride price. After all, he knew of the custom. Rebekah's family had been provided a bride price when she was brought back to him. The sense of urgency in the camp precluded that kind of preparation. This implies that Isaac may have known of the other reason Rebekah wanted to send Jacob away (the threats of Esau). The result was that Jacob had to earn the bride price with his labor (seven years for each of his wives). Whether this was a high price or not,

Jacob endured it for the sake of marrying Rachel. The other wage changes Laban imposed on him apparently were above and beyond the matter of the bride price.

19 Abram built his altar at Bethel prior to his journey to Egypt. When he came back from Egypt, he soon returned to Bethel to, in a sense, renew his acquaintance with the LORD. The two sessions at Bethel provide bookends for Abram's venture outside GOD's provision in Canaan.

20 Hebrews 7:9 states that Levi was in the body (loins) of Abram when Abram tithed to Melchizedek. In a sense, then, the Levitical priesthood was tithing to Melchizedek at that time. If Levi was in the loins of Abram, he was also in the loins of Isaac and of Jacob in turn. In fact, Aaron (the first high priest of the Levitical order) was in the loins of Levi to be born three generations later (Kohath, Amram, Aaron). So, he too was in the loins of Abram that day near Sodom.

21 To whom, or to what institution, would Jacob tithe (Gen. 28:22)? Melchizedek and Abraham were both dead before this time. Who was the "greater" one to whom Jacob could defer in the matter of his relationship with mammon? It would appear that Isaac was now the **primacy** to which Jacob would look.

22 A straightforward reading of the text indicates it took seven years to get to the wedding, at which time Laban deceitfully replaced Rachel with Leah (Gen. 29:19-22). However, only a week passed until the second wedding, where Jacob married Rachel, for whose hand he worked for his uncle another seven years (Gen. 29:27-28).

23 Genesis 29:7-10 presents a scenario in which Jacob took initiative in a very straightforward manner. He hastened the opening of the well and then kissed Rachel as a kinsperson. No one arranged these things for him.

24 Jacob's grandfather Abraham deceived Pharaoh and Abimelech to avoid potential problems related to Sarai/Sarah. His father Isaac deceived Abimelech in order to avoid potential problems related to Rebekah. His mother Rebekah resorted to all sorts of deceit to procure the patriarchal blessing for him as well as his escape from Esau.

25 GOD was not careless when it came to the birth of the son of promise. He had carefully managed events so that the wombs through which the son and grandson of promise were to come forth were honored. In the first case (Isaac), he was simply the only son to leave that womb ever. There was no ambiguity. In the second case (Jacob), GOD permitted the ambiguity of multiple births from the same womb. This allowed a man (Isaac) to confuse the matter of clear **inheritance**. In the final analysis, though, GOD straightened out the matter of the **birthright** and the **primacy** of the designated **patriarch**.

26 Genesis 30:1-2 presents an interesting situation. Rachel was disappointed in her continuing barrenness, so she blamed Jacob for it. He was capable. Jacob could sire sons, as proven by Leah's regular pregnancies. There was some other reason for Rachel to be unable to conceive and bear sons. It was not Jacob; it was the manifestation of the will of GOD. The son of Rachel was not the **patriarch**, but he was a kind of savior.

27 Jacob camped near the Jordan before crossing it for a couple of reasons. First, there was the practical matter of getting all the animals and people across without any losses. There was also the fact that he had left behind the land of his patriarchal leadership education where he had independently acquired wealth. That was now the past. The future was in Canaan, which could be defined roughly in terms of the Jordan River. The crossing of the river was a kind of right-of-passage for Jacob that marked a point of no return. Never

again could he be who he had been. Genesis 32:1 suggests that it was GOD who designated the campsite for that final adjustment in the life of Jacob before he went in to occupy his possession.

28   Genesis 12:6-7 specifies that the first significant stop for Abram was at Shechem. He was 75 years old at the time (Gen. 12:4). Twenty-five years later, Isaac was born (Gen. 21:5). Sixty years later, Jacob was born (Gen. 25:19-26). The total was now 85 years from Abram's entry into the land. Based on the ages of Jacob and Joseph at the time of his entry into Egypt, Joseph was born when Jacob was about 88 years old, and Jacob returned to Canaan when he was about 90 years old. That brings us to about 175 years from the time Abram arrived at Shechem to the time Jacob arrived there.

29   Ephraim and Manasseh were tribes when the Israelites left Egypt (e.g. Num. 1:32-35; 2:18-21; Josh. 14:1-5). Jacob adopted them, in a sense (Gen. 48:5), but they were not included as sons per se in Jacob's patriarchal blessings (Gen. 49) except that they were the sons of Joseph, who was included.

30   This is at least conceivable. The deception itself seems to have been the idea of the whole group of the sons. However, the matter, if joke it was, was born out of deceit (Gen. 34:13-14). Were Simeon and Levi the authors of that request? Scripture is mute on the point but makes it clear they were the leaders, if not the only players, in the subsequent massacre.

31   Genesis 35:6-8 connects the death of Deborah to the events at Bethel. Deborah was the long-term nurse of Jacob's mother, Rebekah. How came she to be with Jacob at Bethel? Of course, he would have known her and been fond of her because she was so close to Rebekah. Perhaps she had even been present when Jacob was born. Her presence in Jacob's camp at Bethel suggests two things: that Rebekah was already dead by then, and that there was

interaction between Isaac's camp and Jacob's camp before Jacob moved to Hebron to be with Isaac.

32 Jacob appears to have ignored the Bilhah incident with Reuben. Later, he clearly attached the blame to Reuben (Gen. 49:3-4). We may assume they exchanged words concerning this transgression, but the blessings in Egypt contain the first recorded words of Jacob on the matter.

33 Why were Joseph and Benjamin not included in this journey? It is likely that Jacob consciously made "camp boys" of them as a comfort to himself. He would not be foreign to the idea of keeping sons close to camp because it was his own nature when he was a youngster.

34 We infer this from Genesis 42:38.

35 (Genesis 41:57; 42:1; 45:11.) The two trips of the older sons of Jacob had to have been completed during the first two years of the famine because Joseph specifically stated there were five years of famine left just before the brothers returned to Jacob after the second trip.

36 Even though the two trips took place within a total of two years, the text implies there was a considerable time lapse between them. The first probably occurred when it became clear there would be no good crops during the first year. The second then probably occurred a year later when the second-year crop was very poor in Canaan. The many-month interval was probably a very emotional period in the camp.

37 Genesis 43:8-9 presents Judah's pledge. We make much of it because he was a son of a very wealthy man. If he gave all that up as a result of failure, he would have nothing; no **inheritance** at all. Hence, he would be no better off than a slave subject to any

arbitrary revenge Jacob might choose to exact. His brothers were witnesses to this sacrifice.

38 Genesis 46:2-4 records GOD's instruction to Jacob to go to Egypt. Surely Jacob knew of the time when GOD forbad Isaac to go to Egypt (Gen. 26:2). He would also have known of the prophesy of GOD concerning oppression (Gen. 15:13-16) that would lead to captivity. But GOD said to go, so he went.

39 Reuben was included in the patriarchal blessings (Gen. 49:3-4) but not in a very positive way. 1 Chronicles 5:1-3 makes it clear that he lost his **birthright** to the sons of Joseph in the sense of the double portion of land **inheritance**, and the rule to Judah.

40 The greater would bless the lesser (Heb. 7:7). Genesis 47:7-10 states that Jacob blessed Pharaoh rather than the other way around. In fact, he did so twice.

41 See note 23. In Genesis 47:29 Jacob required of Joseph an oath as solemn as the one Abraham required of his servant in the matter of the acquisition of a wife for Isaac (Gen. 24:1-4). This oath was taken on the source of human power in the camp, the genitalia of the ruling **patriarch**. Joseph submitted as a son of Jacob, not as the prime minister of Egypt.

42 It is clear that Jacob loved Rachel more than he loved Leah. Leah saw the bearing of sons as a way to draw Jacob from Rachel to herself. It did not work. Leah clearly won in terms of sons born, but Rachel remained the beloved Genesis 35:19-20; 37:3; and 42:38, taken together, make this a very strong argument.

43 This is not a necessary conclusion, but a lot of sons had to be born in an 11 to 13 year time frame. Also, this would be consistent with the principle of the "barren womb."

44 When the father was ready, the son of promise came. When Jacob had matured as leader, Joseph was sent by way of the womb of Rachel, the beloved wife.

45 Did Leah go to Egypt? The text does not say so. She is excluded from the list of those who went (Gen. 46:8-27). The list refers to "Jacob and his descendants," of which Leah was not one. However, the moon in Joseph's second dream (Gen. 37:9-11) was associated with his mother, and Rachel was dead. The question remains unanswered.

46 See chapter 5 in *Birth of the Holy Nation, volume 1* for a discussion of the importance of *b'cʰor.*

47 Genesis 16 recounts the results of Sarai's plan, which resulted in the birth of Ishmael. Genesis 30:3-8 sounds similar. However, GOD was very *particular* about the womb from which the son of promise issued. This was a principle.

48 Four sons had been born to Leah and two each to Bilhah and Zilpah before this dramatic set of events. Again, Rachel was trying to take the place of GOD in the matter of the birth of her first son.

49 We assume the awareness of the famine began early in the year, but its severity would be inferred by the poor crop later in the year. Then came the first trip. When it was apparent the crop of the next year had also failed, the second trip to Egypt took place.

50 Genesis 42:17 says that Joseph imprisoned his brothers for three days. The journey to Mt. Moriah took Abraham and Isaac three days. The dreams of the Pharaoh's butler and baker were three-day dreams (Gen. 40). This three-day motif seems to have been closely associated with Joseph. JESUS was in the tomb three days.

51 Jacob became Israel when he was at the Jordan River just before he returned home to his full inheritance as the son of promise. Before that, he was simply a man of flesh. After that, he was still a man of flesh, but he was also the patriarch of the nation, who began to actualize the plentitude of progeny. This occurred soon after (within two years) of the birth of Joseph, because Joseph would be exiled to save the people for his father. It is beyond the scope of this book to fully explore the distinction between Jacob and Israel, but it is a real distinction.

52 Jacob returned to Canaan from Padan Aram when he was about 90 years old. At that time, Isaac was 150 years old. Since Isaac lived to be 180 years old, he lived for 30 years after Jacob's return. That being the case, Isaac died about the time Joseph was released from prison at age 30 (Gen. 41:46). Isaac was forbidden to go to Egypt (Gen. 26:2). Later, Jacob was told to go (Gen. 46:3-4). Joseph's elevation made it possible for Jacob to go to Egypt, so all these thing fit together quite well chronologically.

53 Isaac died eight to ten years before Jacob received the news that Joseph was alive (see note 52).

54 Consider Joseph's situation. He had been suddenly and cruelly ripped from everything he had known. His entreaties to his brothers fell on deaf ears. He was made a slave in the house of an Egyptian nobleman for a few years. He was then made a prisoner in an Egyptian prison for about ten years. There was nothing to be desired in any of this. One suspects he might have periodically harbored wishes for revenge on his brothers for their treatment of him. When his first son was born after he became prime minister (title approximate), Joseph named him "forgetfulness" (Gen. 41:51).

55 Forgetfulness came to Joseph in Egypt (Gen. 41:39-40). The use of the Hebrew language to name his son Manasseh suggests that

Joseph had not totally forgotten his family or his home. He had used the Egyptian language for a long time by then.

56 Joseph was 17 years old when things went wrong (Gen. 37:2). He was 30 years old when he was released from prison (Gen. 41:46). That is a total of about 13 years. There were then 7 years of bumper crops; 7 years of plenty that Joseph managed with great skill as prime minister of Egypt. That comes out to 20 years for Joseph in Egypt. Then the first two years of the famine came along. Altogether, Joseph was alone in Egypt for about 22 years before he was reunited with his father and Benjamin at the age of 39.

57 With Joseph gone and assumed dead (or as good as dead), it is not surprising that the family soon forgot about his two dreams (Gen. 37:5-11), especially since it seemed impossible now for them ever to be fulfilled. As we are too often, they were somewhat cavalier about the prophetic nature of GOD's word to them.

58 Joseph left in the configuration of his two sons, Ephraim and Manasseh, insofar as tribal designation is concerned. In other words, Joseph did not come out as Joseph. Of course, he did not go down with Jacob, having preceded him by over 20 years. The "adoption" of Ephraim and Manasseh led to Joseph "disappearing" into his sons.

59 The method Joseph used to present his sons to Jacob appears to be an introduction. It is not actually likely that this was necessary, because they were undoubtedly familiar with one another. More likely it was a formality accepted in advance by Jacob and Joseph for the purpose of the adoption (Gen. 48:1-20).

60 The JACOB-JOSEPH dyad was at once very unusual and very affectionate. In the context of that particular relationship, Jacob decided to move the inheritance of the firstborn (the double portion)

through the adoption of the two sons of Joseph and providing each a land inheritance when the tribes came to Canaan in later years.

61 Joshua was undoubtedly an Ephraimite, as revealed in following passages: Numbers 13:8; 14:5-9; Joshua 1:1.

62 The descendants of Judah excelled. His tribe led the other tribes in the desert (Num. 2:3). Caleb, the other hero among the spies, was of the tribe of Judah (Num. 13:6). David was from the tribe of Judah (Ruth 4:12, 18-22; Perez was the son of Judah and Tamar). JESUS was descended from the tribe of Judah (Mt. 1:1-17, the genealogy).

63 Reuben would not have been able to actuate his plan because the other brothers (especially the really angry ones) would not have allowed it. Had that come to pass, Jacob would have inevitably found out. Judah (perhaps accidentally) found the correct solution.

64 Jacob testified to Judah's royal (noble) character in the patriarchal blessings. The blessing for Judah (Gen. 49:8-10) focused on this. Obviously, David and JESUS lived the royal nature of Judah in their times. The southern kingdom was called Judah after this tribal patriarch.

65 Judah went to live among the Canaanites (Gen. 38:1). They were city-oriented people. Judah was a shepherd. He seems to have done quite well in both environments—a handy trait for a ruler.

66 Joseph was not aware of this at the time. He had no idea (although God did) that he eventually would be a "savior" of his own family. By the time they arrived, he was the second most important man in the entire kingdom of Egypt (Gen. 41:39-44), and was perfectly placed to help them.

67 Reuben led the brothers on the first Egypt trip (Gen. 42), not Judah.

68 Judah made the proposition of surety for the safe return of Benjamin by offering all that he was as that surety (Gen. 43:8-9).

69 Judah's bargain was more powerful (more was at stake) than Reuben's bargain, who would still have his inheritance, and could produce more sons. Judah made his own being the guarantee for Benjamin's safety. This was a more noble gesture than Reuben's. Judah would have given his life for his brother. Reuben would only sacrifice for the safety of his brother.

70 Judah would rather have given his own life in Egypt than hurt his father. As far as he knew, he would be treated far worse in Egypt than at home, yet was willing to pay that price in order to spare his father the pain of losing Benjamin.

71 Judah's proposed bargain to Joseph was the final, deciding factor in Joseph's decision to reveal himself to his brothers that day (Gen. 45:1).

72 Genesis 47:13-26. It is not realistic to think that Joseph (Zaphnath Paaneah now) could both manage the affairs of a kingdom AND be re-integrated into the lives of his father and brothers. He was an Egyptian, in essence, with memories of being a Hebrew. This might well have been a part of Jacob's motivation in adopting Joseph's sons to replace him.

73 In Genesis 47:28-31 Jacob required Joseph to take an oath on his father's fertility. (See Note 23 on Genesis 24:9, Victor P. Hamilton, "The Book of Genesis, Chapters 18-50," *New International Commentary on the Old Testament*, (Grand Rapids, MI: Eerdmans Publishing), 624.) No greater vow could be taken. Consider the

indignity endured by Joseph for his father, given his very exalted status in Egypt.

74 See the Occasional Writing, "Four Hundred Years, or So," by C. Gaulden at http://ravensfood.everykindred.com. Click on the "Occasional Writings" link. The paper contains a fairly extensive analysis of pertinent scripture and provides a timeline that resolves certain problems of chronology caused by editorial selections.

75 Exodus 12:40-42 presents 430 years also, but in a different way. Because the purposes of the Exodus and Galatians passages are different, we cannot fully reconcile the two. However, the timeframes are very similar and, more or less, agree. The Exodus passage is interesting because it presents another motive of GOD in the very *precision* of the event. The problem with that one is the identification of the starting point. Also, many manuscripts say Egypt *and* Canaan," where NIV says "Egypt." The former, Egypt *and* Canaan, fits the facts much better. This would require that the Canaan period be first (Abraham, Isaac, etc.).

76 Often prophets address Israel, personifying the people, as Jacob. This is especially true when the matter at hand is related to their flesh nature and not their spiritual destiny. The same device is used in the Psalms as well.

77 Genesis 15:13 presents the phrase "four hundred years" in isolation from the rest of the surrounding text. There is no preposition or other verbiage to tie the phrase to the other ideas in the verse. They were not to be there "for four hundred years" or "during." The four hundred years is information, but is not a statement concerning the duration of the oppression. It seems to be a statement that explains the duration of time from the birth (actually "weaning") of Isaac to the exodus of the descendants.

78 Joseph was about 39 years old when Jacob moved to Egypt. Jacob was 127 years old at the time. With rounding considerations, this means Jacob was about 90 when Joseph was born (perhaps only 88). Isaac was 60 years old when Jacob was born. Round Jacob's age to 90 when Joseph was born. Then Isaac was *about* 150 when Joseph was born. Isaac lived to be 180 years old. Hence, Joseph was 30 years old when Isaac died. That was the age of Joseph when he was released from prison.

79 Sixty-six persons went with Jacob to Egypt (Gen. 46:26). Eleven were his sons, the rest were grandsons. Benjamin had ten of those grandsons for Jacob.

80 Moses was in Egypt for 40 years (Acts 7:23), but lived among the Egyptians, not the Israelites. He returned to Egypt when he was 80 (Ex. 7:7). During the intervening 40 years, he was in the desert, being prepared by GOD for his mission of leading his people out of slavery.

81 Let's be absolutely clear here. The particular human male known as JESUS of Nazareth was "created" (conceived) in Mary's womb by the Holy Spirit. The Son of GOD, the second Person of the Trinity, who was embodied in the human known as JESUS, was not created, but is co-existent, co-eternal, and co-equal to GOD the Father. Upon His incarnation as JESUS, the eternal Son of GOD became eternally the GOD-man.

TO CONTACT THE AUTHOR

Raven's Food
P.O. Box 63002
San Angelo, TX 76906-3002
ravensfood@everykindred.com

Twitter: /ravens_food

Facebook: /ravensfood

Errors, as they are discovered, will appear on the Raven's Food website support section for Birth of the Holy Nation, volume 2. Please refer to that site online from time to time.

eGenCo

Generation Culture Transformation
Specializing in publishing for generation culture change

Visit us Online at:
www.egen.co

Write to: eGenCo
824 Tallow Hill Road
Chambersburg, PA 17202 USA
Phone: 717-461-3436
Email: info@egen.co

 facebook.com/egenbooks

 youtube.com/egenpub

 egen.co/blog

 pinterest.com/eGenDMP

 twitter.com/eGenDMP

 instagram.com/egenco_dmp

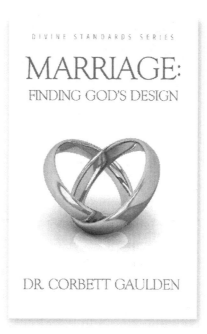

Marriage: Finding God's Design

Traditional marriage is under attack today as never before. Amid the shrill rhetoric and partisan bickering, the need is great for a measured voice to remind us of the fundamental truths. Corbett Gaulden is such a voice.

Deliberately eschewing politics and focusing on Scriptural teachings alone, he takes us back to the beginning, to the origin of marriage in God's design. He then unpacks the distinctive properties that characterize biblical marriage: particularity, oneness, permanency, fidelity, and purity. Regarding roles and relationships, marriage is not about power, but proper function. It is not a political arrangement or a social construct, but a spiritual institution. Biblical marriage is about covenant, not competition. It is about primacy, covering, and order in a partnership of mutual consideration. Ultimately, human marriage is a picture in the natural of the relationship between Christ and His Church in the spiritual.

Scripturally grounded and practical, *Marriage: Finding God's Design* reminds us of what much of modern culture has forgotten, that marriage is God's idea, and it functions properly only when it operates according to His standards.

Available for purchase at:
ravensfood.everykindred.com

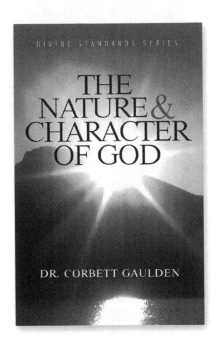

The Nature & Character of God

"Before anything else was, GOD *is*. When all else ceases to have being, GOD will *be*."

This is the simple yet profound premise behind Dr. Corbett Gaulden's brief treatise on GOD the Father. In four short but insightful chapters, he examines certain aspects of the nature and character of GOD as revealed in the specific attributes of His existence, His authority, and His love. Fundamentally, GOD is first in all things. He is first in existence, and by and through Him all else exists. As Father, GOD is first in precedence (though not in essence) over JESUS His Son.

As to authority, GOD's authority is original authority; all other authority, in the spiritual or natural realms, is derived or delegated authority received from GOD.

As to love, GOD is love; all love originates in and emanates from GOD. His love is universal, yet individual; particular and reciprocal, as modeled in the love demonstrated between GOD the Father and JESUS the Son.

Existence, authority, and love originate in GOD the Father and, as He sees fit, emanate from Him to whomever He chooses.

Available for purchase at:
ravensfood.everykindred.com

Made in the USA
Middletown, DE
27 April 2016